MANUEL LONDON
American Telephone and Telegraph Company

STEPHEN A. STUMPF
New York University

Managing
Careers

ADDISON-WESLEY PUBLISHING COMPANY

Reading, Massachusetts · Menlo Park, California
London · Amsterdam · Don Mills, Ontario · Sydney

THE ADDISON-WESLEY SERIES ON MANAGING HUMAN RESOURCES

Series Editor: John P. Wanous, Michigan State University

Fairness in Selecting Employees
Richard D. Arvey, University of Houston

Organizational Entry: Recruitment, Selection, and Socialization of Newcomers
John P. Wanous, Michigan State University

Increasing Productivity through Performance Appraisal
Gary P. Latham, University of Washington, and Kenneth N. Wexley,
Michigan State University

Managing Conflict at Organizational Interfaces
David Brown, Brown University

Employee Turnover: Causes, Consequences and Control
William H. Mobley, Texas A & M University

Managing Careers
Manuel London, AT&T and Stephen A. Stumpf,
N.Y. University

Library of Congress Cataloging in Publication Data

London, Manuel.
    Managing careers.

    (Addison-Wesley series on managing human resources)
    Bibliography: p.
    Includes index.
    1. Vocational guidance. I. Stumpf, Stephen A.
II. Title. III. Series.
HF5381.L656   650.1'4   81-20680
ISBN 0-201-04559-1   AACR2

ISBN 0-201-04559-1
ABCDEFGHIJ-AL-898765432

Series Foreword

Widespread attention given to the effective management of human resources came of age in the 1970s. As we enter the 1980s, the importance placed on it continues to grow. Personnel departments, which used to be little more than the keepers of employee files, are now moving to the forefront in corporate visibility.

The difficulties encountered in effective human resource management are without parallel. Surveys of managers and top level executives consistently show "human problems" at the top of most lists. The influx of the behavioral sciences into business school programs is further testimony to the active concern now placed on human resources as a crucial element in organizational effectiveness.

The primary objective of this Addison-Wesley series is to articulate new solutions to chronic human resource problems; for example, the selection and entry of newcomers, performance appraisal, conflict management, employee turnover, and career management. The aim is to communicate with a variety of audiences, including present managers, students as future managers, and fellow professionals in business, government, and academia.

John P. Wanous
Series Editor

Preface

A book, like a good career plan, should begin with a clear goal. Ours is to provide an overview of managing careers from the perspectives of the individual and the organization. *Managing Careers* covers self-assessment; career and life stages; career issues for minorities, women, and dual-career couples; career planning; training and development programs; organizational staffing decisions; and staffing support systems such as human resource planning, job matching, and mentor–protégé relationships.

In our view, the individual's role in career management is: (1) to examine his or her skills, interests, and potential, (2) to identify realistic career objectives, and (3) to obtain the necessary training and development to prepare for target positions and effectively compete for career opportunities. The organization's role in career management is: (1) to fill positions with the most qualified personnel, (2) to provide challenging job opportunities, and (3) to assist individuals in career planning and development. Individual career management is facilitated by self-assessment, and organizational career management is facilitated by a system of integrated human resource functions.

Managing Careers is for students and young managers who are concerned about career progression. The book is also for human resource practitioners who are, or will be, responsible for organizational career management systems. Experienced managers will also find the book valuable as they make decisions about their careers and those of their subordinates.

An important feature of this book is its summary of recent research and theory on careers, providing readers with a firm grounding in the literature as well as ample references—for those who want more information. We use cases, examples, and exercises to portray realistically the complexity of career issues and provide readers with common experiences for discussion. We also offer guidelines to help individuals formulate and implement their career plans, and to help organizations design and operate career programs.

The book may be used as a supplement in courses on personnel administration, human resource planning, industrial/organizational psychology, and organizational behavior. It may be especially valuable in career decision-making courses often taught in business schools. A recent survey by Francine Hall (1982) asked instructors of career courses to list the topics they covered. Appendix A suggests how *Managing Careers* may be used to cover these topics. This appendix should be helpful to instructors in designing courses and to students in understanding course goals.

Our treatment of careers is intentionally focused toward individuals attempting to manage their own careers and the careers of others. As such, it will have limitations for some readers. Some may view our guidelines as prescriptions for an ideal world. This is the nature of guidelines, and we hope they will serve to direct individuals and organizations in applying behavioral science knowledge. Other readers may feel there are too many research findings. Our goal is to present sound ideas supported by rigorous research in a concrete, practical manner. Others may feel constrained by our focus on management jobs in large business organizations. We believe, however, that many of the concepts apply to other types of employees, such as scientists and other professionals employed by large organizations; and to organizations without profit-centered goals, such as government agencies, the military, hospitals, and universities. Finally, some may feel that career management programs are important during prosperous times but become luxuries at other times. Our view is that career management is always crucial, although it may take different forms in response to changes in organizational and individual needs.

Since we contributed equally to this volume, the order of authorship is alphabetical. Although we are responsible for the book's content, we are indebted to many people for their cooperation, encouragement, and guidance. Many colleagues influenced our thinking during the last four years. Special thanks are due to Doug Bray, Dave Hoyle, Joel Moses, and Bill Regan at AT&T for practical viewpoints on the philosophy and application of career management. The book would never have been completed without Doug Bray's support. We are also thankful to the administration and staff of New York University's Schools of Business for their support in the preparation of *Managing Careers,* and to the NYU students for their cooperation in much of the research and case studies cited.

Several colleagues graciously agreed to comment on drafts of chapters. Francine Hall, Janina Latack, Marilyn Morgan, and Pat Pinto have our thanks for their constructive ideas. Douglas T. Hall, Allen Kraut, Walter Storey, and John Wanous reviewed the entire manuscript. We are grateful for their many helpful suggestions.

Managing Careers is dedicated to our wives and children, Marilyn, David, Jared, Maria, and Eugene, whose presence, patience, and encouragement create a comfortable environment for managing our careers.

Belle Mead, N.J.   **M.L.**
New York, N.Y.   **S.A.S.**

Contents

Section I
Introduction

Career Management: Individual and Organizational Perspectives

1

For most of us, career success is variable; sometimes we feel successful, other times we do not. Few of us have detailed career goals and no one has complete control over career opportunities and outcomes. With changing economic conditions and increased competition among people and organizations, career uncertainty is the rule, not the exception. The ability to seek and select career opportunities requires careful planning and preparation. Our intention is to provide some guidance for both individuals and organizations in managing careers.

Managing careers is a joint process involving individuals and their organizations. By understanding and delineating individual and organizational responsibilities, individuals are better able to manage their careers effectively and organizations are better able to manage their human resources profitably. To accomplish this, individuals should learn and apply techniques of self-assessment, career and life planning, and self-development. Organizations should provide career support systems, such as career planning and development programs, and they should guide supervisors who make staffing decisions. These ideas are developed throughout the book.

In this chapter, we begin by defining several terms pertaining to careers as viewed by the individual and the organization. We discuss individual factors affecting career progression and the concept of individual career management. We next examine organizational factors affecting career progression and the concept of organizational career management. The chapter concludes with an overview of the book.

Defining Terms

Career. A career is the sequence of work-related positions occupied throughout a person's life. A career encompasses those stages and transitions over time that reflect one's needs, motives, and aspirations as well as societal and organizational expectations and constraints. The individual's perspective includes understanding and evaluating his or her career experiences. The organization's perspective includes policies, procedures, and decisions associated with work-roles, organizational levels, compensation, and personnel movement. Matching or synchronizing the individual and organizational perspectives often necessitates work-role adjustments, development, and change.

Career management. Career management involves the interactive processes of developing a concept of self relative to one's work-roles, and being an effective employee. Individuals manage their careers through decisions to seek and accept or reject various work-role opportunities. Organizations manage careers by selectively making such opportunities available to specific individuals.

Career planning. Career planning is the process of generating action steps for individuals to progress along alternative pathways in work systems. For career planning to be effective, it must unite organizational human resource planning with individuals' needs, capabilities, and aspirations. This requires the active participation of both the individual and the organization.

Career development. The activities individuals participate in to improve themselves relative to their current or planned work-roles are viewed as career development. The activities that organizations sponsor to help ensure that they will meet or exceed their future human resource requirements are also labeled career development. While developmental experiences, such as training, job assignments, and job rotations, help meet the organization's needs, individuals need to seek these activities to facilitate their career progression.

Career progression. Career progression encompasses the work-role changes that provide the individual with, on balance, positive psychological or work-related outcomes. We define career progression broadly to include work-role changes that involve more than advancement to higher organizational levels and higher pay scales. Career progression includes any work-role changes resulting in one or more of the following: greater job, career, and life satisfaction; feelings of psychological success and self-worth; feelings of competence, mastery, and achievement; and attainment of organizational rewards such as money, power, prestige, and status.

Changing economic and social conditions require a broad view of career progression. In contrast to the 1960s and 70s, the next twenty years are likely to be marked by slower organizational growth, a larger percentage of mid-career employees (due to the post-World War II baby boom), and lower attrition of senior employees (due to limits on social security benefits and the end of mandatory retirement). Consequently, even talented individuals are likely to be frustrated by fewer advancement opportunities.

This suggests that individuals and organizations may have to alter their conception of career progression from movement up an organizational hierarchy to work-role changes leading to individual growth and organizational effectiveness. While all work-role changes are not career progression, career progression includes promotions, assignment changes, and lateral moves or transfers, if they lead to positive individual outcomes. Changes in the structure and responsibilities of a person's existing job that the individual perceives as positive are also aspects of career progression, and such changes may be a major source of career development in the future. Since each work-role change can affect many career, personal, and family-related outcomes, whether or not a change is positive for an individual depends on how it is perceived, the context of the change, and what transpires over time (Super, 1980).

While the meaning of career progression should not be limited to advancement, it would be unrealistic to believe that talented individuals will no longer seek higher-level positions. Moreover, it would be equally unrealistic to believe that organizations will not continue to emphasize the early identification, development, and promotion of high potential people. Career management processes associated with upward movement must be emphasized if we are to be concerned with individual and organizational effectiveness.

In summary, career management, planning, and development should be viewed from both the perspectives of the individual and the organization. Career progression, which generally denotes upward movement, should be interpreted more broadly to encompass all career moves that generate positive outcomes for the individual. Nevertheless, upward mobility is an important part of career progression for both individuals and organizations.

INDIVIDUAL FACTORS AFFECTING CAREER PROGRESSION

Many factors affect the value a person places on various work-roles. For example, one's expectations regarding the job itself often affect the satisfaction experienced on a job (Wanous, 1980). One's interests, self-identity, and personal orientation affect one's job preferences (Strong, 1943; Super, 1957; Holland, 1973; Hall, 1976). One's socioeconomic background and experiences affect the opportunities that are valued as well as those that are available (Blau et al., 1956).

The career issues most salient to the individual at various times also depend on a person's career and life stage (Levinson, 1969; Super et al., 1957; Super, 1980). Individuals in their early career years are active, exploring career possibilities and trying various work-roles. By their mid-twenties, they are most concerned with establishing themselves in their selected area. Once established, advancement becomes the prime concern. As individuals reach mid-career, their concerns often reflect their changing life situation with greater emphasis on maintenance and

Fig. 1.1 *Individual factors affecting career progression*

stability (Hall, 1976; Stumpf & Rabinowitz, 1981). Hence, career moves should not be viewed as isolated events. They need to be considered in the context of the individual's life, past experiences, and the organization, as suggested in Fig. 1.1. The diversity of factors affecting an individual's career suggests the importance of individual career management.

Individual Career Management

Career progression is likely to be enhanced to the extent that one can accurately perform three tasks: (1) assess one's skills, interests, and potential for various work-roles, (2) identify career objectives and develop a realistic career plan based on self-knowledge coupled with an assessment of organizational job possibilities, and (3) obtain the necessary training and developmental experiences to prepare oneself for target positions and to compete effectively for career opportunities. Each of these individual career management tasks is discussed in subsequent chapters.

Individuals can facilitate their career progression in several ways. Two steps are crucial as a person begins a career. The first is to form a clear, realistic, and accurate view of one's skills, interests, and personal orientation (Kotter, Faux, & McArthur, 1978; Storey, 1976a). This involves examining where one is now and how one got there. The second step is to determine a career direction; that is, establish career goals and work-role preferences. Without these necessary activities, career plans and actions may have little meaning and even less utility.

Once individuals specify career objectives, the objectives must be examined to see if they are attainable. If they are not realistic, they should be revised until they are within reach. A career plan can then be devised which takes into account current skill levels, defines future skill needs, and incorporates developmental activities in areas needing improvement.

However, individuals could do all of the above and still not progress in their career as desired. Few career plans are enacted as written. Organizational realities affect the implementation of one's career plan, and opportunities sometimes arise which are not foreseen (Walker, 1976). Therefore, it is important to understand organizational factors affecting career progression and to incorporate organizational needs, programs, and constraints into individual career management plans and activities.

ORGANIZATIONAL FACTORS AFFECTING CAREER PROGRESSION

Organizational factors that influence career progression include the organization's needs as defined by the job opportunities available and career paths associated with those job opportunities (Walker, 1976; Ouchi & Jaeger, 1978; Blau et al., 1956), the organization's career movement policies and personnel support systems (Ouchi & Jaeger, 1978; Stumpf & London, 1981b), and the individual or group involved in making the decision to offer a particular career opportunity to someone (Stumpf & London, 1981b).

Recent work by Ouchi (1981) and Ouchi and Jaeger (1978) suggests that organizations evolve identifiable patterns of managing their employees. The effectiveness of these patterns for the organization depends on how well the pattern satisfies the demands placed on the organization by its social and competitive environment. Ouchi and Jaeger (1978) label the conventional American organization Type A as one pattern of management, and Japanese firms Type J as another pattern of management. Type A characteristics include short-term employment (i.e., the average employee has limited tenure), rapid evaluation and promotion, and specialized career paths. In contrast, Type J characteristics include secure employment, slow evaluation and promotion, and nonspecialized career paths. A third type of organization, referred to as Type Z, is recommended for many American organizations given recent social changes (Ouchi & Jaeger, 1978). Type Z is characterized by long-term employment (but not guaranteed), slow evaluation and promotion, and moderately specialized career paths. Given such patterns of organizational career management, individuals are likely to experience different career opportunities and constraints as a function of the type of organization.

Careers are also influenced by the human resource management systems that organizations develop to facilitate their decision making about individuals. The more sophisticated and useful human resource management systems include: (1) human resource planning for future labor, technical, and managerial needs; (2) a selection system that results in the employment of competent individuals who have potential and motivation for career progression and who are likely to remain with the organization for several years; (3) an assessment system which appraises current performance, identifies areas in need of improvement, and is able to predict who will perform effectively at higher levels; (4) a career planning process to assist employees in self-assessment and career development; (5) relevant and useful training and development opportunities and experiences; and

(6) staffing support systems and policies to facilitate career progression by providing the enabling information to employees so they can co-manage their careers with the organization. Such systems typically evolve over time as organizations become more precise and systematic in their dealings with their employees. They are also likely to develop in different ways as a function of the culture and industry in which the organization exists (Ouchi, 1981).

Organizational Career Management

From an organizational perspective, career management encompasses (1) moving personnel, usually laterally and vertically, throughout the organization, (2) filling positions with the most

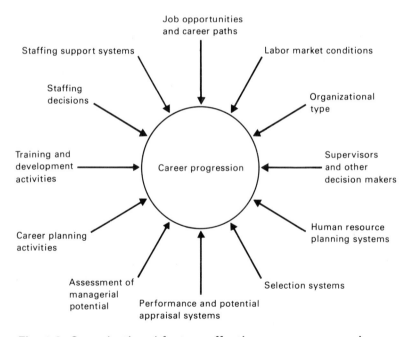

Fig. 1.2 *Organizational factors affecting career progression*

qualified personnel, and (3) providing individuals with challenging developmental experiences. Organization-sponsored career planning programs and training and development activities should be part of the career management process. This process involves supervisors who to some extent are responsible for the development of their subordinates and for making decisions affecting subordinates' careers. It also involves human resource specialists who design and operate career management systems and are responsible for developing and implementing organizational policies regarding career management. Effective career management maintains a standard of excellence at all organizational levels. This is accomplished through the interrelated human resource functions of personnel planning, selection, assessment of performance and potential, career planning, training and development, and staffing decisions (see Fig. 1.2).

SUMMARY

This chapter defined several terms associated with careers and distinguished between the processes of individual and organizational career management. Individuals can facilitate their careers by developing a clear, realistic, and accurate picture of their skills, interests, and personal orientations in relation to career goals and work-role preferences. Career planning should take into account current skill levels and developmental activities to meet future skill needs. At the same time, organizational realities must be recognized. Organizational career management refers to the processes and support systems that affect individual career progression and organizational effectiveness. These include career planning programs, training courses, and staffing procedures for moving personnel.

OUTLINE OF THE BOOK

The chapters that follow expand on individual and organizational career management roles. The general context of each chapter relative to the other chapters is shown in Table 1.1.

TABLE 1.1
Summary of Career Management Activities and Book Chapters

OVERVIEW OF CAREER MANAGEMENT (CHAPTERS 1 AND 2)

Individual Roles in Career Management	Shared Roles	Organizational Roles
Self-assessment (Chapter 3)	Career planning (Chapter 5)	Staffing (Chapter 7)
Individual characteristics affecting careers (Chapter 4)	Training and development (Chapter 6)	Staffing support systems (Chapter 8)

Chapter 2 completes the introductory section by presenting a study of one individual's career and the career management systems in his organization. The case demonstrates the complexity of an individual's career as it evolves over time and the variety of organizational systems and decisions which affect a career. This is valuable in understanding the elements of individual and organizational career management discussed in the remainder of the book.

Section II focuses on the individual's role in career management. Chapter 3 discusses self-assessment and career planning processes and how they guide one's evaluation of career opportunities. Chapter 4 examines the socialization period which follows entry into an organization. It also discusses career management issues which relate to the subsequent years of one's work life with particular attention to individual and organizational career issues dealing with minorities, women, and dual-career couples.

Section III discusses career management activities that involve a sharing of responsibilities between individuals and their organizations. Chapter 5 examines organizationally sponsored career planning programs. Chapter 6 covers training and development activities that are typically available for individuals to enhance their skills.

Section IV extends the discussion of the organization's role in career management by addressing internal staffing decisions. Chapter 7 discusses the promotion and transfer process and establishes several guidelines for organizations to use in making internal staffing decisions. Chapter 8 expands the discussion started in Chapter 7 to include the organizational and environmental context of promotion and other staffing decisions. Support systems such as promotion policies and guidelines, human resource planning, job matching, job posting, and mentors and sponsors are examined as vehicles for facilitating career management. Chapter 8 concludes with several recommendations for improving the effectiveness of the career management process.

The epilogue provides a synopsis of the book and highlights ideal career management behaviors for individuals, and ideal career management practices for organizations.

A Career as a Sequence of Work Experiences

2

A career is a complex set of interrelated work experiences. These are interspersed with behaviors and thought processes involved in searching for and making decisions about career opportunities. One way to understand the potential value of career management is to examine a career in progress. We provide a retrospective analysis of one person's career and its organizational context to convey how career opportunities arise, the role of career planning, and how organizational processes affect career progression. Our purpose in describing an individual's career is to provide a common experience for discussing career activities and issues as they relate to both individuals and organizations.

We begin with a description and analysis of Len White's career. We then examine Metrobank, one of Len's employers.

LEN WHITE'S CAREER[1]

Len White is a vice president and head of the New Services Development Unit (NSDU) at Metrobank. He has been in his current position for two years, with Metrobank for eight years, and out of

---

[1]Readers with substantial organizational experience may skim this chapter without losing the continuity of the book. The case is referred to in chapter 4, so familiarity with Len White and Metrobank will be helpful. We appreciate the cooperation of the individuals and organizations involved in the case. All names are disguised.

college for seventeen years. Reflecting on his career, Len feels that things have progressed well. He earns $60,000 plus bonuses each year, has a budget of $1.3 million, and has the ear of several top managers. Yet, the promotion he is interested in—to senior vice president—still seems out of reach. He is unsure of what he must accomplish to attain his goal.

Len describes his high school and college years as very active. In high school he was involved in many social activities. He participated in sports, and ran for student association president but lost. In college he joined a fraternity and played interfraternity sports, but failed to make the two college varsity teams he wanted. Women moved in and out of Len's life until he met Jan in his senior year. They married two years later.

After receiving his undergraduate degree in liberal arts, Len entered an MBA program at an Ivy League university. He majored in marketing and sought employment in companies with good prospects for expansion. Using the university's MBA placement services, Len interviewed with several firms in the consumer package goods industry (e.g., Proctor & Gamble, General Foods, Lever Brothers). He received job offers from two firms and decided to go with CPH, which was the sixth largest in the industry. Len commented on this decision: "I felt CPH would give me the best training and career advancement opportunities. The company had a formalized career ladder for product managers (i.e., the manager responsible for all marketing, sales, and production aspects of a product), paid well, and was prestigious. Once you made it in CPH, you could go anywhere in the industry."

Len's simple but clear idea of his short-term goal was to become a product manager. His first job was as an assistant product manager on a new bar soap. This position involved substantial numerical analysis of market and competitive information by product, package size, geographical region, type of distributor, etc., and was the first step in the product manager career path. Assuming acceptable performance in a "number crunching" role, one would be promoted to associate product manager within one to two years. A second promotion to product manager normally occurred two to three years later. The responsibility would increase with each promotion so that promotion to product manager gave one primary control over a single product. This included product pricing, distribution, packaging, market segmentation, advertising, and product promotion. Since one's budget and product were part of a group of related products, one's decisions as product manager had to fit the product group manager's strategy.

Although Len felt that his early career goals were clear, he reported that initially he knew relatively little about what an assistant product manager actually did. The stereotype Len had was that of a product manager who would be managing a product, developing it by making changes, and coordinating the efforts of subordinates. Hence Len's first few years, though interesting and developmental, did not meet the expectations he had formed as an MBA.

Establishing Himself at CPH

During his first five years, Len's career was managed primarily by CPH; he was seldom consulted on job changes or career interests. After nine months, Len was moved to another product (a fabric softener) within the same product group but under a different product manager. While CPH referred to the move as a developmental rotation, Len was not sure how to interpret it at first: "Was I being transferred because I was good and needed elsewhere, because I needed additional development not available in my current position, or because my immediate superior did not want me any more?" The skills CPH was trying to develop in Len by the transfer were not made clear.

After a two-month adjustment to his new work associates and the duties of the new position, Len reported that analyzing fabric softener data was really no different from working on a bar soap. The fabric softener was somewhat more interesting to Len, given the newness of the fabric softener market. More judgments had to be made based on less information, and he was involved in some of those judgments.

The Advancement Years

During his second year at CPH Len was promoted to associate product manager on the fabric softener. He was transferred ten months later to a new clothes washing detergent, and moved back after a year to a fabric softener as a product manager. While each move was somewhat disruptive to Len's social relationships at work, he met several people, whom he worked with indirectly during this period, who would subsequently affect other career moves. The most notable of these was a superior, Pete Fallon. "I really enjoyed and learned from Pete. He was one of those people who was always getting involved with new things."

After being in the product manager position for a year, Len examined the aspects of various jobs that he liked and disliked. "I liked the feelings of success, the exhilaration of being promoted and accepted, and the career opportunities CPH seemed to offer." However, several concerns were growing: "Did I want to proceed into management which would involve more attention to financial data, accounting reports, and interpersonal relationships, or should I stay with my marketing specialty? How should I proceed from here—just work hard, conform to CPH, innovate, find and nurture political support, and/or be an outstanding contributor?" A third issue related to managing his family relationships in light of the long hours devoted to CPH. Jan was pregnant.

By the end of his third year as a product manager Len realized that the managerial career path was not right for him. He still wanted the higher salary, power, and prestige associated with managing, but not the day-to-day worries, interruptions, coordination hassles, meetings, and continual firefighting. Working on new products was more exciting, seemed to involve less general management, and was more marketing oriented than working with established products. He felt technically competent in marketing and enjoyed exercising his expertise in new products. Since Len had previously worked with the current group manager for new products, Pete Fallon, it was easy to approach Pete with his career concerns. Several months later when Pete was transferred, he recommended Len as his replacement. Len was subsequently offered the position of group manager for new products. "It was one of the happiest times of my life. My career seemed to be going in a direction that felt good; I enjoyed going to work. My family was settled into a new home. My daughter was four months old and finally sleeping through the night."

Len's job over the next three years included another promotion to senior group manager for new laundry and cleaning products. His most notable project was developing and analyzing the plans for a new plant to manufacture two new products. The plant would cost $20,000,000 to build, involve hiring 2,000 workers, and be the sole producer of two new products as well as have the flexibility to produce several existing products.

Quite unexpectedly, Len was approached by an executive search firm regarding a position in a smaller competing firm (Cleanit) that would involve the strategic redirection and expansion of its household cleaner line. Len's name was given to the executive search firm by an ex-associate at CPH who was now with Cleanit. "With relatively little investigation of the position, I decided to take it. The salary was better, the challenge was clear and entirely marketing related, and after eleven years with CPH I was beginning to feel the need for change." While the position had potential, the rest of Cleanit was not yet ready for strategic redirection or innovative ideas. When an opportunity at Metrobank presented itself eight months later, Len made another career move.

New Roles at Metrobank

Metrobank had been actively recruiting senior product managers from the consumer package goods firms to meet its goal of becoming a national consumer bank. Metrobank's goals required rapid expansion, new banking services, and greater market penetration. It was looking for an experienced and successful senior product manager to start as a vice president.

"I probably would not have changed firms so easily during this period if it had involved relocation. But it did not. Besides, I missed working for one of the top firms in the industry. Smaller firms didn't have the resources I needed to do new product development. Since I was only thirty-six, I felt I could risk another move, especially one that promised opportunities for growth and advancement."

The move to Metrobank was a major one in that the organization, its environment, and its products (actually services) were very different from the organizations, environment, and products in the consumer package goods industry. Yet Len agreed with Metrobank that his marketing and new product development expertise would transfer to banking. Having been disappointed with his brief tenure at Cleanit, Len interviewed with four Metrobank executives.

"It was the discussion with Metrobank's president that convinced me. Metrobank was one of the top five commercial banks in the U.S. It was embarking on a statewide expansion program that could ultimately double its size, and I had an opportunity to be in the middle of it. I would also be doing the kind of work I wanted to do—new product development and marketing."

During Len's first year at Metrobank he was involved in a new retail banking expansion program; he was learning about marketing financial services by being in the field and talking to branch bank presidents, officers, and consumers. About the middle of the year the legal/regulatory environment changed to permit statewide branch offices. The project quickly moved into the "brick and mortar" stage with twenty-three branches being opened throughout the state during the next few years.

By the end of his first year with Metrobank, an even bigger challenge was presented: the use of mini-computer machines to supplement bank tellers. Len became the lead marketing manager on a task force that might revolutionize branch banking. However, there were technical and marketing challenges that could result in millions of dollars of losses rather than a successful new approach to branch banking: "Could we get consumers to use the machines?" Len organized and implemented marketing research which subsequently suggested that consumers would use machines under certain favorable conditions such as low risk of robbery, provision of receipt, easy access and use, and "idiot-proof" transactions. Once it was reasonably clear that consumers would accept the technological change, it was necessary to get senior management's approval.

Len gave several presentations on the project to senior management (John Snow) and business unit managers in the Retail

Banking Department. After several months of discussion, presentations, financial analysis, and market research, the go-ahead was given: (1) to invest $36 million in bank machines, (2) to redesign branches to permit 24-hour access to machines, and (3) to heavily advertise the new service system.

After more than two years of task force development, the new systems were installed in over 200 branch banks. Len moved into the role of market strategy development specialist for the Retail Banking Unit, Consumer Banking Division (CBD), of Metrobank. After six months Len's role was changed as part of a divisionwide reorganization. Len subsequently became Head of Marketing, CBD.

During the development of the machine banking system, Len first met John Snow, head of CBD. When CBD was reorganized, Len began to report directly to Snow at Snow's request. Over the next three years, Metrobank continued its efforts to become a national consumer bank by offering banking services via direct mail (e.g., card products such as VISA and MasterCard, traveler's checks, etc.). Federal regulations prevented branch banking across state lines, hence efforts to become a national bank lacked the physical presence offered by a branch banking system. Len's role as head of division marketing was to provide marketing guidance to the various businesses within CBD on their development of new services.

After three years of working with the CBD businesses with some notable new service successes and failures, Len White suggested to John Snow that "the business units (e.g., Retail Banking, Card Products, Traveler's Checks) just don't know how to develop and integrate new services into their businesses. They are consumed with day-to-day operations; new services get second shift. What is needed is a new services development unit to help institutionalize the new services development process and pass along expertise."

After hearing such suggestions several times, John Snow created the New Services Development Unit (NSDU) as a temporary unit with an expected life of two to three years to get new services developed and implemented throughout CBD. John Snow commented on his decision to create such a unit: "We have been trying to develop new products for several years with only moderate success. Len knew more about new product development than any of the business unit managers or other staff members. The time was right to create a task force to improve our hit record with new products. I might have acted on Len's suggestion earlier except that Len has not always worked effectively with the business unit managers in his role on CBD staff. Sometimes his marketing expertise is perceived to get in the way of running a business. Len does not have 'bottom line' responsibility; whereas, the business unit managers do. Since it is difficult to determine the cost effectiveness of marketing methods and activities, ideas get suggested that are not easy to evaluate. When a business unit manager rejects marketing ideas or, more typically, stalls action on them, Len has been known to get upset. Hence, this new position should give Len some autonomy to get the job done."

During his first two years as head of NSDU, Len and his staff of fourteen banking professionals and six clerical assistants developed four new services. Two were implemented, and two were placed on hold by senior management pending a change in the legal/regulatory environment. Four other new services had been conceptualized and looked favorable based on initial qualitative research on marketability. The NSDU was doing well. However, the latest reorganization of Metrobank and CBD resulted in two layers of management now separating Len White from John Snow. John Snow had been promoted and a new layer of management had been created.

The success of NSDU and the Metrobank reorganization stimulated Len's thoughts regarding his career. "Where do I want to go from here? Have I leveled off at age forty-four? Am I beginning to stagnate? Should I redirect my efforts to teaching others and pass my expertise on to my subordinates? What can a staff person do to continue to progress in a line-oriented organization?"

ANALYSIS OF LEN WHITE'S CAREER PROGRESSION

Len White's career progression is a sequence of positions as outlined in Table 2.1. His career progression has been neither completely fortuitous and random nor intended and systematic.

TABLE 2.1
Len White's Career

AGE	CAREER RELATED EVENTS
14–17	High school; socially active, sports.
18–22	College; liberal arts, fraternity, sports, met Jan.
23–24	Graduate school; MBA, marketing, married Jan.
24	Joined CPH; assistant product manager on bar soap.
25	CPH; moved to fabric softener.
26	CPH; associate product manager on fabric softener.
27	CPH; moved to clothes washing detergent.
28	CPH; product manager on fabric softener.
29	Questions product manager role, Jan becomes pregnant.
31	CPH; group manager for new products.
34	CPH; senior group manager for new laundry and cleaning products.
35	Cleanit; manager responsible for product and market strategies.
36	Metrobank; retail banking expansion program.
37	Metrobank; marketing manager for task force on computer banking.
39	Metrobank; market strategy development in Retail Banking.
40	Metrobank; head of marketing, Consumer Banking Division.
43–44	Metrobank; head of New Services Development Unit.

Several individual and organizational factors affected each career move, and the salient factors influencing one move were not generally the same factors influencing the next move.

Len White's experiences suggest several issues that one must address for effective individual career management. These include: (1) the need for self-assessment, (2) the need to develop realistic career goals, (3) the need for specific career plans, (4) the need for training and development activities to prepare for target positions, and (5) the need for lateral as well as vertical job mobility. These issues are identified below as we analyze Len's career progression.

Len's initial entry into product management was the culmination of his interests and educational training coupled with CPH's recruiting and selection system. Whether Len would advance in CPH depended on his performing effectively as an assistant product manager and exhibiting potential to continue to do so in the product manager's role. Had his self-perception of his interests and abilities been inaccurate, he might have performed below standard and/or felt dissatisfied or unfulfilled by his work at CPH.

Given his effective performance at CPH, Len received two promotions in four years to reach the product manager level. CPH had also provided Len with two developmental experiences during this period through lateral transfers to a fabric softener and then a new detergent. Both product-related transfers were intended to broaden Len's experience base and expose him to additional CPH managers. When the fabric softener product manager left CPH, Len was considered for the position. He had experience on the product, was evaluated highly by the three supervisors he had reported to since joining the company, and was seen as having potential to perform effectively as a product manager.

It was not until after Len had been a product manager for a year that he seriously reflected on his work experiences. As a result, Len decided to seek a position that involved marketing new products. Since Pete Fallon, one of his previous superiors, was involved with new products, Len decided to share some of his career goals with Pete. These conversations influenced Len's decision to attend a Management Skills Development Program offered by a nearby university, and also led to Pete's decision to recommend Len as his replacement.

Len achieved substantial success while working on new laundry and cleaning products. When an opportunity was presented at Cleanit, Len felt he could be even more successful if he had broader product and market responsibilities. Len left CPH with little investigation of Cleanit, only to discover that the other Cleanit managers were resistant to new product and marketing ideas.

Len's opportunity to move to the banking industry after eleven years in the consumer package goods industry stimulated considerable thought. Were his skills transferable? Where might a career path in banking lead? How will this change affect family and life-style? Hence, Len considered what his career plan would be for the next several years. The plan would have to include developmental assignments to learn the banking industry.

From Metrobank's perspective, Len White was an interesting prospect. He had demonstrated skills and abilities in marketing, was familiar with new markets and motivated to attack them by developing new services, and had experience in the type of marketing organization (CPH) that Metrobank aspired to be. Metrobank's challenge was to provide Len with a guide and a thorough introduction to banking so he could apply his marketing expertise.

Len's first few years at Metrobank involved developmental experiences via job assignments just as the transfers he received at CPH were intended to be developmental a decade earlier. By his fourth year at Metrobank, he had worked his way into a division level staff position reporting directly to John Snow, one of the top twelve executives at Metrobank. While his relationship with Snow was exceptional, Len's ideas often failed to influence the business unit managers who reported to Snow. Snow provided the business unit managers with ample discretion to manage their units as they desired, as long as profits were forthcoming and the behavior of one unit did not adversely affect the others. This profit center approach taken by Snow resulted in few new products, and virtually no new products that crossed business unit lines. Len saw an opportunity to move out of his staff role into a position that had some line responsibility and was more closely linked with the business units. It also provided him with the opportunity to do more of the activities he enjoyed, offered him greater opportunity to influence new services development, and at the time seemed to be a strategic move with respect to his career plan. As head of the New Services Development Unit, he would share responsibility for new services with the business unit managers. Metrobank tended to promote more line than staff personnel, and this move provided Len with more line responsibility and exposure to line activities.

Len's move from head of Division Marketing to head of NSDU is an example of career progression that involves a lateral move. Len's pay increased marginally, and his status became more tenuous as his reporting relationship with John Snow was replaced with two intermediate reporting relationships. His influence on some issues increased (e.g., new services), while it decreased on others (e.g., existing services and marketing strategy in general).

METROBANK AS AN EMPLOYER

Two years prior to Len's employment at Metrobank, the bank began to design and implement a human resource planning and career development system which would provide: (1) a personnel data base to identify and categorize top talent, (2) a management information system to make use of the data base in filling critical jobs, and (3) a career development program to ensure that the careers of the most talented individuals were being managed effectively.

The need for a personnel inventory, allocation process, and career development program stemmed from rapid growth and market expansion into additional consumer banking services. Managerial jobs at all levels were being created due to the expansion, and there was insufficient talent within the organization to fill the newly created positions. This lack of available talent from within heightened the need for future human resource planning. Scores of management trainees were hired, many with MBA degrees from top ranking universities. While the management trainees progressed rapidly to the junior officer level, there was still a gap in managerial talent in middle management. Hence, Metrobank began recruiting middle level managers from outside.

Len White was hired at a time when Metrobank was hiring many middle level managers from *outside* the banking industry. Based on an analysis of current and future needs, top management identified two areas of expertise that were needed but not currently available within the banking industry: marketing managers and operations managers. The former were recruited from major consumer package goods firms, the latter from manufacturing organizations such as Ford and General Motors.

Metrobank followed the strategy of hiring highly skilled middle managers to reduce their training costs and shorten the amount of time required for a new hire to become effective. The underlying assumption was that it would be more efficient to transfer marketing or operations management skills to banking than to train bankers in marketing or operations management. Given this strategy, it was necessary to develop the new hire's knowledge of banking.

New middle managers and college hires were typically assigned to several projects and rotated through several positions in their first few years to provide developmental experiences. However, the dramatic growth of Metrobank made adhering to historic career paths difficult. The results of this unilateral organizational career management with little regard for individual career plans did not become clear for several years. Many individuals were progressing rapidly; middle management was viewed as effective, and Metrobank was rated as one of the best managed corporations in the United States by *Dun's Review.* While some managers were highly committed to Metrobank, others were not and quietly waited for an opportunity to leave. Turnover among recent college hires was higher than the industry average. This increased the costs of recruitment and selection, and lowered productivity at the junior officer level.

Metrobank recently estimated the cost of management trainee turnover to range from $20,000 to $100,000 *per person* depending on the type of position and amount of formal in-house training required. Given the turnover of high potential individuals whom Metrobank had hoped not to lose, the cost of replacing management trainees was several million dollars per year.

SUMMARY

Len White and Metrobank provide a context for examining individual and organizational career management issues. No attempt is made at closure by providing career direction for Len White or by resolving Metrobank's turnover problems. Clearly, Len is at another pivotal stage in his career. We will meet Len again in Chapter 4 when we present the case of one of his subordinates. Metrobank is also at a pivotal stage in designing and implementing career management systems. The decision to select and train experienced marketing and operations managers was linked with growth and change in the bank. The decision seemed to pay off, yet new problems apparently emerged when individuals were not involved in making decisions affecting their careers.

The next section of the book covers individual career management processes and discusses problems faced by several subgroups. Section III presents organizational strategies for facilitating individual career management, specifically career planning programs, and training and development activities. The final section deals with internal staffing processes and organizational career management support systems.

Section II
The Individual's Role in Career Management

Establishing the Groundwork for Individual Career Management

3

The last two chapters introduced individual and organizational career management concepts and provided a comprehensive example. The next two chapters focus on the individual's role in career progression. Chapter 3 describes the processes of self-assessment and developing realistic career objectives and plans. Special attention is given to assessing prospective positions and to understanding how organizational recruitment and selection practices affect individual career actions. Appendix B provides exercises for self-assessment and establishing career objectives. Chapter 4 discusses career management throughout one's career and bridges the gap between the individual and the organization by reviewing issues both must face.

In Chapter 1 we suggested that three things are essential for effective career progression. First, one must have an accurate view of where one is now; specifically, knowledge of one's skills, interests, and preferred life-style. Second, one must have a personal definition of career success. This includes having an idea of the work-roles and activities that lead to feelings of success and the future jobs or positions that may satisfy career, social, and family needs. It also entails having a realistic set of plans and action steps to progress from where one is now to where one wants to be in the short and long term. To the extent that the plans and actions are flexible and sensitive to organizational opportunities and constraints, they are more likely to result in effective career progression.

These three elements—self-assessment, establishment of career objectives, and career planning and actions—are the essence of individual career management. They reflect a dynamic process whereby each element interacts with and affects the others. As suggested in Fig. 3.1, one cannot establish personally meaningful and feasible career objectives without an accurate self-assessment and a review of environmental opportunities and constraints. For example, establishing a career goal of becoming a medical doctor when one dislikes and does poorly in science courses, does not enjoy helping others, and prefers a 9-to-5 workday hardly seems feasible. However, it is often necessary to consider one's ideal career objectives in order to stimulate an assessment of the skills and interests relevant to such a career preference. As one develops a career plan and begins to take career actions, information is acquired which can alter one's self-assessment and/or career objectives. Although the career management process is dynamic, one must start somewhere in order to improve one's career progression possibilities. We begin with self-assessment.

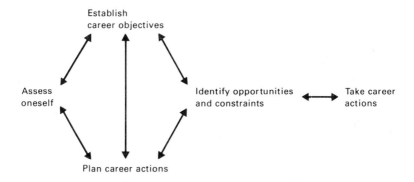

Fig. 3.1 *The groundwork for career progression*

HOW TO CONDUCT A SELF-ASSESSMENT

Self-assessment involves a systematic process of generating data about oneself and analyzing that data to provide guidance for career and life decisions. Such guidance should take the form of specific self-identity statements which capture accurate aspects of one's identity vis-à-vis one's ego, affiliations, family, and work-roles. Self-assessment typically leads to greater personal awareness and understanding. Self-assessment can be used to define possible career work-roles, identify training and development needs, and guide one's career progression. An accurate self-assessment provides an information base on which to make such career decisions as:

1. Which jobs and positions to seek or avoid.
2. What strategy to employ for getting a particular job.
3. Selecting a job from among alternative job offers.
4. Accepting assignments, transfers, and location changes.
5. Selecting a sequence of job moves to attain one's preferred position.

Self-assessment provides the information necessary, although not sufficient, to facilitate a better match between the individual and the job. Holland (1973) proposes a theory and substantial empirical evidence supporting the value of a personality–vocational choice match. O'Reilly (1977), Stumpf (1981b), and others support the benefits of a person–job match with respect to both job attitudes and performance variables. Cobrun (1975) reports similar findings demonstrating that feelings of person–job incongruence are related to negative job attitudes and perceptions of ill health. Hence, the value of self-assessment is in improving the *likelihood* of seeking and selecting jobs that fit one's skills, interests, and personality. One must act on the insights and plans formulated as a result of self-assessment in order to manage effectively his or her career.

Given the potential benefit of self-assessment, it is not surprising that there are dozens of books that advocate self-assessment as part of career planning (see Bolles, 1980). Yet, different authors recommend different self-assessment processes. While each self-assessment process encourages an accurate self-appraisal, some fail to provide the tools, structure, or methods necessary for one to accomplish the task. Since exemplary self-assessment workbooks are available in most bookstores (Bolles, 1980; Crystal & Bolles, 1974; Kotter, Faux, & McArthur, 1978), we focus on general guidelines for self-assessment. Examples of self-identity statements and their use in career decision making are also discussed. Exercises are provided in Appendix B as well as in the above-mentioned workbooks.

Our focus is on an individual conducting a self-assessment; however, it is possible for one to obtain an accurate and meaningful assessment without doing the entire analysis oneself. Career and vocational counselors and centers can provide an assessment based on valid and reliable instruments and years of clinical experience. Supervisors and peers can contribute meaningful information with respect to job-related skills and abilities (Storey, 1976a); family members may be able to assist in defining career interests and goals. Quite possibly, the most accurate assessment would involve a combination of sources of information and multiple analyses.

GUIDELINES FOR EFFECTIVE SELF-ASSESSMENT

Developing an *accurate* self-assessment is difficult because one is so intimately familiar and involved with the data. For example, self-perceptions of performance and others' ratings of one's performance often do not agree (Klimoski & London, 1974; Thornton, 1980). The differences between self and others' perceptions of performance are that: (1) individuals rate themselves higher than they are rated by others, and (2) individuals' ratings often do not agree with ratings made by peers or supervisors. However, individuals seem to be better able to distinguish among their own performance attributes than peers or supervisors (Thornton, 1980). This suggests that methods need to be followed in performing a self-assessment that reduce leniency in self-appraisal, increase agreement between self-assessment and other relevant raters of one's performance, and maintain or increase discrimination among dimensions describing oneself. We offer the following guidelines.

1. *Generate information without evaluating it.* The most common problem individuals have in self-assessment is that they do not make use of all available and relevant information. For example, if self-assessment indicates that an individual has many personal contacts each day, there is a tendency to evaluate that data without looking further. The person who stops here and describes him or herself as "highly social," may overlook the real meaning behind "many personal contacts." "Many personal contacts" may actually be more supportive of a concept relating to "enjoys many activities" or a "people-centered leadership style." Without further data, inaccurate conclusions may be drawn. Hence, the process followed should be first to generate information fully and completely, then to analyze it for meaning.

2. *Generate useful information from multiple methods and sources: don't worry about redundancy.* The more data you have on yourself, the more likely it is that you will have tapped most aspects of your identity. However, every method used to collect data and every source of information has its limitations. By using several methods and sources of information, each may partially compensate for the weaknesses of the others.

Table 3.1 lists several useful self-assessment exercises and instruments offered by different authors. Kotter, Faux, and McArthur (1978) suggest that one begin the self-assessment process by writing an autobiography which focuses on past activities, acquaintances, and work-roles. Several additional methods can be used to augment or support aspects of one's autobiography. A values instrument (e.g., the Allport-Vernon-Lindsey *Study of Values*) and an interest inventory (e.g., the *Strong-Campbell Interest Inventory*) provide self-report information which can be compared to others in the form of percentiles or norm scores (see Appendix B for sources of these instruments). Additional

TABLE 3.1

Exemplary Self-Assessment Exercises and Instruments

From Kotter, Faux, and McArthur (1978)

1. Write an autobiographical summary including a general scenario of your life, the people in your life, feelings about the future, the major changes which have occurred, the turning points, and the pros and cons of various career-related decisions.
2. Complete the Allport, Vernon, and Lindsey (AVL) *Study of Values.* The values indexed are theoretical, economic, aesthetic, social, political, and religious. (See Appendix B for information on where to obtain this instrument.)
3. Maintain a 24-hour diary of what you do over one (or more) 24-hour periods.
4. Complete the *Strong-Campbell Interest Inventory.* (See Appendix B.)
5. Develop a representation of your life-style (i.e., a pictorial, graphic, or written representation of your current life-style).
6. Document your feelings immediately after completing instruments and exercises.
7. Review your college application.
8. Summarize your biographical data.

From Bolles (1980)

1. Develop an inventory of functional/transferable skills along such dimensions as machine or manual, athletic/outdoor/ traveling, detail/follow-through, numerical/financial/ accounting, influencing/persuading, leadership, developing/planning, language/reading, instructing/ interpreting, serving/helping, intuitional and innovating, artistic, and so forth.
2. Document memories of the past.
3. Focus on your feelings about the present.
4. Stimulate visions of the future.

From Storey (1976a): Career Dimensions II

1. Document life/career concerns.
2. Document and reflect on past work experiences and attitudes, career tasks and interests, and career actions and reactions.
3. Complete a career choice/prediction grid which reviews your valued accomplishments and valued achievement skills.

TABLE 3.1 (continued)

4. Conduct conversations with select others to examine the validity and reliability of the predictions made from your examination of your valued accomplishments and achievements.

methods suggested by Kotter et al. and others include: keeping track of the activities one engages in for some period of time (e.g., a diary), displaying graphically one's visions of the future, reviewing past goal statements (e.g., the essays on a college application), generating a list of goals, documenting major accomplishments and analyzing them along a set of skill dimensions, and so forth (see Table 3.1 and Appendix B). When performing a self-assessment, use as many methods and sources of information as possible.

3. *Interpret information in the form and context in which it is generated.* While prematurely evaluating one's data is the foremost problem in developing an accurate self-assessment, misinterpreting the data is another common problem. Misinterpretation occurs when the information generated by a particular method is misunderstood or the context in which it was generated is ignored. For example, a frequently used self-assessment instrument is the *Strong-Campbell Interest Inventory* (SCII) (Campbell, 1977). This inventory provides an analysis of a person's interests based on preferences for various occupations, school subjects, activities, amusements, types of people, and so forth. It provides *no* information on the user's skills, abilities, or values. SCII results reflect a person's interests and compares them to the interests of people in various occupations. Therefore, interpreting SCII results as an indication of which occupations one could perform well or should pursue would be erroneous (Campbell, 1977).

In addition to understanding what a method or instrument is capable of measuring, the context in which one behaves and generates data must be considered. For example, after completing the SCII, several individuals commented that they responded to the items as *future* interests rather than current interests. If the SCII is responded to in such a context, it no longer provides the proper self-assessment information.

4. *Organize information into identity statements.* The most difficult and rewarding process in self-assessment is analyzing the data. Kotter, Faux, and McArthur (1978) refer to this as thematic analysis (p. 8): "It starts by focusing on specifics (information generated by the various devices) and from that slowly develops generalizations (themes). It involves sifting through large amounts of information looking for clues, drawing tentative conclusions, and then testing those conclusions against still more data."

Because the analysis starts with specific bits of information and moves to generalizations, it is important to stay close to the data, making as few inferences and assumptions as possible until a tentative identity statement is defined and substantially supported. Table 3.2 provides information supportive of a "Need for Diversity" identity statement written by Mary Johnson.[1] She generated this data following procedures outlined by Kotter et al. (Table 3.1). This included writing a 28-page autobiographical paper, generating a 24-hour diary, completing the SCII, drawing a life-style representation, maintaining a record of how she felt when completing various instruments in her self-assessment, and reviewing her college application. The results of her analysis were twenty-one identity statements, of which "Need for Diversity" was one.

The analysis process used by Mary Johnson was first to cluster her data into tentative identity groups, then to label each group completely, descriptively, and nonevaluatively with an identity statement. By postponing the labeling process until all the data were reviewed several times, it was easier to avoid evaluating the data prematurely. It was possible to search for patterns rather than impose them on the basis of preconceptions. Inferences and assumptions could be checked by reviewing the data listed together to see whether the information converged. Contradictory bits of information could be identified and used to challenge the integrity of an identity statement.

---

[1]We appreciate Mary Johnson's (disguised name) willingness to share her self-assessment.

TABLE 3.2
Support for Mary Johnson's "Need for Diversity" Identity
Statement

Quotes from her written autobiographical paper

My career position was too stagnant (after 1 year).

I wanted to make a move.

I became involved in all activities from softball to the Spanish Club, drama, class president.

Lifeguard during summers; would have preferred a variety of experiences.

I was anxious to leave Jonesville.

I always wanted to study abroad.

Denver opened up new opportunities.

I became more inclined to try new things.

My existence revolved around myself which I found very depressing.

Split with boyfriend who never liked to do anything different.

I learned how important "mixing" is to me.

Went to Paris and Madrid alone to pursue activities and friends which I chose.

Attracted to Denver and college by new and interesting people and experiences.

Second job at NBC represented an exciting world.

Changes refer to new environment, opportunities, challenges.

24-hour diary

Didn't finish class assignment—too boring.

Noted over 15 different activities within 24 hours.

Changed activities quickly once closure was obtained.

College application

Included many diverse activities.

Feelings record

Written autobiography: Got bored with writing about myself.

Life-style representation: Relief at present life-style, more time for friends and other activities.

The development of identity statements is a time-consuming, emotionally demanding process that involves substantial analytical skill. Unfortunately, not all people are good at self-analysis; some need assistance in the process. Two forms of assistance are usually available: practice with feedback, and counseling. Self-assessment and career planning books such as those mentioned above provide exercises to guide one's analytical thinking, encourage one to work with others (classmates, work associates, a supervisor, friends, family), and identify sources for career counseling.

5. *Assess the accuracy and importance of identity statements.* Once self-assessment information has been generated and organized into tentative identity groups, the data within each group are reviewed, and a descriptive, nonevaluative label is applied. The labels provide a way of concisely communicating one's identity to others. The accuracy of a label can be estimated by examining the homogeneity of the data supporting it. If there are many bits of information from many sources that tell a consistent story with few contradictions, then the identity statement is likely to be both accurate and important. In contrast, if there are relatively few bits of information from few sources which give a mixed or contradictory message, the identity statement is likely to be less accurate and less important. Reviewing identity statements for accuracy and importance makes it possible to refine the self-assessment.

6. *Cluster identity statements to facilitate drawing implications for career decision making.* Just as several bits of information provide greater support for an identity statement, clusters of identity statements provide greater support for the work-role and life implications drawn from those statements. Mary Johnson's identity statements are presented and clustered into five groups in Table 3.3. These were developed by her, without counseling, as the output of her self-assessment.

While Mary Johnson developed this set of twenty-one identity statements which she grouped into five categories, other self-assessments identify different statements and different groups. After reviewing several hundred self-assessments, we

TABLE 3.3
Mary Johnson's 21 Identity Statements as Developed and Grouped by Her

Artistic interests and inclinations

1. Attraction to aesthetically pleasing elements in life.
2. Desire for attractive surroundings.
3. Importance of money as a vehicle for aesthetic satisfaction.
4. Fascination with and desired exposure to foreign cultures.

Maintain control over life's many facets

5. Balance of work, social, and family.
6. Control over time and activities.
7. Need to be focused to accomplish tasks.
8. Need for diversity to enrich life's activities. (See Table 3.2 for support for this identity statement.)

Strong internal pressure to accomplish things

9. High need to achieve.
10. Expected high performance in all tasks.
11. Challenging activities take priority.
12. Will take initiative to get things done.
13. Need to be recognized for performance.
14. Attracted to symbols of prestige.

Must operate from a secure position

15. Strong affiliations with family as source of support.
16. Resist unfamiliar situations which seem to have high risk.
17. Avoid conflict in favor of compromise.

Need for social interaction and influence

18. Relationships with colleagues affect career decisions.
19. Influencing others through social interaction is fulfilling.
20. Often express opinions and feelings to influence others.
21. When influence attempts are ineffective, prefer to perform alone.

believe there are over one hundred possible themes of which twenty to thirty characterize each individual.

7. *Draw implications for career decision making.* The self-assessment process is of little value unless reasonable career

TABLE 3.4

Excerpts from Mary Johnson's Career Implications Based on Her Identity Statements

On the basis of my self-assessment, I believe that my career is the logical focus of my life. It has the potential to satisfy my need to accomplish things and need for security as well as my aesthetic interests, if managed effectively.

I plan to seek positions in a creative industry such as cosmetics or advertising. While the industry should be creative, the position needs to be creative only to the extent that I can engage in many different types of activities and interact with different people.

While my career should be demanding in order to fulfill my need to achieve and be recognized, it should not run me. I must be in control and able to establish a balanced life. Although I would probably not be satisfied with a "9-to-5" job, I must feel free enough to help my spouse in his career, manage our home, and devote attention to our marriage. I would not mind working late, but not for show. Time wasted is time I could spend achieving a balance.

I would probably be more satisfied with a medium-size rather than a large institution. I need a place to shine, seek out challenges, and demonstrate my abilities. A medium-size, though still prestigious, organization might be more impressed with my credentials and give me the opportunity to influence others and form relationships.

I have a strong need for "people contact," and in fact, dynamic interaction with people has often served as a prime source of satisfaction. However, I don't prefer to work on a team. Therefore, I should engage in work which I can accomplish alone, but which requires a large degree of interaction with people.

In order to satisfy my desire to influence people, I should be in a position to provide input to my boss, who presumably would be effective with his or her boss. I must be able to function individually and express my opinions so that they will be heard.

I would prefer to have friendly, although not close, relationships with people at work. I fulfill my needs for closeness through my family, and I am not inclined to devote the time to becoming close to many people outside that sphere. However, I find friendly relationships gratifying and I prefer to work in a warm atmosphere where conflicts can be easily resolved.

implications are drawn from one's identity statements. Therefore, identity statements must be used to analyze the feasibility of various career possibilities. Excerpts from Mary Johnson's career implications are presented in Table 3.4. She has begun to focus her attention on industries that involve creativity, on medium-size organizations, and on positions where she can engage in many different activities and interact with people. She is also interested in a position where she can maintain control over her hours, activities, and affiliations, and thereby balance work and family roles.

Self-assessment has several benefits: (1) It allows identifying strengths and weaknesses which help establish realistic career objectives. (2) It provides an information base from which to present oneself on a resumé and in job interviews. (3) It provides a framework for generating questions to be answered in the career exploration process. (4) It suggests compatible and incompatible work-roles. Some benefits of self-assessment are discussed below in the context of establishing career objectives, career planning, assessing organizations and positions, and taking career actions.

BENEFITS OF CAREER OBJECTIVES

As Cheshire Puss said to Alice, it doesn't much matter which path you follow if you don't know where you want to end up. But of course we all know where we want to end up—or do we? When asked what their career goals are, most people respond in socially acceptable generalities. Responses we have heard from students and young managers include: "A high level position in either marketing or finance." "An accountant and general partner at a big eight public accounting firm." "The president of my own firm." "A high level manager in a Fortune 500 company." While these are career objectives, they are generally sought with relatively little idea of what work-roles and activities are associated with these positions.

Few people systematically investigate and collect extensive information on target jobs and the possible career paths to attain them (Ullman & Gutteridge, 1973; Posner, 1981). Establishing career objectives is more than stating a possible target job. It is knowing: (1) the work-related activities one is seeking, (2) the social and political aspects of the position, (3) the demands the position will place on one's personal time and family, and (4) the series of possible positions which would prepare one to perform effectively. A process of organizational assessment, suggested later in this chapter, indicates methods of learning about organizations and positions that permit one to collect information on the four aspects of positions suggested above.

Self-assessment, however, provides the data on which to establish tentative objectives and outline questions for exploration. Each identity statement indicates an area of strength, weakness, or interest. Does the target job utilize one's strengths, minimize one's weaknesses, and conform to one's interests? Information seeking questions can be tailored to a person's needs and asked in interviews with friends, associates, and individuals in the target job. By exploring the target job, it is possible to refine one's career objectives, evolve a career development plan, and take positive career development actions.

PLANNING YOUR CAREER ACTIONS

Career planning involves defining a series of activities that facilitate career progression. Before such activities can be planned effectively, possible paths between where one is now (using self-assessment) and the objectives one would like to attain must be explored (Stumpf, Colarelli, & Hartman, 1981; Colarelli, Stumpf, & Hartman, 1982). A number of possible activities, career planning methods, and developmental experiences are discussed in Chapters 5 and 6. The active involvement of one's current organization and supervisor is generally essential for effective career management; discussion of the organizational processes and individual career management activities relevant for those seeking to advance within their organization is deferred until the next chapter. Here we focus on career planning for entry level jobs.

Career planning for an entry level position begins by using the knowledge gained through self-assessment to examine various career options and then narrowing the search to the few most desirable possibilities. This involves focusing on an occupational area, then a job type, and finally the type of organization (Stumpf & Colarelli, 1980). This process is exemplified in the following case of Steve Wilson who is about to graduate with an MBA degree.[2] Steve performed a self-assessment as part of a career decision-making course and subsequently developed a career plan.

Steve Wilson's Self-Assessment and Career Development Plan

"During the past six months I have thought about who I am, what I like and dislike, what makes me happy and unhappy, when I am comfortable or uncomfortable, and what I want to do with my life. I do not believe that I will ever come to firm conclusions since I am constantly changing. But some things are relatively static, and I have some definite preferences.

"I want to work in a people-oriented task environment in which I can assume responsibility and avoid technically-oriented procedures. This partially limits my career options and excludes careers which are numbers-oriented or highly analytical. I am not inclined to pursue a career in accounting, finance, or computer science. Instead, I consider line management, consulting, or personnel as viable alternatives. I have never really considered marketing. My educational training in marketing is limited. Furthermore, when I think of marketing, I picture the highly ambitious manager who is actively monitoring the activities of both colleagues and competitors to make sure that he/she is a step ahead at all times. I envision a successful marketer as having deceived the public, something which is contrary to my values. I enjoy interacting with people in a helping mode. I am concerned with getting along with others, and I am influenced by them in my decision making. Although I realize that my characteri-

---

[2] We appreciate Steve Wilson's (disguised name) willingness to share his career plans and actions.

zation of a marketing professional is a stereotype, I believe these qualities were instrumental in my disassociation with this field of business.

"Line management is a viable career alternative, but I am eliminating it from consideration at this time. On the positive side, I evaluate a career in line management as providing the interactive environment I desire. It would give me a chance to assume responsibility as well as the opportunity to motivate others. On the other hand, line management also means maintaining an operation in a line environment. This would require such activities as developing budgets, maintaining equipment, and forecasting future needs. The people-side of the job is, therefore, consistent with my self-assessment, but the equally important operation-side of the job deviates somewhat from my interests.

"Management consulting is another option I am currently eliminating. As a management consultant I would be analyzing management and business problems. This would allow me to be actively involved in critical decision making and planning, which is consistent with my enjoyment of responsibility and setting and achieving high work standards. These factors seem to indicate a good individual—career fit, but there is more to the consultant's job. A good consultant is a confident decision maker and able easily to confront others and sell ideas. I am not that self-assured. While a consultant interacts with people in a helping fashion, much of the work is individual and project-oriented. Affiliations with other people will play a subordinate role in my job responsibilities in this type of work. Interaction with clients is limited during the first few years as a management consultant. Extensive travel is also typical. While travel is consistent with my preference for an active schedule, it would also create some inner tension, since it would disturb my close ties with family and friends.

"A consultant functions in a relatively unstructured environment and usually works on several projects simultaneously. This characteristic of the job is also inconsistent with *my self-assessment. I prefer structured and organized activities.*

"I have decided to pursue a career in human resource administration. Specifically, I am looking for a position with a large company, where I will be able to gain experience in each of the functional areas that compose the human resource department. I would like to be part of an on-the-job training program which will allow me to work on three or four separate assignments in a variety of task areas during my first two years. Initially I hope to gain a generalist background in the areas of labor relations, equal employment opportunity, compensation and benefits, wage and salary administration, training and development, and recruitment and selection. This short-term career objective provides me with an optimal type of experience, for after this generalist training I would be better equipped to make an educated decision to either remain a generalist (and supervise a personnel department) or specialize in a specific functional area.

"Personnel administrators need to be able to communicate effectively and work with people at all levels of education and experience. They also must be able to see both the employee's and the employer's points of view. In addition, they should be able to work as part of a team. I enjoy affiliations with people and am concerned about getting along with them. A personnel administrator must also be a good businessperson and manager. He/she needs supervisory abilities and must be able to accept responsibility. I like responsibility and the chance to assume a leadership role. In addition, my MBA degree has given me a general understanding of business. The informational interview I had with the employment specialist at General Foods indicated that human resource management positions generally required one to be flexible and able to handle a dynamic, fast moving, challenging, work environment. I enjoy a busy schedule, but sometimes resist change. However, I adjust rapidly once a change is accepted. This past summer, for example, involved lots of activity and changes. I was usually on the go,

interviewing different corporate executives and placement directors.''

Steve Wilson's Career Management

The above scenario is an excerpt from Steve Wilson's career development plan. Steve's thinking and analysis reflect his self-assessment and career objectives *as interpreted by him.* He has a reasonable idea of what he is looking for and has tested some of his assumptions and stereotypes regarding human resource management by interviewing an employment specialist at General Foods and working as a summer intern in personnel.

Steve began to enact his career plan by tailoring his résumé and cover letters to the human resource area. Many past activities, projects, and work-roles were reanalyzed for elements of, and accomplishments in, human resource management. His career objective was clearly indicated on his résumé, and the experience/qualifications listed highlighted human resource functions. Such targeting of one's résumé and cover letters is generally recommended (Bolles, 1980; Kotter, Faux, & McArthur, 1978).

Relatively few organizations recruited for human resource management positions at Steve Wilson's graduate school, so Steve decided to augment his five on-campus interviews with a letter campaign. Steve mailed out thirty-five letters to Fortune 500 companies headquartered in the New York City metropolitan area. His cover letter indicated his career preference for on-the-job experience in several human resource functions over the first two years.

His thirty-five letters generated ten interview offers. Of the ten interviews requested, Steve accepted eight. He also went on the five interviews set up by the college placement office. From thirteen first interviews, he received eleven call-back interviews. He accepted six of these and obtained four competitive job offers from which he selected the one which he felt best fit his career plan.

The exceptional success of Steve Wilson's job search may be due to his efforts in self-assessment, establishing career objectives, developing a workable career plan, and taking targeted career actions. Steve also developed and enacted a job-finding strategy that eliminated many organizations from more than casual consideration. He focused his efforts on those organizations that offered him the career opportunities he wanted. In so doing, he did not waste time and energy generating career opportunities that were inappropriate for him.

Some individuals who form accurate self-assessments do not receive as many or as favorable job offers because their search is poorly focused, the opportunities in their preferred area are few, or their record and their job-related abilities are not favorable. Others lack the necessary job-search skills. Still others are unable to form meaningful self-assessments due to a lack of patience with the process. However, recruiters report favorable reactions to individuals who have specific career goals, and unfavorable reactions to those who have vague or ambiguous goals (Kotter, Faux, & McArthur, 1978).

EVALUATING ORGANIZATIONS AND POSITIONS

After acquiring an understanding of one's identity and goals, the implications of identity statements can be refined by systematic examination of prospective employers and positions. Just as individuals have several aspects of their identity, so do organizations and positions. Organizational attributes are often defined by the organization's work and social climate; authority, task, reward and power structures; policies; and decision-making methods. Positions can be characterized by functional area, various dimensions of work, and reporting relationships. Part of managing one's career involves the investigation of organizational and position-related attributes so that one's goals, job assignments, and developmental activities reflect organizational reality. Organizations and positions that do not fit one's goals or assessed skills and interests can be avoided; those that do fit can be sought.

The process of organization and position assessment follows the basic guidelines outlined for self-assessment, with one notable addition: analyze the fit between you and the organization or position (see Table 3.5). Information should be collected from many sources with little evaluation during the collection phase. Once a substantial amount of information is available, it should be examined and compared with one's self-assessment.

In order to collect useful information about organizations and positions, one should sift through the volumes of written material in libraries, annual reports, etc., and then focus on the organizations and positions of interest. One of the more effective ways of investigating organizations and positions is to conduct *informational interviews* with current employees, job incumbents, or other knowledgeable individuals. Informational interviews differ from job interviews in that one seeks information, not a position—yet! (Kotter, Faux, & McArthur, 1978; Bolles, 1980) When one does not have personal knowledge of organizational members or job incumbents, referrals from someone one knows to someone in the relevant organization or position generally result in the desired informational interview (Granovetter, 1974).

Exemplary sources of information about organizations and positions are shown in Table 3.6. The usefulness of the various sources of information is suggested in Table 3.7. Written material and information from nonemployees is most useful in defining general dimensions of an industry or company. Interviews with potential supervisors and peers and direct observation provide

TABLE 3.5
Guidelines for Assessing Organizations and Positions

---

1. Generate information to fit your career identity without evaluating it.
2. Generate information from multiple methods and sources.
3. Interpret information in the form and context in which it is generated.
4. Analyze information into organizational attributes.
5. Assess the accuracy and pervasiveness of the attributes relative to your self-assessment.
6. Analyze the fit between your identity and the organization's attributes.

TABLE 3.6
Sources of Information and Referrals

Friends and family
- Who work in industry or company of interest
- Who know people in industry or company of interest
- Who know people with contacts

Written sources
- Career libraries
- Placement offices
- Dept. of Labor *Occupational Outlook Handbook*
- Corporate annual reports
- Investment analyst reports
- Trade publications and directories
- Journal articles about companies (e.g., *Forbes*)
- Recruiting brochures
- Advertisements
- Newspaper articles
- Industry/company case studies

People in industry and professions
- Alumni
- Trade associations
- Professional societies
- Visiting speakers
- Chamber of Commerce

Social, religious, and political organizations
- Kiwanis, etc.
- Rotary Club
- Church groups
- Political parties

People with contacts
- Bankers
- Doctors, dentists
- Lawyers
- Accountants
- Insurance agents
- Investment analysts

the richest information on career possibilities and the actual job activities that need to be performed (Colarelli, Stumpf, & Hartman, 1982; Granovetter, 1974; Reid, 1972; Jacoby, 1976).

Two examples of informational interview summaries are presented in Table 3.8. The framework used to generate these summaries is presented in Exercise 3 of Appendix B. The first example focuses on a senior financial analyst position in Metrobank; the second relates to a product manager position in a multinational manufacturer. Both provide a detailed summary of

TABLE 3.7
The Relative Usefulness of Information Sources

TYPE OF INFORMATION OBTAINED	WRITTEN MATERIAL FROM LIBRARY NEWSPAPER, TRADE JOURNAL, ETC.	INFORMED NONEMPLOYEES	POTENTIAL SUPERVISORS	POTENTIAL PEERS AND OTHER EMPLOYEES	DIRECT OBSERVATION
Industry characteristics	Most useful	Good	Adequate	Adequate	Limited usefulness
General organizational characteristics (products, location, markets)	Most useful	Good	Good, but why waste your time or their time when written material is available	Adequate	Good
Organization climate, structure, functioning	Limited usefulness	Good	Good	Good	Good
What it is like to work for this organization	Limited usefulness	Good	Adequate	Most useful	Most useful
Job characteristics	Limited usefulness	Limited usefulness	Good	Most useful	Adequate
Career possibilities	Limited usefulness	Adequate	Most useful	Most useful	Limited usefulness

Kotter, Faux, and McArthur, *Self-Assessment and Career Development: A Systematic Approach to the Selection and Management of a Career*, 1978, p. 121. Adapted by permission of Prentice-Hall, Inc., Englewood Cliffs, N.J.

TABLE 3.8
Exemplary Informational Interview Summaries

Case 1: Senior financial analyst, Metrobank

Primary functions and responsibilities:

Direct financial management accounting activities to ensure records are accurate, properly prepared, and maintained.

Monitor the accounts payable functions, which includes development and implementation of the procedures, exercising direction over the workflow, review of daily work, and related policies and practices.

Coordinate the preparation and consolidation of all budget, forecast, and reforecast information into meaningful forms for presentation to senior management.

Perform budget-related projects such as profitability analysis, and cost of product/service promotions.

Monitor the consolidation of all elements needed to produce monthly, year-to-date, and forecasted management profit reports and legal financial statements.

Analyze budgetary and monthly information and assist department managers in the preparation and interpretation of same.

Interact with internal and external auditors in their performance of their tasks.

Managerial roles performed:

The primary managerial roles of this senior financial analyst and examples of each include: *Interpersonal roles* providing challenging assignments to subordinates, encouraging subordinates, selecting personnel, training new employees, attending staff and professional meetings, and meeting with managers of other departments. *Information sharing roles* include monitoring work flows, auditing expense control statements, reviewing exception reports, disseminating results of meetings, transmitting policy letters, briefing subordinates, sending out copies of information, and posting schedules and forecasts. *Decision-making roles* include cost control, reorganizing the department, redistributing work during "crash programs," resolving personal conflicts, budgeting, program scheduling, assigning personnel, strategic planning, and resolving jurisdictional disputes with other departments.

Qualifications and requirements:

a. Education: MBA in finance, BS in accounting desirable.

b. Experience: 5+ years in financial analysis and planning.

TABLE 3.8 (continued)

c. Other requirements:
   1. Good organization planning and analysis skill.
   2. Good decision making.
   3. Good leadership and communication skills.
   4. Highly motivated and able to work independently.

Case 2: Product manager

The first thing I noticed as I stepped into the reception area were the fresh flowers on the receptionist's desk. The people seemed very friendly toward each other. The product manager's (PM) secretary came to the reception area and led me to the PM's office. I noticed that all the product managers' offices had doors but none of them were closed.

I asked the PM several questions that I generated from my self-assessment. The PM seemed very enthusiastic about sharing information about his work. He showed me some of the tasks he was currently working on. We had four interruptions (people popping in) and one phone call during the interview. I guess a few adjectives to describe the atmosphere are active, alive, and even fun. He said that his primary functions are scheduling and coordinating. He has to work 4–6 months ahead in scheduling new advertising material. Working with a future time frame, he often loses track of what day it is. He works closely with the advertising agency representatives who visit at least twice a week, and different people within his firm such as purchasing agents, sales people, market researchers, legal professionals, and production people. He tries to keep formal meetings to a minimum, 5–10% of his time, so that he can devote more time to what he calls "massive coordinating." Since 90% of his work gets done through other people, he said that flexibility is very important.

He stressed that a PM is a conductor, or a manager of other people's talents. Teamwork is very important and the PM must make decisions as to how to get things done through these people. He also said that he must develop people who work under him. His evaluation is in terms of his ability to meet schedules and whether he is consistently producing outstanding work compared to the competition. He is also evaluated in terms of his ability to interact with the advertising agency, including his ability to provide them with good direction. A small part of his evaluation deals with his ability to generate new ideas.

The PM said he likes to start work early; his weekdays at work normally run from 7:30 a.m. until 6:00 p.m. He likes to write all important memos and letters before noon so that he can review and revise them in the afternoon and also devote time for meet-

TABLE 3.8 (continued)

ings. He stated that he is a family oriented person and tries to get home by 7:00. He does not usually work on weekends unless he is on a business trip or has a deadline to meet. He said that he likes a balance in life and takes pleasure in the husband/father roles. He consciously makes an effort so that his work does not interfere with his family life, even at the expense of advancement if necessary. Through the course of a year he usually spends about 50 days traveling. He travels to supervise the production of advertisements, visit test markets, and visit actual markets to compare and contrast good markets from bad. He feels that it is extremely important to keep close contact with the field to know what is going on, rather than just interpreting the data he gets from market research.

When I asked him what qualities he looks for in job candidates he said verbal communication and confidence. He also said that he looks for people who seem willing to do anything to get the job done, not necessarily a superstar but a well-rounded person. Common sense is stated as the key to success in marketing. Once an entry level person is hired, he or she would go through training for a period of 1–2 years in different departments such as market research, field sales, headquarters sales, product management, promotion programs, and field support. After initial training is completed, there is high turnover because people trained here are highly marketable. However, once people decide to stay after training, there is little turnover. He felt that this was a good company to work for, the management was not petty, and it gives recognition to its employees.

---

the activities, responsibilities, and work-roles of the position analyzed and are exemplary of similar positions in other organizations in the respective industries.

The senior financial analyst example is a fairly objective account of the position—relatively little information is reported that suggests the interviewer's career concerns. In contrast, the scenario written on the product manager reflects the self-assessment of the interviewer, is a more subjective view of the position, and includes life-style issues as well as information on job content. Both informational interviews provide salient information needed for making job choice and career development decisions.

Examining Job Content

As the examples presented in Table 3.8 suggest, knowing what one is likely to do at work is important for identifying career goals that reflect salient aspects of one's identity and developing career plans and actions to achieve these goals. Several researchers have investigated managerial roles across many positions to identify the most germane activities, behaviors, and skills necessary to perform effectively (Mintzberg, 1973; Mitchell & McCormick, 1979; Tornow & Pinto, 1976). McCall (1979) summarizes the characteristics of managerial work as:

1. Very active, varied, and interactive.
2. Fragmented and brief activities.
3. Much time spent in oral communications.
4. Little reflective planning.
5. Information is the central ingredient.
6. Long work hours.

Managerial work has been classified by Mintzberg (1973) into three general categories of work-roles: interpersonal roles, informational roles, and decisional roles. The interpersonal roles involve representing the organization or work unit as its figurehead, leading, and liaison work with other business units, functional areas, or outsiders. Informational roles include monitoring the organization and its environment, disseminating information to subordinates, and acting as the unit's spokesperson to senior management and outsiders. Decisional roles include entrepreneurial activities, handling disturbances, allocating resources, and negotiating agreements. Some of the behaviors associated with these roles are suggested in Table 3.8 with respect to a senior financial analyst position. While each role is not likely to be salient in every managerial position, most roles are performed by managers in the course of a few weeks.

Other researchers have analyzed managerial work and evolved descriptive and evaluative dimensions such as planning, controlling, monitoring, supervising, and coordinating (Mitchell & McCormick, 1979; Gomez-Mejia, Page, & Tornow, 1979; Tornow & Pinto, 1976). To the extent that individuals have preferences for various tasks or activities, managerial roles and dimensions can be used to direct one's career exploration. Questions that reflect one's preferences can be generated for informational interviews. Knowledge of different positions can subsequently help in career planning. By knowing the salient dimensions of various managerial positions, individuals can direct their career actions toward positions that utilize their skills and minimize their weaknesses.

Common Preferences for Job Attributes

Self-assessment leads to the development of identity statements that reflect or suggest preferences for job attributes. While each person's self-assessment is likely to suggest specific job attributes that others may not prefer, there is likely to be some commonality across individuals in their preferences. Research on job preferences indicates three general findings: (1) a small set of job attributes are repeatedly identified as salient preferences, (2) individuals weight the importance of these attributes differently, and (3) there is only modest agreement between the attributes people say are important and the attributes they actually use in making decisions (Zedeck, 1977).

The job attributes viewed to be important by many individuals include opportunities for task accomplishment, opportunities for advancement, salary level, continued knowledge and skill development, possibilities for recognition, opportunities to be creative, congenial interpersonal relationships, flexible task assignments, security, and opportunities to assume responsibility (e.g., see Manhardt, 1972; Jurgensen, 1978). The relative importance of these attributes depends on a person's sex, age, career interests, and amount of past work experience (Manhardt, 1972; Zedeck, 1977). However, the largest differences seem to be idiosyncratic. Further, individuals who have not conducted extensive self-assessments seem to have a limited ability to state their preferences and then choose positions that fit those preferences, even when given clear lists of how specific jobs vary on the job attributes of interest (Zedeck, 1977).

Job Search and Choice Actions

An assumed benefit of self-assessment is that once individuals have evolved an accurate picture of their strengths, weaknesses, and preferences, they will be able to explore the labor market and generate job opportunities that fit their needs. The career exploration literature does not test this assumption directly due to its fragmented and often atheoretical nature (for reviews see Colarelli, Stumpf, & Hartman, 1982; Stumpf, Colarelli, & Hartman, 1981; Super & Hall, 1978). The evidence that exists suggests three possible job search and choice models: (1) a *maximizing* approach whereby individuals explore extensively and follow a subjective expected utility decision-making model (for a review, see Wanous, 1980), (2) an *unprogrammed* decision-making process whereby search is limited to the generation of a few alternatives, and choice typically involves only two competitive offers (Soelberg, 1967), and (3) a *satisficing* process whereby the information obtained is imperfect and choice is often constrained to a single offer (Simon, 1957; Dyer, 1973; Lippman & McCall, 1976).

Individuals in a favorable labor market or having a clear competitive advantage over others are likely to follow either the maximizing or unprogrammed decision-making job search and choice process (Wanous, 1980). However, individuals who face highly competitive labor markets may not be able to generate job opportunities that fit their preferences. This leads to satisficing behavior, or the acceptance of an undesired job alternative with the intention to quit as soon as a satisfactory offer is generated.

The above does not imply that self-assessment and the evaluation of organizations and positions are unnecessary under unfavorable job search and choice conditions. Job seekers cannot know whether or not labor market conditions are unfavorable in their preferred area until they have assessed their strengths, weaknesses, and preferences, and have explored the environment for opportunities. If one is unable to generate career opportunities in one area, self-assessment may suggest alternative areas. While most job seekers will *not* search for a position until a perfect match is found between their preferences and job attributes (Dyer, 1973; Lippman & McCall, 1976; Horwitz & Stumpf, 1981), person–job congruence is desirable (Stumpf, 1981b). Matching individuals to jobs is likely to be an iterative process whereby individuals redefine and refine their self-images as they explore career possibilities and experience specific work-roles (Schein, 1978). Greater person–job congruence is likely to evolve through changes in preferences, changes in jobs, and changes in one's work-roles in a given job over time.

ORGANIZATIONAL RECRUITMENT AND SELECTION PRACTICES

Up to this point, the individual's role in collecting relevant information on him or herself and on organizations and positions has been emphasized. The other half of the information and choice process involves what organizations do to recruit and select employees (Wanous, 1980). Recruitment involves sharing information on the organization and positions with people who are believed to have the relevant skills and motivation to perform well if hired and who will remain beyond a few years. The goal of recruitment is to attract suitable job candidates; the goal of selection is to evaluate the candidates and subsequently employ those who are most qualified. We review these practices here and then examine them with reference to individuals' job-seeking actions.

Recruiting Methods

A recent Bureau of National Affairs survey (1979) asked a sample of 188 organizations to indicate the recruiting methods used to identify candidates for managerial jobs. Newspaper advertising and private employment agencies were each used by more than 75% of the responding organizations. Referrals by current employees and advertising in special publications, search firms, colleges, and universities were used respectively by between 50 and 75% of the responding organizations. Other sources used less frequently were walk-ins to the employment office, professional societies, community agencies, and the U.S. Employment Service. Thus, organizations may use a number of methods to recruit college graduates and managers. This suggests that job seekers may increase the likelihood of generating viable alternatives by matching their methods of seeking job opportunities with the methods used by employers.

When asked which recruitment methods are most effective, 35% of organizations in the survey indicated that newspaper want ads are the most effective method of recruiting managers. The response to advertisements tends to be high and the costs low. Twenty-seven percent believed that private employment agencies are most effective, while 17% cited search firms as most effective. Only 2% of the organizations labeled colleges and universities as the most effective recruiting source for managers. Many organizations seek experienced managers who would generally not be available through college placement services.

A review of the recruitment literature found that new employees were likely to stay with the organization longer when they were referred by other employees compared to those who walked into the employment office or were recruited from want ads or private employment agencies (Schwab, 1982). One explanation for these results is that different recruitment methods tap job seekers from different applicant populations (Schwab, 1982). This suggests that job seekers should be aware of which sources organizations use to find different types of people. It also suggests that organizations should use methods directed to the populations they want to attract. Research is needed, however, to determine which recruitment methods are most appropriate for different populations.

Another explanation for the differential effectiveness of various recruitment methods is that some methods provide more accurate information about the job than others (Schwab, 1982). Applicants referred to the organization by current employees, for example, may have a more realistic picture of what it is like to work in the organization (Colarelli, Stumpf, & Hartman, 1982). Other applicants, influenced by overly favorable descriptions given by recruiters or described in newspaper ads, may have unrealistically favorable expectations. These individuals may be more inclined to leave when their expectations are not met (Wanous, 1980). Some organizations use films or company tours to generate realistic expectations prior to or just after extending an employment offer. These methods intentionally depict both positive and negative aspects of working for the organization.

Recruitment methods and information may affect applicants' attitudes and job choice behaviors in other ways. Rynes, Heneman, and Schwab (1980) suggest the following general conclusions about recruitment: (1) the recruiter's behavior and knowledge of the job and applicant affect the applicant's attitudes and choices; (2) time delays in organizational decisions regarding applicants reduce the applicant's expectations that an employment offer is likely; (3) employment interviews and pre-employment tests that are job or position related generate more favorable applicant attitudes. Another conclusion is that recruiters who have more job information make better recruiting decisions (Weiner & Schneiderman, 1974). These results suggest the obvious importance of selection methods.

Selection Methods

Job seekers are likely to face a variety of methods intended to evaluate their skills and predict their potential in the organization. Organizations often use a combination of devices in selection including multiple interviews, ability tests, personality measures, and business simulations.

A method that combines interviews, paper-and-pencil measures, and the simulation of work behaviors is the assessment center. The success of assessment centers in predicting advancement stems from the use of evaluations of behaviors that are directly related to the job rather than inferences about behavior or perceptions (Bray, Campbell, & Grant, 1974; Campbell et al., 1970). The high cost of conducting an assessment center and the logistics involved in assembling a group of applicants for one or more days makes this process less practical for selection than for determining the advancement potential of current employees. (See Chapter 5 for a discussion of the use of assessment center results in career planning.)

A review of selection devices, how they are combined, and their validity is beyond the scope of this book. The reader should be aware that a number of factors may influence the accuracy of a selection method. These include the applicant's age, race, and sex; nonverbal communication in an interview; decision-maker characteristics; and the hiring environment (e.g., the organization's equal employment opportunity-affirmative action policies). Interested readers should refer to a text on the subject such as Arvey (1979) or Cascio (1978).

Integrating Job Seeking Actions with Organizational Recruitment and Selection Practices

Individuals and organizations need to share relevant information to facilitate effective career decision making. Several aspects of effective job search behavior can be related to effective organizational recruitment practices. We offer the following guidelines (after Wanous, 1980):

1. Entering an organization is a *dual* matching process between human capabilities and job requirements, and between individual needs and organizational climates. Matching only capabilities to requirements is likely to lead to dissatisfaction for either the organization or the individual.

2. Job seekers often have inflated expectations about what their work-roles will be. These expectations are most seriously inflated for job content, responsibilities, and activities. Individuals fail to investigate opportunities extensively enough, and organizations fail to share the necessary information with job seekers. The best sources of information for job seekers are those from which the job seeker will develop realistic expectations, such as current and former employees.

3. Ineffective job search behaviors and organizational recruitment and selection can affect newcomers' *performance* and/or their *job satisfaction* and *organizational commitment*. The primary impact of job search and organizational recruitment is on voluntary turnover via low job satisfaction and commitment.

Organizational selection practices are more closely linked to job performance.

4. Realistic job previews can improve job search and organizational recruitment outcomes. Providing realistic job previews generally does not reduce an organization's ability to recruit newcomers; it deflates the job seeker's expectations. In deciding whether or not to use realistic job previews, an organization should consider the type of job and the likely ratio of job seekers to position openings. Realistic previews are most cost effective for positions in which turnover is high and costly and when the ratio of job seekers to position openings is high.

These four points suggest that accurate job information is likely to facilitate more effective career management decisions by both individuals and organizations. This applies to entry level personnel and those in later career stages (Wanous, 1980). For instance, accurate performance feedback is important at all career stages. Research has found that employees receiving a poor performance appraisal are likely to voluntarily leave the organization (Wanous, Stumpf, & Bedrosian, 1979; Stumpf & Dawley, 1981). This suggests that when given accurate job information, individuals may adjust their career paths without organizational intervention.

SUMMARY

This chapter argues that self-assessment, establishing career objectives, and career planning are the essence of individual career management. They provide the framework for identifying opportunities and constraints that lead to effective career actions. Self-assessment is the process of generating information on oneself and analyzing that information for career and life themes. As demonstrated in the self-assessment guidelines and the examples, self-assessment contributes to establishing career objectives and planning for one's early career actions. The case of Steven Wilson demonstrates how a job finding strategy helps one focus on organizations that offer desirable career opportunities. Assessing prospective employers and positions helps one to identify career actions that reflect important life goals. Organizational recruitment and selection practices have implications for job seeking behavior. Realistic job information obtained in the recruitment process as well as throughout one's career can facilitate effective individual career management.

Issues in Individual Career Development

4

The last chapter examined the early career period of people as they explore their vocational interests and needs, begin to define their career goals, identify job opportunities, and join organizations. This chapter continues our discussion of careers by considering career development once the individual has joined an organization. Career development issues related to one's career stage, race, sex, family situation, and nonwork activities are addressed. The experiences of Len White, introduced in Chapter 2, and Len's subordinate, Diane Jackson, introduced in this chapter, provide examples of development concepts at various career stages. Attention is given to career development problems faced by minorities, women, and dual-career couples. We then discuss the implications of nonwork involvement for career development. Finally, we review the need for organizational career planning and development programs.

THE CASE OF DIANE JACKSON

After receiving an undergraduate degree in mathematics, Diane Jackson started work at Metrobank in computer services. She left after one year to get her MBA. She worked as a summer intern the following year in a different Metrobank division. By the time she completed her MBA, she had developed an interest in marketing and received several job offers. She chose Metrobank because she was familiar with the company and felt that Metrobank offered the combination of financial analysis, computer applications, and marketing that she wanted. Her first post-MBA year with the bank involved financial analysis work within the Consumer Banking Division (CBD). She was given an opportunity to work on the minicomputer banking machine task force when the machines were first considered for in-branch use. The assignment "sounded like fun" so she took it. This was Diane's first contact with Len White.

Diane worked on the banking machine task force for nearly two years and was promoted to assistant vice president in the process. Since it was a task force, it was to be disbanded upon successful implementation of the systems and services. This meant that task force members needed to find positions in other CBD business units. In her task force work, she developed contacts with officers in the Credit Card Services Unit and they subsequently offered her a position. She was also offered an opportunity to manage a branch within the Retail Banking Unit which she turned down. "I didn't want to manage a branch, or even a group of branches. I figured Retail Banking was probably the way to progress quickly in Metrobank, but I didn't want that job." The position Diane accepted involved new services development work for Credit Card Services (e.g., VISA, Master-Card). Diane again crossed paths with Len White while working in this department. Now Len was head of CBD marketing.

Diane worked in Credit Card Services for six months before being transferred to the newly created New Services Development Unit (NSDU) headed by Len White. She reported to Len through an intermediate superior who was in charge of two new service concepts. Diane's responsibilities were to develop the service concept, prepare a test market plan, and coordinate marketing efforts with the customer services and systems managers. The NSDU's goal was the quick development of new services which would be handed off to the relevant business units within Metrobank.

The service concept Diane worked on for a year was one of the NSDU's two implemented successes. The service provided consumers with higher interest on savings than the usual passbook rate. Diane's performance was rewarded by her assuming responsibility for one of the four new service concepts NSDU had defined, but had yet to market. Diane indicated that she felt good about her new role, but really would like to be promoted to the vice president rank by year's end. This desire was made more salient by unsolicited interest on the part of another organization. She interviewed with a large electrical and appliance manufacturer's credit business for a position as head of new services development. The offer would be a promotion and included a 25% increase in salary and "the promise of a line job in eighteen months." "But I didn't want a line job in eighteen months. I like new services development work and want to progress in management along a staff route. I might like to run a business someday, but not by working my way up from the production floor through line positions. I talked to Len about this. He thinks that it's possible to advance in Metrobank to a VP level in a staff role, but he is not so optimistic about promotion to senior VP. Len has worked with some high level people like John Snow and knows a lot about Metrobank. Yet, the bank is so large it's hard to know what career information is really relevant to me. Len may not have the power to get things to really happen."

Len's conversation about his own career concerns (see Chapter 2) closely paralleled his concern over Diane's career. "What is the best career pattern for good people like Diane? She has the ability to be a top level manager in Metrobank, but chooses not to take the conventional route of becoming a line manager in a branch bank. Her promotion would reward a high performer and possibly attract other good people into New Services Development. However, it may be difficult for her to move into a line unit as a VP without previous line experience. Yet, she has been with Metrobank almost five years, has done an outstanding job, and deserves the promotion."

INDIVIDUAL DEVELOPMENT DEFINED

Individual career development consists of the work experiences and related activities that occur throughout a person's career which contribute to positive career outcomes and effective performance. Both the individual and the organization should be concerned with performance effectiveness. Individuals rely on organizations for income, identity, and opportunities to use and expand their skills. Organizations rely on individuals to conduct their business. Career development helps individuals use their personal resources to achieve their goals and, in the process, contribute to the organization's goals.

Organizational career development includes job assignments, training programs, interactions with co-workers, and other experiences designed to help attain career goals. Admittedly, chance affects career progress. We never know what experiences will have an impact on later events. Career development, nevertheless, is controllable and can help the individual progress in a desired direction or achieve explicit goals. Career development, which includes career planning, is a continuous process of related events whereby each work experience and training course builds on others.

Analysis of Diane Jackson's Career

Diane Jackson's career progression exemplifies the career development process. After completing her undergraduate degree she began work in computer services at Metrobank. Diane's training in mathematics provided a foundation for computer work, but left the computer applications up to Diane and her employer. After several months of on-the-job training and developmental work assignments, Diane decided that she needed additional formal training to expand her career opportunities.

Diane's interests and career goals changed as she earned her MBA and learned more about business. By the end of her MBA she was favoring a position in marketing that would capitalize on her skills in finance and computer science. The Metrobank position seemed to fit her career needs.

The bank's offer to Diane to work on the banking machine task force was not as casual as Diane might have thought. One of Metrobank's corporate policies was to challenge new management trainees with special assignments. While the task force position was not part of a formal career development plan, it was considered developmental.

Metrobank's decision not to place Diane in a business unit after completion of the banking machine project put all the career management responsibilities on Diane. To the extent that she was not managing her career and planning her next assignment, her career movement would have been either random or entirely fortuitous. While the move to the Credit Card Unit to work on new services was viewed by Diane as continued development, Metrobank had temporarily abdicated its career management role. Len White took up this responsibility again in his offer to Diane to join the New Services Development Unit; he subsequently designed a role for her to further her development in marketing new services.

As suggested by Diane Jackson's experiences, career development is not likely to be a programmed process mutually agreed on beforehand by the individual and organization. Some opportunities arise; others need to be created. A personal career development plan provides the framework from which to judge opportunities and developmental assignments. Diane evolved her plan a year or two at a time. It was not until she joined the NSDU that she formalized her career development plans in writing and shared them with management.

Career Development Concepts Suggested by the Experiences of Len White and Diane Jackson

Both Len White's and Diane Jackson's career histories suggest several concepts in career development that become relevant at different career stages. The concerns and aspirations of employees at age twenty-five are not likely to be identical to their concerns at age fifty. People change, organizations change, and life−family situations change. Career development must be considered in the context of other life interests and events. Five concepts suggested by the careers of Len White and Diane Jackson are identified below and discussed later in this and other chapters.

Is Len White a "plateaued" manager?   Possibly the most unpalatable thought for aspiring executives is that they will plateau at a level below their potential. Some individuals are organizationally plateaued, meaning they have the ability to perform well in higher level jobs, but the organization lacks top level openings (Ference, Stoner, & Warren, 1977; Veiga, 1981b). In contrast, personally plateaued employees are seen by their organizations as either lacking the ability for higher level jobs or not desiring further advancement. Both organizationally and personally plateaued employees can be effective in their current position (Ference, Stoner, & Warren, 1977). In these cases, their plateauing is more a personal concern than an organizational one until their performance deteriorates or they terminate.

Whether or not Len has plateaued is difficult to answer without knowing his superior's views and something about the mobility pattern for middle level managers in Metrobank. Since Metrobank is attempting to expand nationally, new senior level management positions may be created. Thus, if Len is plateaued, it would likely stem from his superior's perception that Len lacked ability for the next higher level.

Mentors can influence one's career.   The relationship John Snow developed with Len White closely parallels that of mentor and protégé. Mentors typically suggest developmental experiences and provide advice about how to succeed in the organization (Shapiro, Haseltine, & Rowe, 1978). Len's relationship with John, and John's power in the bank can be seen in the establishment of the New Services Development Unit. However, the recent reorganization in Metrobank which resulted in two additional levels of management between John Snow and Len may weaken the previously strong relationship. No doubt this is one of Len's current career concerns.

The sponsor-protégé relationship between Len White and Diane Jackson.   Similar to mentor-protégé relationships, sponsor-protégé relationships facilitate the career development of junior employees. However, sponsors are generally less powerful than mentors in promoting and shaping their protégé's career (Shapiro, Haseltine, & Rowe, 1978). Sponsors act as sounding boards for an employee's ideas and issues. They may guide their protégés and provide examples of what one can and should do to advance in the organization. Len seems to be serving in this capacity for Diane. (Mentor and sponsor roles are discussed in Chapter 8.)

Present career stage affects future career development.   Len is in the "maintenance" stage of his career (Hall, 1976). He has made a stable and productive place for himself. Career concerns tend to center on holding onto what he has accomplished and continuing along established lines. While hierarchical advancement is still possible in this career stage, younger employees are often considered and selected for higher level positions. Diane Jackson is a case in point. Twelve years Len's junior, she is in the "advancement" stage of her career. She has found a viable career field and continually strives to make a permanent place in it. While her career concerns a few years ago were to establish herself by building skills and developing competence in organizational roles, her present concerns center around upward mobility, independence, mastery, and achievement (Dalton, Thompson, & Price, 1977; Stumpf & Rabinowitz, 1981).

Life, family, and career issues need to be integrated.   Len's interorganizational mobility was limited to the geographic area where he first worked for CPH since he preferred not to relocate for personal and family reasons. This is just one example of how individuals deal with multiple aspects of life, family, and work as part of managing career progression. The growth in the number of women in managerial and professional roles has resulted in an increase in the number of families that must be managed around two careers. Such career management often requires substantial commitment to the dual-career reality, flexibility in the work and family situation, high energy levels, and effective coping methods (Hall & Hall, 1978).

RELATIONSHIPS BETWEEN CAREER STAGES AND CAREER DEVELOPMENT

The cases of Len White and Diane Jackson suggest that career development depends on the situation and the individual. One important individual variable implied in these cases is the person's career stage. A stage model labels different events in one's life corresponding to one's age. For example, a person progresses from childhood to adolescence, becomes an adult, and eventually achieves senior citizen status. In the process, the individual typically receives an education, chooses an occupation, is employed, marries, raises children, and retires (Super, 1980). Other major events may include military service, divorce, physical or mental illnesses, purchasing a home, relocating, and changing jobs.

Clearly all people do not experience the same events, nor must certain events occur at a specific age. Some people marry early while others marry late or not at all. Some work all their adult lives while others stay at home to care for children or aging parents. Moreover, all individuals are not affected in the same way by the same events. A period of unemployment may be devastating financially and psychologically to some but not to others. Nevertheless, defining career stages and the major events associated with them can be helpful in specifying the different tasks individuals accomplish, the conflicts they face, and the choices they make during their lives. This, in turn, can be

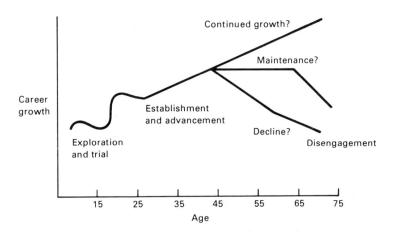

Fig. 4.1 *The career growth curve (From* Careers in organizations, *by D.T. Hall (p. 57). Copyright © 1976, Goodyear Publishing Co, Inc. Reprinted by permission.*

useful to organizations in helping individuals manage their careers.

Career stage models resemble biological growth and decline curves, beginning with an early period of exploration and trial, moving to a period of growth and stability, followed by decline and withdrawal from the work environment (Hall, 1976). Such a model is present in Fig. 4.1. While the stages shown generally correspond to a person's age, some individuals may repeat the cycle more than once. Each stage is discussed below along with implications for development. The relationship between career stages and career development are summarized in Table 4.1.

Stage 1: Exploration and Trial

During exploration and trial an individual searches for, and is recruited by, prospective employers (Schwab, 1982; Stumpf, Colarelli, & Hartman, 1981; Stumpf & Colarelli, 1980). After screening and selection by the organization, job offers are extended, and the individual makes a choice. Next, the person either participates in a formal training program or is placed in a first assignment. Several transfers and promotions may occur during the first few years. If the individual decides to leave the organization, the exploration and mutual choice processes resume.

Career development requirements prior to and during exploration and trial include self-assessment as discussed in Chapter 3, developing a preliminary understanding of the occupation and the organization, and having a formal or informal job preview. Wanous (1978) reports that a realistic job preview prior to or just after entering an organization lowers expectations, increases job satisfaction, and decreases turnover (see Chapter 3). Vardi (1980) suggests that new employees should be given information about career opportunities as a realistic career preview. Company recruiters should avoid promising more than they can deliver in terms of type of assignment and rate of advancement.

The trial stage requires time for reality testing, orientation to the organization, technical and supervisory training, and socialization. Experiences that are important during this stage for later success include early job challenge (Bowen & Hall, 1977), de-

TABLE 4.1
Relationships between Career Stages and Planning and
Development Requirements

Stage I: Exploration and trial

Elements:

Mutual recruitment; testing and screening; accepting a job; experiencing the first assignment; early transfers and promotions; deciding to stay or change organizations and repeat Stage I.

Requirements:

Developing an image of the occupation and the organization; previewing the job/career; taking a job offer; going through orientation and training courses; experiencing early job challenge, goal setting, and feedback.

Stage II: Establishment and advancement

Elements:

Having special assignments; being transferred and/or promoted; becoming visible to those at higher levels; establishing one's worth to the organization; receiving offers from other organizations.

Requirements:

Setting goals and receiving feedback; developing expertise; having a feeling of success or failure; reassessing self-image in line with opportunities; forming a career strategy; finding a mentor.

Stage III: Mid-career

(a) GROWTH

   Elements:

   Promotions, new experiences; being given greater responsibility and higher status positions.

   Requirements:

   Having the feeling of having "made it"; evaluating goals; fearing stagnation; needing change; adjusting career direction; working through mid-life crisis.

(b) MAINTENANCE

   Elements:

   Remaining in same job; possibly being transferred.

   Requirements:

   Realizing the value of job security; fearing the risk of change; expressing loyalty to the organization; having a feeling of pride in professional accomplishments; becoming a mentor; developing nonwork interests; planning a second career.

TABLE 4.1 (continued)

(c) DECLINE

Elements:

Being considered "surplus" by the organization; possibly being demoted.

Requirements:

Sensing failure, insecurity, and crisis; anticipating early retirement with few plans; disengaging from work and non-work prematurely; developing physical and/or mental illness.

Stage IV: Disengagement

Elements:

Assuming advisory role; mentoring; preparing for retirement.

Requirements:

Being concerned with teaching others; psychologically preparing for retirement; finding new interests and sources of self-improvement; learning to accept a reduced role.

Adapted from Van Maanen and Schein (1977) with permission.

veloping feelings of psychological success (Hall, 1976; Stumpf, 1981a), role modeling (Bandura, 1971a; Brief & Aldag, 1981), goal setting (Latham & Yukl, 1975), and feedback (Nadler, 1977). These experiences are discussed in Chapters 5 and 6 in relation to career planning and development programs. The socialization process is examined below as it relates to the exploration and trial stage of career development.

Socialization refers to how organizations attempt to change employees. Socialization efforts during the exploration and trial stage are aimed at newcomers as they enter the organization (Feldman, 1980). Newcomers typically experience a major change in role requirements, such as from being a student to becoming a financial analyst. The various work-role changes experienced by the newcomer are contrasted with what one expected upon entry. This leads to either confirmed expectations or surprise (Louis, 1980; Wanous, 1980). Louis (1980) suggests that surprise stimulates the cognitive process of "sensemaking." This process is one of attributing meaning to surprises by: (1) examining past experiences with similar situations to reduce the surprise effect, (2) interpreting the surprise relative to its immediate stimuli and context, and (3) seeking information and interpretations from others. As one is able to make sense out of the surprises, one attributes meaning to the events that led to the surprise and selects various behavioral responses. To the extent that the organization's socialization practices are effective, job-relevant skills are identified, work motivation and commitment to the organization are enhanced, and the role expectations the organization has for the newcomer are communicated (Wanous, 1980).

Unfortunately, the information gained in career exploration and the socialization practices used by organizations are not always adequate or effective. Webber (1976) identifies several common difficulties experienced by young specialists and managers, including: (1) early frustration and dissatisfaction due to conflicting expectations and an inadequate developmental relationship with one's first supervisor, (2) insensitivity to the political environment and insufficient probing of the work context, (3) ignorance of real performance criteria, (4) confusion over what loyalty means (e.g., obedience, effort), and (5) excessive personal anxiety. Being aware of these common difficulties can assist one in coping with them during this critical career stage of exploration and trial.

The job experiences one encounters during this stage provide a basis for further self-assessment and increased self-knowledge, particularly in the area of self-perceived skills. As one's self-concept evolves to encompass motives, values, and abilities, one develops what Schein (1978) refers to as a "career anchor." Career anchors are the result of the early job experiences and interactions between the individual and the organization. One's career anchor is viewed as a stabilizing force within oneself which encompasses motives, values, and abilities. Career anchors relating to technical/functional competence, managerial competence, security, autonomy, and creativity have been suggested as the guiding and constraining forces in different individuals' careers (Schein, 1978). Identifying one's career anchor and then using the anchor to guide and constrain career decision making begins in the exploration and trial career stage and continues in the next stage: establishment and advancement.

Stage 2: Establishment and Advancement

The second stage, establishment and advancement, often involves new experiences such as special assignments, further transfers and promotions, offers from other organizations, chances for visibility at higher organizational levels, and establishing one's value to the organization. Feedback and goal setting continue to be crucial as the individual develops a feeling of success or failure. This is also a period of establishing oneself as a professional and developing a level of expertise that is valuable to the organization and contributes to self-worth.

An individual's potential for advancement in an organization generally becomes apparent during the first few years (Howard & Bray, 1981). Individuals who are seen as having high potential should be given experiences that allow them to compete for positions at higher levels. Those who are good performers but do not have potential for high or middle level positions need to resign themselves to the fact that their hopes for advancement may never be realized. Most individuals, however, are neither stars nor failures. They anticipate future promotions and transfers, hoping to attain responsible positions in middle management. Forming a career strategy is as crucial for these individuals as it is for the "rising star." Establishing a mentor or sponsor relationship with one's boss or a higher level individual may be essential during the establishment stage.

Individuals can facilitate the process of establishment and advancement in several ways. For example, they can try to be at the right place at the right time by volunteering for visible assignments, requesting challenging tasks, and developing themselves for target positions. Individuals who rely on the organization to manage their careers are less likely to achieve their career goals than those who use some initiative. While realizing this is easier than doing it, risking interaction with others and seeking new experiences becomes easier with practice.

Stage 3: Mid-Career

Development in this stage depends on the direction the individual's career takes and the strength of his or her career anchor. Continued growth encompasses more promotions, new experiences, greater responsibility, and higher status. The individual may have the feeling of "having almost made it." But this does not necessarily mean contentment. Fear of stagnation may continue to drive one to reach the top, or it may lead to a reevaluation of career goals and redirection of one's career. A mid-life crisis, while not inevitable, is not a myth for many individuals who feel discontent (Levinson, 1978; Korman & Korman, 1980). Creatively resolving a mid-life crisis and constructively dealing with needs for control and affiliation are necessary during this stage (Korman, Wittig-Berman, & Lang, 1981).

Individuals who seem to be in a maintenance mode in mid-career are those who remain in the same job for many years or have had several transfers but few meaningful changes in responsibility or job function. Such individuals often value job security, fear change, and are loyal to the organization. They take pride in professional accomplishments, such as being recognized as the organization's expert in a particular area. Some may become mentors to others, passing on their expertise and showing newcomers the ropes. Developing interests outside of work and/or planning a second career may become concerns during this stage.

Transfers, job enrichment, special assignments, and other work-role changes may increase a manager's career interests during mid-career. Howard and Bray (1980), however, are pessimistic about the value of these attempts in mid-career, particularly for those in the maintenance mode. Expanding opportunities for achievement and autonomy assume that lateral transfers and job restructuring are possible. Even if transfers are available, they may involve relocating one's family, which the individual may not want to accept and the organization may be unwilling to pay for (considering that the average move in 1982 will cost the organization about $30,000). Enlarging the scope of a person's present assignment requires a willingness on the part of supervisors to alter subordinates' jobs, and doing this without affecting other positions may not be possible. Further, added responsibility and authority often entails sacrificing personal time which may be undesirable. Howard and Bray conclude that career planning for middle-aged managers is most worthwhile for those who have the ability, motivation, and opportunity to advance. For others, career planning may be busywork.

Some individuals face decline during mid-career. A demotion, being labeled surplus, or simply feeling obsolete are signs of decline. This is often accompanied by a sense of failure, insecurity, and crisis. Early retirement may be necessary, but planning for retirement may be particularly difficult. The individual mentally, if not physically, disengages from work activities and possibly nonwork activities as well.

Stage 4: Disengagement

All individuals eventually disengage from work. This occurs suddenly for some; it is gradual for others. It may encompass assuming an advisory role, mentoring, and/or preparing for retirement. However, teaching others is a role that does not always come naturally, and preparing for retirement raises psychological and financial concerns. Finding new sources of interest and self-improvement, and learning to accept a reduced role, may require considerable adjustment. Thus, life planning and development may be helpful during disengagement.

To summarize, each career stage contains different developmental issues and requirements. Exploration and trial is a process of developing one's self-image, testing reality, and developing commitment to the organization. Some of the career requirements at this stage are realistic job and career previews, training programs, and goal setting. Organizations typically try to socialize new employees to meet their work standards. The establishment and advancement stage requires a reassessment of one's self-image, forming a career strategy, and establishing a support system. Mid-career is a time for growth, maintenance, decline, or perhaps a combination of these. Growth requires evaluating one's goals while dealing with fear of stagnation and need for change. Adjustment in career direction may be necessary. Maintaining career stability requires expressing one's loyalty to the organization while developing outside interests, planning alternative career paths, and/or becoming a mentor to others. Decline requires dealing with a sense of failure and preparing for early retirement. Disengagement requires learning to accept a reduced role and finding new interests, a process which may be difficult for individuals who have continued to grow throughout most of their careers.

SPECIFIC CAREER DEVELOPMENT ISSUES

Now that we have examined the meaning of individual development and relationships between career stages and career development, we discuss career development issues for specific groups: minorities, women, and dual-career couples. We selected these groups for special attention since considerable evidence indicates that being in one or more of these groups can present some major career difficulties. This section concludes with an examination of the importance of balancing career development with nonwork activities and goals.

Just as different aspects of career development relate to various life and career stages, different subgroups of employees may experience or need different developmental opportunities. To assume that minorities and women require or seek the same career paths and developmental programs is an oversimplification not supported by organizational realities.

Career Issues Minorities Often Confront

Racial and ethnic discrimination is a serious problem in many employment settings. Minorities, especially blacks and Spanish-speaking Americans, face role stereotypes and a history of limited educational and career opportunities. Increases in the percent of blacks in managerial and administrative positions, for example, have been small. Blacks comprised 4% of this group in 1972 and 5% in 1978 (U.S. Bureau of the Census, 1979). Other minority groups have also experienced discrimination, although to different degrees and in different ways.

Judicial rulings, laws, and executive orders have limited the white male majority's power to control the jobs available to minorities and women. Fernandez (1981) interprets such recent developments as resulting in a power struggle between white males, who make up 37% of the population and who have dominated 95% of the managerial positions, and minorities and women, who make up 63% of the population and who have only 5% of these positions. The prevalence of racism in the United States calls for new insights and strategies if the consequences of equal employment opportunity-affirmative action efforts are to be fruitful (Alderfer et al., 1980). The causes and consequences of employment discrimination are too complicated to review in depth here. Below we explore general explanations for discrimination and implications for managing careers.

Forms of discrimination.   Fernandez (1975, 1981) described two forms of racism in organizations. One is individual white racist attitudes against blacks, what Blauner (1972) termed neoracism. The other is institutional racism. This refers to exclusionary procedures, rules, and regulations which have the effect of barring minorities from desirable positions.

Most often such rules were formulated without the specific intention of excluding blacks. It is simply that in our white-oriented society, most institutionalized procedures and rules have been made with whites in mind, especially white males. This has resulted in the almost total barring of blacks from equal and full participation in the society in which they are nominally full citizens (Fernandez, 1975, p. 197).

Fernandez (1975) provides several examples:

The most usual, time-honored way to advance within a corporation has been the slow one of gradual rising from the lowest ranks to the higher managerial levels. The fact that until recently all but a few blacks have been barred from the low levels of management means that this convention of promotion from within has become an effective means of institutional racism that keeps whites exclusively at the top (p. 200).

Racism also operates when higher level managers fill positions from outside the organization. Friends and other contacts are a prime source of candidates. Because most managers are white and have little contact with blacks, whites tend to be recommended for the vacancies. Another barrier is the importance placed on overqualification when it comes to hiring and promoting blacks. Fernandez (1975) found that many white managers believe blacks must be better than whites to get ahead and/or that organizations try to be more careful in promoting blacks because they want to be certain the blacks will succeed. Fernandez also points out that qualified blacks who are hired may not succeed because of the reluctance of whites to treat them equally.

Another career concern facing minorities is the lack of role models and sponsors in senior management (Sarachek, 1974). Past discriminatory practices have resulted in few minorities reaching senior management positions. As minorities now advance, they do not have others to look to for subsequent career guidance. This suggests that organizations need to offer career development experiences that compensate for the inherent lack of role models. Special assignments, involvement in task forces, and committee work with higher level managers may facilitate the development of minority group members.

Motivational differences.   Howard and Bray (1981) conducted a study of 204 college recruits in the Bell System during 1977 through 1979. The purpose of the study was to understand the career aspirations and motivations of recently hired young managers. Several of the analyses dealt with differences between minorities and whites. About one-half of the sample were female and a third were minorities (blacks, Spanish-speaking Americans, and Orientals).

The minorities scored significantly higher than whites on a questionnaire measure of motivation for upward mobility. The minorities were higher on motivation for money, suggesting that their higher career expectations were, in part, financially motivated. The minorities were less motivated than whites on task accomplishment. These results are consistent with research on black-white differences: "blacks have higher occupational aspirations than whites, . . . and do not have as high a degree of achievement motivation" (Kirkpatrick, 1973, p. 356). Kirkpatrick's (1973) review of literature on black-white differences in occupational aspirations, opportunities, and barriers also indicates that in the face of past and possibly still present realities, black job expectations are lower than their aspirations, and correspondingly lower than white job expectations. The primary reasons suggested include entry discrimination, advancement discrimination due to differences in seniority, and nepotism.

Minorities bring values to the workplace that are disconcerting to many whites. Minorities have developed operating and survival behaviors that often conflict with the traditional corporate value systems and modes of operation (Fernandez, 1981).

> They are much more likely than white men are to be forthright in their corporate dealings and to be more critical of corporate policies. Many will openly challenge supervisors, a practice traditional managers find to be a sign of disloyalty. They are more likely to take risks and to seek new directions. . . . By contrast, many white men . . . are more likely to be indirect, more conforming, set in their ways, and less likely to take risks (Fernandez, 1981, pp. 295–296).

Assuming that differences in aspirations, motivations, and behavior persist into the 1980s, organizations need to develop policies and systems for dealing with minority differences. Minorities need to develop realistic career goals, establish plans for attaining those goals, and then take relevant career actions.

Organizational policies and racial discrimination in employment. A step companies often take to help ensure that blacks receive equal opportunities is to establish goals and timetables for employing and advancing minorities. Fernandez (1975) emphasized that white executives should realize that such special efforts are not reverse racism but necessary actions to achieve real nondiscriminatory policies. Actions that seem like reverse discrimination should be considered compensatory until equal employment opportunity is achieved.

Jones (1973), a black executive writing in the *Harvard Business Review,* noted that most companies fail to recognize the crucial difference between recruiting blacks with executive potential and providing the needed organizational support to help them realize their potential. Based on his own experience, he made the following suggestions to help management overcome the subtle ramifications of racial differences within organizations: (1) Top management should be involved in, and committed to, an affirmative action program to hire, train, and promote minorities; (2) Direct two-way channels of communication should be established between top management and black trainees; (3) Managers should be evaluated and rewarded for their contributions to the company's equal employment objectives; (4) The temptation to create special showcase black jobs (e.g., "Director of Community Relations") should be avoided; and (5) Assignments for new black managers should be challenging but not likely to increase their chances of failure. These suggestions involve career development activities and assignments which would begin to overcome past discrimination. If applied equally to *all* newcomers, they are likely to help individuals of all races and ethnic groups develop in their careers.

Career Issues Women Often Confront

The number of women in the work force has increased considerably, from 18 million in 1950 to over 42 million in 1978 (National Commission on Working Women, 1979). The percentage of women managers and administrators rose from 15.9% in 1970 to 23.1% in 1978 (Employment and Training Report of the President, 1979). The number of women in these positions rose 79% between 1970 and 1978, while the number of male managers and administrators rose by 11%. Women workers, however, are concentrated in a few job categories, primarily clerical, sales, and service positions. These positions are often dead-end, highly structured, low status jobs with little career development potential (Powell, 1980; Terborg, 1977).

Two general types of discrimination face women in the work force: (1) job entry discrimination, and (2) treatment discrimination (Terborg, 1977). These are discussed below.

Restricted entry.   Restricted entry refers to bias in the selection of women for entry level jobs. Terborg and Ilgen (1975) cite three forms of job entry discrimination. The first is rejection of women applicants for non-job-related reasons. Sex discrimination is illegal in the United States, and women who have been discriminated against have successfully sued potential employers (Arvey, 1979).

A second type of job entry discrimination is failure to recruit women for certain positions. This subtle form of discrimination may be difficult to recognize, and it may not be evident to the women affected by it.

A third type of discrimination is lower starting salaries for women (Stumpf, Greller, & Freedman, 1980). Again, this form of discrimination is illegal and those who have been discriminated against have successfully sued their employers (Arvey, 1979).

Many women have varied career patterns, working for several years, taking time off, or working part-time as they raise children and later re-entering the work force full time. Yohalem's (1979) study of business and professional women found that such broken patterns of employment did *not* bar access to top positions. It took additional time, however, to facilitate career advancement after a period of unemployment.

Differential treatment.   Once women enter the work force, they may be subject to discrimination in how they are treated in such areas as job placement, promotional opportunities, salary increases, and other personnel decisions. The newcomer to an organization must be given opportunities to learn about the organization and master new skills. Women may be discriminated against when they are not given sufficient information about the organization and their job duties or when they are isolated from other workers without the opportunity to learn the technical and social aspects of the job (Terborg, 1977). Further, they must cope with conflicting behavior and performance demands associated with family responsibilities, which men often have to a lesser degree. For example, when a woman adds the role of a business career, she may not be able to reduce the role demands of housewife or mother. This can result in role conflict or role overload. Women who choose traditional, male-dominated careers, such as industrial sales, engineering, or product management, are less likely to receive support for their choice and may actually be discouraged by family members (Crawford, 1978).

Yohalem (1979) found that 53% of the professional women she sampled believed they had not received equal treatment as workers. Paradoxically, successful workers (especially those in male-dominated occupations) were more likely to report discriminatory treatment in salary and promotional opportunities than women with less occupational attainment. Harlan and Weiss (1980) studied managers in two retail organizations. They found that women in one company felt they were not considered for some managerial positions. Yet subjective ratings of female work performance generally indicate that women can be effective managers (White, DeSanctis, & Crino, 1981).

A more subtle form of differential treatment appeared to be operating in another company in which women received less critical and constructive feedback from their supervisors than men. Women also faced barriers involving formal and informal training. Men were automatically brought into the informal "how to" network, while women had to make a conscious effort to establish themselves in the network (Harlan & Weiss, 1980).

These studies suggest that professional success for women entails the ability and willingness to withstand discriminatory treatment. Yohalem (1979) recommends that women assess the value of a profession to them and not undertake a profession simply because it is traditionally male (or female) dominated. Encouraging women to bypass traditionally female fields may not take into consideration the value of these occupations to society and to the women themselves.

Explanations for sex discrimination. Different explanations for sex discrimination entail different strategies for dealing with it. One explanation is person-centered, arguing that female socialization practices from childhood encourage the development of personality traits and behavioral patterns that are contrary to the demands of male-dominated work settings (Riger & Galligan, 1980). One implication of this perspective is that women who behave more like men are less likely to be the objects of discrimination in performance assessment (White, DeSanctis, & Crino, 1981).

The second perspective is situation-centered. Research has found that sex differences may reflect differences based on factors that vary with gender but are inadequately controlled in the research design or nature of the situation (Terborg, 1977). According to Riger and Galligan (1980, p. 905):

> Some studies note that women tend to over-emphasize the task at hand, as opposed to seeing it as a stepping-stone to further achievement. According to person-centered explanations, women do this because they have not learned to set goals or plan ahead. According to situational explanations, because women are not promoted within organizations, they over-emphasize the job at hand.

Another situationally based explanation is that control mechanisms for women such as salary increases often reward conformity and discourage independent action. Such controls, Acker and Van Houten (1979) argue, may be more effective if they are consonant with controls women experience outside the organization.

A greater need for career development. Career development strategies for women vary depending upon the explanation accepted for sex discrimination. Powell (1980) suggested two strategies:

1. Women should rely on their social sensitivity, interpersonal awareness, and other characteristics stereotyped as feminine to gain management positions in socially directed functions.

2. Alternatively, women should adopt masculine behaviors.

Powell also suggested a more situationally based development strategy:

3. Women should seek entry into existing informal networks or establish their own networks through formal and informal channels.

Viewing sex discrimination as a problem of role management suggests several other career development strategies for women (Terborg, 1977). These include: (1) structural role redefinition—actually changing the demands of a role (e.g., not working overtime in order to meet the needs of one's family); (2) personal role redefinition—setting priorities on meeting role demands and otherwise learning to live wth role conflict; and (3) reactive role behavior—attempting to meet the demands of multiple roles. Hall (1972) found that structural role redefinition was positively related to career satisfaction and was probably the best strategy in the long run, while reactive role behavior was negatively related to satisfaction.

Organizational responses to sex discrimination. The burden of alleviating sex discrimination in the workplace should not fall on women. Yet, organizational initiatives designed to recruit, support, or improve the performance of women managers are not common (White, DeSanctis, & Crino, 1981). Riger and Galligan (1980) suggest five approaches organizations should take to increase the upward mobility of female workers.

1. Train managers in the uniform use of objective rating scales and specific decision rules.

2. Present affirmative action policies in a noncoercive manner.

3. Change the distribution of opportunities and power and eliminate women's token status.

4. Reduce the salience of gender and stereotypes by increasing the amount of information on which decisions are based.

5. Severely sanction those who discriminate and tangibly reward those who sponsor women's entry into managerial networks.

Yohalem (1979) suggests several other organizational interventions to increase opportunities for women:

1. Base performance evaluation on professional competence not seniority.

2. Provide flexible work schedules and shorter work weeks.

3. Focus equal employment opportunity-affirmative action on advancement opportunities as well as hiring practices.

Suggestions such as these recognize that eliminating sex discrimination is not just the individual's responsibility and not one that can be tackled by development alone. The problem is that past individual prejudices and organizational practices often represent the formalization of attitudes, and the attitudes that originally led to the discriminatory policies continue even when the policies no longer exist (Stumpf, Greller, & Freedman, 1980). Therefore, much time and persistent effort on the part of organizations and individuals are necessary to avoid sex discrimination (Bryson & Bryson, 1978).

Many of the organizational strategies mentioned above are valuable for decreasing sex discrimination as well as for improving the quality of work life for all employees. Changing work schedules and role demands, in particular, recognizes the need for individuals to cope with multiple, often conflicting roles (Ronen, 1980). This leads to our next topic: managing dual careers.

Managing Dual Careers

As noted earlier, the number of women in the work force has increased dramatically in the last thirty years. According to data from the U.S. Bureau of Labor Statistics, 55.6% of wives with school-age children and 37.4% of wives with preschoolers were employed in 1977 (Bryson & Bryson, 1978). Many married women leave the work force when they have children, ironically just when they have acquired experience and are becoming most valuable to their employers (Hall & Hall, 1979). However, over one-third remain in the work force.

Dual-career couples face problems of managing family and work responsibilities. Career planning and development may be meaningless without considering a person's role as a family member, especially when this role conflicts with work activities (Smith, 1981). In their book on dual-career couples, Hall and Hall

TABLE 4.2
Characteristics of Early Career Couples

1. The need for both partners to develop skills, gain experience, and establish themselves.
2. Career opportunities force family decisions which primarily benefit one partner's career.
3. Mutually intense commitment to respective careers.
4. Little knowledge of managing a two-career family.
5. Lack of experience in problem solving around career or family problems.
6. Fear of the organization, job insecurity, and treating the organization as if it is totally inflexible to individual needs.
7. Willingness to evolve a flexible family relationship.

Reprinted with permission from F.S. Hall and D.T. Hall, *The two-career couple.* Reading, Mass.: Addison-Wesley, 1979, pp. 44–45.

(1979) contrast couples in the early career stage with those in mid-career. Their points are summarized in Tables 4.2 and 4.3.

Issues early career couples experience. Couples in their early career are "breaking in" and "learning the ropes." Becoming established in their fields may mean working long hours, traveling, and a high degree of job involvement. A financial analyst, for example, may be expected to spend long hours developing an analytic program, working with specialists, and preparing research reports, all of which are new experiences. An assistant account executive in advertising may work long hours in developing a client presentation, writing a competitive product analysis, and traveling to the client's headquarters.

Marriage introduces additional demands—yet may also provide the support and encouragement needed during the establishment stage. A dual-career relationship may require moving in different directions geographically or in settling for a less than optimal position so that one's spouse can take advantage of an excellent job offer. Comparatively simple problems of coordinating work activities, such as working late and scheduling a trip,

TABLE 4.3
Characteristics of Mid-Career Couples

1. Career versus family conflicts over children and relocation.
2. Alternative career paths which accommodate family needs are viewed as viable.
3. More clearly defined career and family priorities and goals.
4. Commitment to the family unit.
5. Improved ability to plan and cope as a function of experience in problem solving career-family issues.
6. Less fear of the organization, more sharing of career-family concerns, and willingness to test the organization's flexibility.
7. Acceptance of the career as flexible and the family as a given.

Reprinted with permission from F.S. Hall and D.T. Hall, *The two-career couple.* Reading, Mass.: Addison-Wesley, 1979, p. 46.

can become major issues for dual-career couples. Young couples are becoming quite flexible in their willingness to explore non-traditional alternatives such as living apart, long-distance commuting, and sharing responsibility for child care and household maintenance.

Issues faced by mid-career couples. Mid-career couples often view the family's needs as primary. They may refuse added work responsibilities or other opportunities for career advancement if it means relocation or interference in the lives of other family members. Decisions must be made within the parameters of the activities of one's spouse and one's children. Many couples delay making career moves until the children finish high school. Others move for the sake of the children (for example, moving to a particular city so that a talented child can take advantage of a special preparatory program). These decisions may involve changing jobs or may have other effects on work activities such as spending more time commuting and, as a consequence, having less time available for other tasks. Mid-life couples have had more experience planning and solving problems together. They tend not to live in fear of their employer or unemployment, and they are more willing to ask supervisors for help in solving work-family difficulties.

Hall and Hall (1978) identify several factors that contribute to successful management of a dual-career family. There needs to be substantial flexibility, mutual commitment to both careers, several coping mechanisms, and development of the competencies to manage one's career through career information, goal setting, career planning, and problem solving.

The individual coping mechanisms referred to earlier in the section on sexual discrimination also apply to dual-career couples (Hall & Hall, 1978). Role redefinition entails agreeing not to engage in certain time-consuming activities (such as volunteering to serve on committees), enlisting help from others for cleaning, babysitting, etc., and integrating careers by working in related fields so that two careers become more like one. Personal role definition involves establishing priorities, ignoring less important role activities (e.g., dusting), separating roles (e.g., not bringing work home from the office), seeking self-fulfillment, and satisfying personal interests. Reactive role behavior means accepting all role demands as given and finding ways to meet them. This requires organizing and planning, working harder, or simply taking care of things as they come up (probably the least satisfying approach).

According to Hall and Hall (1978, 1979), organizations need to: (1) provide assistance for couples attempting to manage dual careers, (2) allow flexible work schedules, (3) offer couple counseling, (4) train supervisors in career counseling skills, and (5) establish support structures for transfers and relocations.

The last point regarding transfers and relocations has been investigated by Veiga (1981a) and Brett and Werbel (1980). Veiga (1981a) found that 51% of the 6332 job changes he studied were viewed as transfers by the organizations. The typical manager averaged a career move every 3.5 years; mobility was highest in the early career stages. The more mobile managers (i.e., those experiencing more job moves than average) relocated more often than the less mobile managers, earned comparable pay, expressed less satisfaction with their salary, and more satisfaction with their advancement. Veiga (1981a) concluded that job mobility per se has dysfunctions which might be overcome by organizational support systems and more careful career management.

Brett and Werbel (1980) examined the effects of job transfers involving relocations on employees and their families. The degree of mobility had little impact on employee and spouse self-concepts, their health, or their attitudes toward life. Mobile employees were more self-assured than comparably less mobile individuals. They were also more satisfied with their marriages and families, but less satisfied with friendships and nonwork activities. The latter point suggests the importance of balancing one's career actions with nonwork activities.

Balancing Career Development with Nonwork Activities and Life Goals

An issue related to managing dual careers is the importance of nonwork activities to the individual and the relationship between work and nonwork spheres of life. Nonwork activities include, but extend beyond, the family to encompass involvement in leisure, religion, politics, the community, home maintenance, and so forth. Some nonwork activities are necessary (such as shopping); others are purely voluntary and done for personal satisfaction. In most cases, nonwork activities do not receive monetary reward. There are, however, examples when work and leisure are not easily separated, as when an amateur pilot charges for rides or when business is discussed on the golf course. Some people argue that their work is their leisure. Most people, however, would probably agree that leisure activities are voluntary, and done for personal satisfaction; they do not involve maintenance and are not a prime source of income (Kabanoff, 1980).

Work activities affect nonwork behavior and vice versa. There is a substantial body of literature on the relationship between work and nonwork. Work affects political behavior, leisure behavior, and family relationships (Near, Rice, & Hunt, 1980). Moreover, nonwork factors such as demographic characteristics, community involvement, health, and nonwork activities can affect work behavior and attitudes. While the nature of work affects job satisfaction (Hackman & Oldham, 1980), nonwork factors have also been found to be important to job satisfaction (Rice, Near, & Hunt, 1979). If living conditions affect job reactions, efforts to improve job performance through only career planning and development may have limited success (Near, Rice, & Hunt, 1980; Kabanoff, 1980; London, Crandall, & Seals, 1977). Moreover, individual differences may moderate the relationship between work and nonwork. Nonwork activities may be more important than work for some individuals while the reverse may be true for others.

Developing an effective pattern of work and leisure.   Kabanoff (1980; Kabanoff & O'Brien, 1980) identified four work/leisure patterns on the basis of five attributes: autonomy, variety, skill utilization, pressure, and interaction. These patterns are shown in Fig. 4.2.

The first pattern consists of individuals who have low levels of one or more of the five attributes in both work and leisure. They tend to be males with low education, low income, and low intrinsic work motivation but high extrinsic work motivation.

The second pattern reflects a high level of an attribute in leisure but a low level in work. Individuals characterized by this pattern tend to be females who are internally controlled, have low income, and low extrinsic work motivation. Family commitments and other nonwork activities are their central life interest. Also included in this category are those who are younger, work shorter hours, have higher intrinsic work motivation, and have leisure activities that are high on pressure and skill. These individuals apparently compensate for a less interesting job in their leisure time.

The third pattern consists of individuals with a high level of an attribute at work and a low level in leisure. They tend to be predominantly male and more concerned with the economic outcomes of work than its intrinsic value.

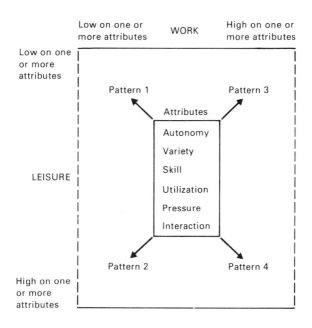

Fig. 4.2 *Patterns of work and leisure (After Kabanoff, 1980)*

The fourth pattern reflects a high level of an attribute in both work and leisure. This group tends to have high income, be better educated, and be motivated by the intrinsic nature of the work rather than the pay and benefits it provides.

These different patterns of work-nonwork behavior and attitudes suggest that job success does not necessarily imply an impoverished personal life, and that different individuals exhibit different work-nonwork patterns. While time spent working means less time available for other things, several studies have dispelled the popular belief that the successful executive inevitably pays a price for career success. In Vaillant's (1977) study, successful managers who became company presidents also enjoyed good marriages and rich friendships; whereas many of those who did not reach middle management had unstable marriages and short-lived friendships. Bartolome and Evans (1980) found that executives whose private lives deteriorated were subject to the negative effects of emotional spillover in which work consistently produced negative feelings that overflowed into private lives. Successful executives learned to manage their work and careers so that the negative emotional spillover was minimized, and thus they achieved a balance between their professional and private lives.

Bray and Howard (1980) found a weak relationship between career success (organizational level achieved after twenty years with the company) and life satisfaction. Contrary to the conclusions of Vaillant (1977) and Bartolome and Evans (1980) that career success and life satisfaction are positively related, Bray and Howard concluded that "the most successful at work are no more likely to be the most successful in marriage and family life or in recreational pursuits. Nor are they more likely to feel more positive about life and the nature of man or be able to avoid the feelings of crisis that sometimes accompany middle age" (1980, p. 286). "On the other hand," they continue, "there are no apparent detrimental effects of career success on life satisfactions" (p. 287). All three studies fail to support the common belief that success in one's vocation can be achieved only by sacrificing aspects of one's personal life.

This suggests that individuals must learn to manage both their work and nonwork activities to achieve life goals. One's self-assessment is likely to identify many family- and leisure-related identity statements in addition to career identity statements. One's career objectives need to be expanded to include other life goals. Career plans should be developed in conjunction with leisure and nonwork plans.

Shifting patterns of commitment.   A cross-cultural study of middle managers revealed changes in sensitivity to, or preoccupation with, marriage, leisure, and work at different points in the life cycle:

> *This changing pattern of pre-occupations appears as a rhythm that runs through the lives of many of our managers. It is a rhythm that probably in part reflects psychological*

developmental processes as well as the structure of careers and families in modern industrial society. But it is not a deterministic rhythm. It is not a rhythm that says, "Launching your career will be a tense and painful process in your 30's," or "You would have a mid-life crisis!" Instead it is a pattern whereby a person's sensitivity to different areas of life changes. It is a rhythm whereby certain events, if they happen, have great significance at one stage of life, but are of subsidiary significance at another stage (Bartolome & Evans, 1979, p. 26).

Thus, work and nonwork activities have different meanings for individuals depending on the nature of the work, the nature of nonwork demands, and leisure interests at different points in time.

Implications for career planning and development.   The effects of a career planning and development program may be limited unless the relationship between work and nonwork is taken into account. Self-selection is one way to do this. That is, when individuals can choose to participate in a career planning and development program, those who are not interested can choose not to participate. Nonwork goals may influence what people hope to gain from their careers. Career advancement may be a dominant concern simply because it provides the income and benefits that allow individuals to pursue certain leisure activities. Some employees may wish to plan for delayed advancement—postponing added work responsibility until the children are older and relocation becomes easier. Others may wish to wind down their work involvement as self-development and leisure activities become more important.

THE NEED FOR ORGANIZATIONAL CAREER PLANNING AND DEVELOPMENT PROGRAMS

The above issues suggest that career planning and development is a complex process that needs continual attention from both individuals and organizations. Formal planning and development programs create a basic structure and process for integrating individual needs with organizational requirements. Such programs are discussed in the next two chapters. Here we examine the need for career planning and development programs and their potential disadvantages in light of the individual concerns discussed above and the benefits to the organization.

Career planning and development programs help employees influence their organizational roles and career paths. These programs allow individuals to build into their career opportunities to satisfy their needs while fulfilling the demands of their jobs. The rapid rate of organizational and technological change necessitates career development for one to stay competent, avoid obsolescence, and manage mid-career change (Kaufman, 1974). Rather than imposing rigid structure, career development can create viable alternatives for adapting to change.

Social and economic changes also suggest the need for organizations to introduce career planning and development programs. Individual values have evolved over the past two decades placing emphasis on psychological returns from the job in addition to economic gains (Miller, 1978). Economic stabilization and in some cases economic decline have forced individuals to seek alternatives to advancement as acceptable career paths. Rapidly changing environments have made the early identification of high potential employees essential if enough individuals are to have the necessary work experiences to meet future leadership needs. Increased educational opportunities for more people and corporate commitment to equal employment opportunity have increased the competition for promotions.

Walker and Gutteridge (1979) studied why organizations value career development by surveying 225 companies on their career development practices. Over 80% indicated that a major factor influencing their firm's career development program was the desire to develop and promote employees from within. Other major reasons included the shortage of promotable talent (63%), the desire to aid individual career planning (56%), and the desire to improve management productivity (39%). Additional factors considered by over 70% of the respondents included the strong expression of employee interest in career development, affirmative action program commitment, concern about managerial turnover, the personal interest of unit managers, and the desire for a positive recruiting image.

Robinson and Glueck (1980) examined the value of career development activities from the organization's viewpoint. These activities help young managers confront multiple, dysfunctional career problems. They reduce managerial obsolescence and prevent "hoarding" of good employees. They also reduce high executive turnover and excessive, costly recruitment of executives from outside the organization. Another advantage is that career development activities make better use of women, expedite meeting equal employment opportunity guidelines, and break down dysfunctional stereotypes of female employees. Moreover, they result in a closer match between the individual and the organization.

Potential Disadvantages

Career planning and development is not without its potential disadvantages. Ackerman (1976) warns that career development may "prepare round pegs for square holes" by training individuals for opportunities that will never be available. This, however, may be overcome by good human resource planning (see Chapter 8).

Career planning and development may be disruptive for those who are content in a secure, unchanging environment (Pinto, 1980). This is particularly likely in lean and stable organizations where there is little room for movement between positions. A guiding principle in implementing career planning might be, "If it ain't broke, don't fix it" (Pinto, 1980). Howard and Bray (1980) convey this message in their warning, "Don't inveigle the system by dangling promotions in front of those who don't really want them and those the organization shouldn't really want at higher levels" (p. 6). They also suggest that we should not feel sorry for individuals whose careers have plateaued. Howard and Bray's (1980) longitudinal data on managers indicate that many managers in mid-career have reached the level to which they aspired. Other plateaued managers are frankly relieved they don't have to aspire to higher levels. Still others either adjusted long ago to the fact that they are not going any higher or have the defense mechanisms to keep from experiencing a mid-career crisis.

SUMMARY

Career development consists of experiences occurring throughout a person's career which contribute to more effective performance for the individual and the organization. The experiences of Diane Jackson and Len White demonstrate the importance of career goals and managing one's career, the meaning of plateauing, the concepts of sponsors and mentors, the relationship between present career stage and future development, and the integration of life, family, and career issues. Career stages pull together these processes by specifying different events, conflicts, and choices facing people during their careers. Four stages were described: exploration and trial, establishment and advancement, mid-career, and disengagement. Mid-career can be a period of continued growth, a period of maintenance, or a period of decline. Though factors beyond one's control influence one's career, some individuals effectively position themselves to accomplish their career goals.

Issues influencing career direction include minority discrimination, discrimination based on gender, dual careers, and nonwork activities. Minorities have different motivations and place different values on job outcomes than whites. The solution for the organization is to find minorities with relevant abilities and work-related motivation, or to change its expectations of minorities. Also, organizational policies prevent minorities from developing and using their skills and advancing in the organization. Strong affirmative action policies and rewarding managers for developing minorities will help alleviate racial and ethnic discrimination in employment.

Women face problems of entry and treatment discrimination. Person-centered perspectives suggest a need for women to change to fit into male-dominated organizations. Situation-centered perspectives view sex discrimination as a function of sex-role stereotypes and call for changing organizational policies and providing career opportunities to allow women to maximize their professional competence. We feel that this latter approach will be more effective.

Managing dual careers is another issue which must be considered in relationship to career planning and development. Couples starting out have different career concerns from those in mid-life who have had experience coping with career and family demands. On the one hand, career changes often involve changes in responsibilities, travel requirements, relocation, and other factors affecting one's life. On the other hand, family demands, especially children and a spouse's career, affect the time and effort available for work. Career planning and development that ignores the demands of dual careers may not be effective.

The individual must balance work and nonwork activities including, and extending beyond, one's family. Nonwork factors may be more important to life satisfaction than work factors. This implies that the direction a person's career takes will depend on nonwork interests, and that career planning and development must take these interests into account.

Career planning and development programs create a structure for integrating individual needs and organizational requirements. Such programs may not be relevant for everyone and may take different forms depending on their purpose. The next section discusses these programs by examining career planning and development activities sponsored by organizations.

Section III
The Organization's Role in Career Planning and Development

Organizational Career Planning Programs

5

In the last two chapters we defined individual and career development and discussed how they vary in different career stages. We explored career issues for racial and ethnic minorities, women, and dual-career couples, and found that career progression may be affected by how individuals balance work and nonwork activities.

We now define areas of organizational, individual, and shared responsibility for career planning. Career planning activities are then discussed. We describe organizational career planning programs which are part of the ongoing career development process used by organizations to provide career management services. Behavioral science research is summarized with respect to the elements necessary to design and evaluate effective career planning programs. The chapter concludes with a review of research evaluating career planning and a discussion of some points to consider in the design and implementation of such programs.

DEFINING RESPONSIBILITIES

For career planning to be effective, it is necessary to determine which responsibilities should be assumed by the organization, which should be primarily the individual's, and which are best shared. We address these organizational, individual, and shared responsibilities below along with survey results of current practices in American business.

In an American Management Association survey, Walker and Gutteridge (1979) identified career planning responsibilities. The 225 responding companies represented 10 major industrial groups, and each had 500 or more salaried employees. Respondents reported on the career communications and career planning practices which were applicable to the salaried personnel of their company.

Organizational Responsibility: Communicate Career-Related Information

Walker and Gutteridge (1979) found that most companies with career planning programs provided substantial career-related information to employees. For example, 93% of the respondents indicated that they provided information on EEO and affirmative action programs and policies, and 85% provided information on the company's condition and economic situation. Information on other personnel functions was also communicated by most firms. Salary administration information was communicated by 76% of the respondent firms, job requirement information by 71%, and training and development options by 64%.

Providing information specific to individual career progression was less common. Only 54% of the respondents used job posting or provided job vacancy information, and 39% communicated career paths or ladders. Furthermore, the above responses indicated that such information was communicated, not that the information actually reached the majority of employees or their supervisors. To the extent that such career communications are provided only by the companies in the survey, and then only to a fraction of each company's employees, substantially more can be done by organizations to keep their employees informed.

Individual Responsibility: Self-Assessment and Career Planning

Self-assessment and the development of career and life plans are the responsibility of the individual. However, several of the organizations surveyed by Walker and Gutteridge provided assistance in these areas. Psychological testing and assessment activities were conducted by 35% of the companies and 33% provided testing and feedback regarding aptitudes and interests. Individual self-analysis and career planning workbooks were available in 16% of the companies, and life and career planning workshops were offered by 11%. Specialized workshops focusing on retirement (34%) and outplacement (37%) were also offered on an intermittent basis in response to specific needs.

Shared Responsibility: Balance the Needs of the Individual and Organization

A "person-centered" approach to career planning attempts to balance the needs of the individual and the organization, in contrast to a "manager-centered" approach which highlights selecting the best people for each organizational position without regard to individual needs (Storey, 1978). The latter approach is what managers generally believe they are already doing (Walker & Gutteridge, 1979).

The person-centered approach implies that individuals are responsible for developing their career plans while the organization provides the information and resources that make this possible. Some companies, for instance, develop a career planning program with the philosophy that the primary responsibility for individual career planning lies with the employee. The company carries the responsibility to compile and share the relevant information needed by the employee for planning and by the company for decision making. This suggests that a viable career management system requires both information about the company to help employees plan and make decisions and mechanisms to communicate information between the company and its employees.

Shared responsibility between the individual and organization is necessary for the development of career plans that can be translated into meaningful career actions. Career planning includes two areas of shared responsibility: (1) counseling and coaching for development while on the job, and (2) specifying relevant training and development activities to prepare employees for target jobs (Walker, 1977).

Career counseling generally involves discussions of current job activities and performance, individual job and career development objectives, and action plans (Walker & Gutteridge, 1979). While many of the companies responding to the career planning practices survey provided informal counseling by the personnel staff (89%), few utilized specialized staff career counselors (21%) or referred employees to external counselors and resources (29%). Supervisors were typically considered a primary source of career counseling information (56%).

Many of the organizations studied offered and encouraged managers to participate in various training and development activities to facilitate targeted career progression (see Chapter 6). The widespread existence of tuition refund arrangements offered by corporations is indicative of the shared responsibility for training and development. Organizations and individuals need to work together to identify relevant areas for development and programs to meet their developmental needs.

Workshops were also offered as part of the career development process. Approximately half of the firms in the Walker and Gutteridge study reported holding interpersonal relations workshops and job performance and development planning workshops. However, life and career planning workshops were offered in only 11% of the firms. In general, the workshops were more likely to focus on job-related outcomes than on personal outcomes.

CAREER PLANNING ACTIVITIES

Before describing how various methods are combined in career planning programs, we examine different types of career planning activities more closely. Bowen and Hall (1977) described four types of career planning activities: individual activities, counselor-client activities, boss as counselor or coach, and group activities. Potential advantages and shortcomings of each are discussed below and summarized in Table 5.1.

Individual Activities

These involve personal planning—perhaps with the aid of self-help materials—but without the aid of company officials or external counselors. The information used in developing a career plan would generally be uncovered through self-assessment and/or be available as part of the feedback provided by the performance appraisal system or an assessment center.

Popular workbooks designed to facilitate individual career planning include Bolles's (1980) *What Color Is Your Parachute,* and Kotter, Faux, and McArthur's (1978) *Self-Assessment and Career Development.* People who are motivated and persistent often find this material valuable in setting their goals. Self-assessment, as discussed in Chapter 3, is a difficult part of career planning. It is especially difficult for those who are not motivated or who require feedback and social support. These people need additional career planning assistance before meaningful plans can be established.

Counselor-Client Activities

People seeking advice often use professional counselors available through guidance centers, local colleges and universities, community associations (e.g., the YMCA, YWCA), and private counseling organizations. Counselors help clients explore their needs through interviews and by interpreting and feeding back the results of vocational interest and aptitude tests. These procedures tend to be moderately expensive and of most benefit when integrated with life and organizational goals. Since people are likely to resist results that disconfirm self-concepts, skilled counseling is necessary for meaningful career management activities.

Clinical assistance in career development offers advantages in information gathering, employee acceptance, and relevance for subsequent planning. For example, one consulting firm offers a program of clinical evaluation, immediate feedback, and development planning (Hellervik, 1981). An interview, conducted by a manager with interviewer training, a human resource professional, or a psychologist, is used to determine an individual's

TABLE 5.1
Characteristics of Various Career Planning Activities and Probable Contribution to Career Success

ACTIVITY	POTENTIAL ADVANTAGES	POTENTIAL SHORTCOMINGS	PROBABLE IMPACT ON PSYCHOLOGICAL SUCCESS AND IDENTITY INTEGRATION
Individual Activities			
1. Personal planning with possible aid of self-help materials.	a. For persons with strong motivation and adequate sources of information, may be adequate for goal setting. b. Cost is minimal.	a. Most people need interpersonal feedback to develop a complete and accurate self-evaluation. b. No built-in mechanism for checking completeness of information on occupational opportunities or for correcting distorted views of self. c. No opportunity to explore new occupational possibilities.	Considerable potential contribution because individual sets own goals. Actual contribution likely to be minimized, however, because the activity lacks mechanisms for exploration of new potentials, interpersonal feedback, and social support to maintain motivation.
Counselor-Client Activities			
2. Testing Approach: Guidance counselor administers vocational interest and	Test results and information supplied may be of considerable value for client.	a. Usually expensive. b. Client has no way of testing validity of counselor's views or	Since people do not readily accept disconfirming data in situations where there is no

	Advantages	Limitations	Comments
aptitude tests and feeds data back to client—may also provide information on occupations, job market, and job-hunting techniques.		test results. c. Interpersonal feedback likely to be minimal.	opportunity to validate the information, contribution may be relatively limited.
3. Counselor Approach: Emphasis on interpersonal exploration of client's needs with counsellor.	Skillful counselor may provide valuable input for self-assessment.	a. No mechanism for checking validity of counselor's perceptions. b. Most helpful in exploring personal needs; minimal stress on occupational information. c. Usually expensive.	Potentially helpful, subject to the limitations that client must experience insights produced as valid and must check validity with other persons outside of the counseling situation.
4. Combination Testing and Clinical Approach.	a. Combines benefits of both Testing and Counseling Approaches. b. Checking test results against perceptions of counselor provides some mechanism for "validating" information.	a. Potentially very expensive. b. Most counselors are not equally proficient in both approaches. c. Counselor may experience a need to see client in a manner consistent with test results.	Essentially the same as for #3.

TABLE 5.1 (continued)

ACTIVITY	POTENTIAL ADVANTAGES	POTENTIAL SHORTCOMINGS	PROBABLE IMPACT ON PSYCHOLOGICAL SUCCESS AND IDENTITY INTEGRATION
Boss as Counselor or Coach			
5. Superior regularly or periodically assesses subordinate's performance and provides feedback and suggestions for improving performance and/or career opportunities.	a. Superior may have an excellent opportunity to observe subordinate's behavior in a number of work activities. b. Superior knows career opportunities within the organization. c. Superior can provide assignments to expand subordinate's capabilities.	a. The superior's power can be highly threatening, causing subordinate to be defensive, cautious, and closed to feedback. b. Superior's first loyalty is likely to be seen as to the interests of the organization, not subordinate. c. Not likely to integrate nonwork aspects of subordinate's life with career issues.	a. If done as a part of performance appraisal, depends on format. Traditional performance appraisal unlikely to be productive. MBO with substantial self-evaluation by subordinate may be helpful, since subordinate sets own goals, etc., and takes lead in assessment. b. If done as informal coaching, can be very effective to the extent that superior provides relatively nondirective assistance which maximizes subordinate's freedom to choose.

Group Activities

6. Assessment Center: Usually conducted by or sponsored by employer. Employee is tested by a number of pencil and paper tests and is presented with situational tests and interviews where performance is observed and evaluated. Evaluators are often other managers trained in the technique. Psychologists design Center and interpret test results.

a. Substantial amounts of data can be developed quickly.
b. Multiple judges on panel and results of several tests provide variety of perspectives for candidate.
c. Moderate cost—usually borne by employer.
d. Some evidence for more valid predictions than available through counselor-client approaches.

a. High threat situation:
1. Employee likely to feel "on the spot" and anxious about results—not an optimal situation for feedback.
2. Center serves interests of employer first, which may be incompatible with interests of employee.
b. Primary emphasis is not on setting personal goals.
c. Data generated primarily applicable to career with employing organization only.
d. Interpersonal feedback frequently not a prime or major objective.
e. Does not provide information on other job possibilities especially outside of employing organization.

a. Likely to be minimized to the extent that employee:
— Cannot really choose not to attend.
— Is not involved in design of activities.
— Is threatened by long-term career implications of evaluation.
— Receives minimal or threatening feedback.
b. No explicit provision for goal-setting.
c. No support group for planning or dealing with career crises.

TABLE 5.1 (continued)

ACTIVITY	POTENTIAL ADVANTAGES	POTENTIAL SHORTCOMINGS	PROBABLE IMPACT ON PSYCHOLOGICAL SUCCESS AND IDENTITY INTEGRATION
7. Life Planning Workshop: Conducted within organization. A set of semistructural experiences are presented which encourage participants to assess their values, situation, etc., to set goals, and to develop greater self-awareness through interpersonal interaction with other participants.	a. No cost to participant. b. Encourages personal goal setting. c. Wide exploration of self and needs encouraged. Copious interpersonal feedback generated. d. Supportive environment. e. Development of "supportive groups" and opportunities to assess and develop job-relevant skills possible. f. Other participants are frequently valuable sources of information on career alternatives. g. Goals developed and development needs	a. Normally does not provide occupational information, especially for careers outside of the organization. b. Employers leery of processes which may encourage employees to leave organization. c. Provision for periodic follow-up probably necessary to maximize value to most participants. d. Participants may not be encouraged to explore changing jobs or careers.	a. Specificlly designed to provide identity integration and psychological success through personal goal-setting and enhanced self-awareness. b. If conducted within organization benefits may be somewhat limited by need for program to serve employer's needs and by reluctance of employees to open up in groups of colleagues. c. Only design which explicitly requires small group design to maximize feedback and opportunity to validate data.

	Advantages	Limitations
	can be integrated into parallel organizational programs. h. Can be a part of an organization development effort.	a. See *a* and *c*, above.
8. Life Planning Workshop: Conducted outside of organization.	a. Same as *b* through *g*, above. b. Low threat situation. c. Potential for developing job-hunting skills possible.	a. Moderate cost to participants unless underwritten by employer. b. Normally do not provide occupational information on job markets, nature of jobs, etc. c. See *b* and *c*, above.

From D. Bowen and D.T. Hall, Career planning for employee development: A primer for managers. © 1977 by the Regents of the University of California. Reprinted from *California Management Review,* vol. 20, no. 2, pp. 33–35 by permission of the Regents.

strengths and weaknesses along a set of career relevant dimensions. By focusing on past behavior, the interviewer assists the individual in identifying what the individual can do when he or she exerts maximum effort. The rapport between the interviewer and the individual facilitates acceptance of feedback. Such rapport and acceptance of feedback, coupled with the interviewer's knowledge of the organization, helps the person develop realistic career plans. The result is a development program that capitalizes on opportunities, personalities, relationships, and activities specific to the work environment.

Boss as Counselor or Coach

This activity relies on supervisors to appraise their subordinates' performance and provide them with feedback, suggestions for improvement, and information on career opportunities. Supervisors are generally in a position to observe and evaluate their subordinates' behavior, to know about available career opportunities, and to provide assignments that expand the individual's capabilities. However, some supervisors lack the ability or willingness to appraise and discuss such information with their subordinates (Walker & Gutteridge, 1979). Supervisors may not have sufficient influence to fulfill promises regarding future developmental assignments. Moreover, subordinates may be defensive when faced with a negative evaluation and/or have difficulty discussing their feelings with the supervisor. Guidelines for more effective performance reviews and feedback are available (Carroll & Tosi, 1973; Raia, 1974). A management by objectives approach which integrates self-evaluation with goal-setting is a widely recommended procedure; however, it requires substantial commitment on the part of both the supervisor and the subordinate.

Several seminars and workshops help individuals manage their personal growth by integrating self-assessment with supervisor judgments. One such seminar, developed by a firm specializing in career development programs, uses different methods to help individuals understand their work-related values and assess their skills in relationship to job requirements

(White, 1980). The central technique in the seminar is a rating form consisting of seventy skills. Participants rate the extent to which each skill is required on their jobs and the extent to which they possess the skill. Each participant's supervisor separately rates the extent to which each skill is required on the participant's job and the extent to which the participant possesses the skill. The participant and the supervisor then hold a developmental discussion. A comparison of the two rating forms results in the following types of information:

1. *Job characteristics*—skills that the supervisor and subordinate agree are required on the job.

2. *Job gaps*—skills that the supervisor and subordinate disagree are required on the job.

3. *Talents*—skills that the supervisor and subordinate agree are the subordinate's strong points.

4. *Developmental needs*—skills that the supervisor and subordinate agree are not strengths.

5. *Appraisal gaps*—skills that the supervisor and subordinate disagree are strengths or weaknesses.

The developmental discussion results in a training agenda and plans for coaching, feedback, further discussion of development needs, and progress reviews. An action plan resulting from such a program consists of a written statement of the participant's and the supervisor's commitments.

Group and Other Activities

Assessment centers, business simulations, and life planning workshops may be conducted within or outside the organization to generate relevant career management information. Assessment centers, which are discussed later in this chapter, use group discussions, individual decision-making exercises, and paper and pencil tests as data generating devices. The results are suggestive of advancement potential and identify strengths and weaknesses for developmental purposes (Boehm & Hoyle, 1977;

Bray, Campbell, & Grant, 1974; Freedman, Stumpf, & Platten, 1980; Freedman & Stumpf, 1981).

A program designed by the Center for Creative Leadership for work-related skill assessment allows individuals to manage a simulated organization, "Looking Glass, Inc." (McCall & Lombardo, 1978) Trained staff observe the Looking Glass participants, evaluate the decisions made (or why they may not have been made), and provide group and individual feedback on more than a dozen managerial skills. As applied by Union Carbide Corporation, individuals volunteer for the program to learn more about their skills; no evaluative information is reported to the participant's supervisor or otherwise retained within the corporation. Since the simulation includes roles for twenty top level managerial positions across four hierarchical levels, three divisions, and three functional areas, there is substantial variation in the role requirements for each position. Prior to attending this program, participants complete a managerial position description questionnaire which indexes the extent to which various job dimensions are salient in their Union Carbide position. The Looking Glass, Inc. positions were analyzed using the same dimensions permitting a high degree of matching of actual positions to the simulated position (Page & Gomez, 1979; Colarelli, Stumpf, & Wall, 1981; Stein, 1980). Feedback is subsequently tailored to the areas the participants view as most relevant to their current job and career growth.

Life planning workshops attempt to develop greater self-awareness through interaction with other participants. Groups may discuss cases or simulated problems with which group members identify. Discussion may also deal with participants' problems. Aspects of group activities that facilitate more effective life planning are: the availability of more information and sources of information, shared concerns which facilitate openness and realistic discussions of career plans, norms for helping others, and the opportunity to develop social skills. In contrast to assessment centers and business simulations, life planning workshops are generally low pressure situations oriented toward discovering and revealing one's feelings and goals. Voluntary participation and confidentiality are ground rules for most life planning activities.

Before sponsoring life planning workshops, organizations should ask whether this is a necessary or desirable activity. One view is that work and nonwork are integrally related, and career planning will not be effective if it does not take a holistic approach (see Chapter 4). Another view is that life planning is solely the individual's responsibility (Blessing, 1979) and that the organization's role should be limited to helping individuals identify their basic motivators and the constraints they put on themselves. Perhaps the best approach is to offer life planning aids that allow individuals to determine the extent of their involvement and to take responsibility for outcomes of the experience.

Special career planning problems demand unique efforts. For example, companies may develop "outplacement" programs to deal with surplus or ineffective managers (Abdelnour & Hall, 1980). Such programs may offer crisis-oriented workshops or counseling services to help the individuals find new positions in other organizations, help them cope with family and financial difficulties, and reduce the effects of anxiety and weakened self-esteem (Freedman et al., 1981). Retirement workshops and mid-career clinics may also provide valuable assistance in examining and reorienting one's career. Several such programs have been devised in business organizations as well as in educational institutions, government agencies, and professional associations (Ferrini & Parker, 1978).

ORGANIZATIONAL CAREER PLANNING PROGRAMS

Career planning programs generally integrate several activities. The activities chosen depend on the purpose of the program. Some career planning programs are intended to have universal applicability; anyone who wishes, regardless of career stage, ability, organizational level, and job function, may take advantage of the program. Other programs are meant for high potential individuals—those who are identified early in their careers as having potential for advancement. This section provides examples of these two types of career planning programs.

Universal Programs

The emphasis in universal programs is on self and organizational assessment. Participants want to learn about themselves, the opportunities available to them, and what actions they can take to avail themselves of these opportunities. Participation is voluntary and the outcomes depend on the individual's commitment and motivation. Such programs may be offered by organizations that are not affiliated with the individual's employer. Career planning, however, is probably most successful when it is linked to the employer's management staffing procedures and policies (see Chapters 7 and 8).

A person-centered workshop. One career planning program that provides an example of a person-centered approach was developed by Benson and Thornton (1978). Their approach integrates self-understanding, setting goals, and methods of acquiring skills. The program encompasses three stages centered around a workshop. Stage I (pre-workshop) consists of completing self-descriptive instruments and obtaining the perceptions of friends and peers for later feedback to the participants. Stage II (workshop) is a four-day, off-job site meeting held on company time (two work days) and the employees' personal time (a weekend), thus emphasizing the joint responsibility of the organization and the individual for career planning. Group and individual activities use experiential learning techniques. Tasks include assessing skills, planning alternative future life and career activities, and having personal time to integrate self-evaluations, test results, and inputs from other participants. Planning short- and long-range goals is a major function of the workshop. Stage III (follow-up) includes informal and formal meetings to assist in regular assessment of progress toward goals. Benson and Thornton recommend that companies train supervisors in coaching and reinforcing the career planning activities of subordinates who participate in the program.

Career planning at Polaroid. A career planning program developed by Polaroid shows that organizational concerns can be addressed within a career planning system, and that career planning can be integrated with other personnel functions (Ferrini & Parker, 1978). In designing their Career Development Series, Polaroid's Education Department staff focused on the ability of employees to set realistic career goals as a key outcome of the career planning process. This involves getting employees to understand the value of lateral moves, identify skills that are transferable between job families, and take initiative in making career contacts. The Career Development Series consists of a group orientation session and four voluntary career workshops: Career Awareness, Résumé Organization, Interview Skills, and Career Search. The first workshop focuses on self-assessment, the next two on building skills, and the last on how to gather information about Polaroid job opportunities and how to best use Polaroid's Job Posting and Education Systems. The Career Development Series often results in additional management training and development for the user. It also helps establish more systematic staffing decisions via the job posting system.

GE's Career Dimensions system.   The General Electric Company provides a third example of a career planning program (Brewer et al., 1975; Storey, 1976b). The program is divided into four workbooks, entitled *Career Dimensions I, II, III,* and *IV,* published by the General Electric Company (Story, 1976a). *Career Dimensions I* and *II* are self-directed workbooks designed for employees with optional supervisor support. *Career Dimensions III* is a how-to-do-it guide for managers to use in coaching employees about their careers and for dealing with the difficult career questions often asked by subordinates (e.g., Why was I passed over? What's my career path?). *Career Dimensions IV* is a handbook for professionals in human resource management to use in implementing career planning programs.

Several thousand GE employees and many individuals outside the organization have used the system. The reactions have been positive. "Experienced benefits for the business have included improved fitting of jobs to people, higher quality of data for manpower reviews, development of a framework for affirmative action, and allocation of scarce dollars for employee education" (Storey, 1976b, p. 12). Managers also report several personal benefits; for example, they feel less threat and emotion in conducting career discussions, the process provides a comfortable and effective way of helping or redirecting an employee, and the process encourages the employee to assume the proper share of responsibility for career planning. Individuals report "having effective career discussions with their manager, identifying and taking prompt and specific professional development actions toward the achievement of specific goals, and developing a pattern of skills for career-long use" (Storey, 1976b, p. 12).

The career planning process at GE is closely related to its annual manpower review, which includes a review of performance, career interests, developmental needs, developmental actions, and projections of career directions. "The process helps identify individuals of high-growth potential for managerial positions, with emphasis on the higher organizational layers, and encourages the development and proper placement of all employees in the exempt salaried segments of the workforce" (Storey, 1976b, p. 13).

Bell of Pennsylvania's career development program. This is a four-unit sequence conducted on a voluntary, confidential basis. The program is aimed at managers in low and middle management positions regardless of years of experience in the company. Supervisors of those who choose to attend are also offered a one-day workshop to help them participate in career development discussions with their subordinates.

Invitations to participate are sent to the managers, and those expressing interest are sent the first unit: a self-assessment workbook with exercises on identifying personal values, assessing training and job experiences, and relating these to general skills. Individuals also assess their managerial potential. The final exercise in the self-assessment workbook helps identify career goals and subgoals and establish a reasonable schedule for meeting these goals.

The second component is a career exploration guide. Here, attention is given to clarifying career goals and using company-provided information on potential opportunities. It also discusses how to obtain help from career development coordinators, and how to use other company-provided resources, such as the tuition aid program and company training courses.

The personal development plan is the third unit in the sequence. This is a workbook which helps participants prepare for a career development discussion with their supervisors. Participants develop a preliminary work action plan, summarize their talents, and list plans for developmental experiences including the job assignments they would like. An example of a personal development plan is shown in Table 5.2.

TABLE 5.2
Excerpt from a Personal Development Plan

Goal: To progress from a first-level supervisor of a research project team to a second-level manager and assistant director of the Research Department.

PLANS FOR DEVELOPMENT

Talents	Experiences	Job Assignments
Knowledge of technical domains	Develop oral communication skills; attend 2-day workshop.	Volunteer for role of presenter at project review.
Good co-worker relationships		Move to group leader of several project teams.
Forcefulness	Learn more about work scheduling; attend a course in operations management.	Seek task force leader role on XYZ project.
Effective written communications	Develop performance appraisal feedback skills; seek coaching from superiors.	Transfer for six months to Technical Development Department to broaden perspective.

The products of the career development discussion comprise the fourth unit in the program. They include a five-year personal development plan and a corresponding work preference document. This latter document contains one's preferences for desired transfers corresponding to developmental needs. This is input to the company's personnel data base for use in job matching when vacancies occur.

A typical program and its potential problems. A universal career planning program is summarized in Table 5.3. As might be

TABLE 5.3
General Structure of Universal Career Planning Programs

PHASE	ACTIVITIES	TIME FRAME
I	Self-assessment and obtaining peers and friends' perceptions of your skills, interests, values.	One to two weeks prework plus one workshop day.
II	Skill assessment exercises, establishing goals.	One to two workshop days.
III	Integration of information and initial career and life planning.	One workshop day.
IV	Skill building in the areas of résumé writing, interviewing and exploring career possibilities.	One to two workshop days.
V	Development of a personal development plan and work preferences.	One day.
VI	Sharing relevant information with supervisors, family, and peers. Identification and enactment of career actions.	Immediately following the workshop and intermittently thereafter.
VII	Routine examination and re-evaluation of career progress.	Once every several months.

expected from the institutionalization of such programs, career planning experiences can affect behavior and aspirations; however, the effects are likely to be temporary unless follow-up is provided. Precautions must be taken to avoid becoming bogged down in the self-assessment and goal-setting phases of a program and never following through on planning and development phases. While lectures and techniques of self-behavior modification such as those used in the Benson and Thornton (1978) program may help, routine periodic examination and evaluation of career progress is essential. Managerial career planning and development is best viewed as a process of continual incremental change.

Supervisors should be trained to provide ongoing career counseling. Moreover, supervisors must actually use the career planning information in making staffing decisions. The Work Preference Documents in the Bell of Pennsylvania plan, for example, would be of little value if managers filling job vacancies did not access such information to identify which individuals are interested in the positions or which individuals designated the positions as part of their long-term development plan.

Career Planning for High Potential Employees

Programs for high potential employees require identifying participants and then providing planning and developmental activities which accelerate their movement in the organization. Some programs focus on the early identification of talented individuals with the intent of developing that talent to the fullest. Other programs focus on identifying talented individuals who may have been with the company for several years and may have been overlooked. Another approach is to focus on high potential middle level managers with ability for officer level positions.

The most thorough strategy is one that encompasses all three possibilities. High potential employees are identified early in their careers and placed in an accelerated development program. They, along with additional talent identified later, serve as the pool of employees who may have potential for even higher levels. This approach begins with young, high potential employees at a time when they are adaptable and sensitive to the nature of their jobs. Focusing on individuals in their early career stage combines many ingredients which are associated with later success: ability, job challenge, feedback, and early success (Hall, 1976; Stumpf, 1981a).

Identification methods. There are two basic approaches to selecting high potential employees. One involves rating managerial potential by recruiters of job applicants or by supervisors of their subordinates. The other involves an assessment center. In general, potential should be clearly distinguished from performance. *Performance* is a judgment of the employee's outputs, while *potential* is an evaluation of the quality of the process used to obtain those outputs. Performance is rated on the basis of fulfilling job requirements or meeting prestated objectives. Potential is rated on the basis of the skills necessary to advance to higher levels. While an individual with high potential usually performs well, this is not necessarily the case. Some individuals may not perform as well as possible due to a person–job mismatch or for reasons beyond their control. Nevertheless, they may have the skills necessary to perform at a higher level. On the other hand, some individuals may perform well in their current position but not have potential for advancement.

1. *Potential ratings.* The person rating another's potential should have knowledge of the job requirements at the target level. Supervisors, therefore, should be able to evaluate the potential of their immediate subordinates to advance to their level. A second level manager should not evaluate the potential of first level managers for third level. When it is desirable to evaluate the potential of an employee to advance more than one level, other methods, such as an assessment center, need to be used.

One approach to obtaining potential ratings requires the supervisor to collect critical incidents reflecting each subordinate's behavior throughout the year and then to use this information in rating the subordinate's potential. The measure could be a single, overall rating or multiple ratings on dimensions associated with organizational advancement, such as ability to make effective decisions, interpersonal skills, and administrative ability (Brush & Schoenfeldt, 1980).

Several companies rely on committees to assess the advancement potential of subordinates. This process has the advantage of providing different viewpoints and helps committee members compare their judgments with those of others. Individuals also have to justify their judgments. This system works particularly well when most committee members have contact with subordinates in other units and can share opinions of others' subordinates.

Recognizing the advantage of multiple judgments, Exxon requires that once a year each of its management and professional employees be assessed by at least four different supervisors (Career Success at Exxon Corporation, 1980). The pooled judgments are filed on standardized forms which also include suggested training, recommended job assignments, ultimate potential (i.e., the level the individual is expected to reach), and a projected career path covering the next five years.

Supervisor training is an essential component of a system to appraise managerial potential. The raters must know how to observe and evaluate critical employee behaviors. The training should: (a) provide information on the general content of the subordinate's job (e.g., making presentations, interacting with clients, coordinating work activities, etc.), (b) help build skills in observing and evaluating behavior, and (c) provide practice in giving feedback to employees.

2. *Assessment centers.* Assessment centers are often used to evaluate managerial potential. The results may help determine who should be promoted, selected for an accelerated advancement program, or receive developmental experiences.

An assessment center is a standardized program consisting of a series of individual and group exercises administered over several days. The goal is to simulate critical situations in order to observe behaviors related to managerial success (Moses, 1977). Procedures may include a personal interview; personality and intelligence tests; a leaderless group discussion; an opportunity to analyze a problem, present a solution to the problem during an oral presentation, and discuss the different solutions with a group; and an in-basket exercise requiring the participant to deal with information, problems, and issues left in a manager's in-basket.

The assessment center staff, usually higher level managers and psychologists, observe the participants and write a formal report about each one. Staff members also make an overall judgment of each participant's potential.

The philosophy underlying the assessment center method is that dimensions of managerial potential, such as leadership, decision making, interpersonal skills, oral and written communication skills, and organizing and planning, can be identified by observing behaviors in management simulations. Managerial skills evidenced during an assessment center have been found to remain stable for as long as twenty years (Howard & Bray, 1981), and the predictive validity of assessment center judgments has been well documented (Bray & Grant, 1966; Bray, Campbell, & Grant, 1974; Moses & Byham, 1977). In addition to having high validity, assessment centers are generally accepted by employees as a realistic simulation of job behavior and a fair opportunity to exhibit one's abilities. (For a more thorough discussion of the assessment center process and research results see Moses & Byham, 1977; Finkle, 1976; Cascio & Silbey, 1979; Bray, Campbell, & Grant, 1974; and Wanous, 1980. For a critique see Klimoski & Strickland, 1977.)

3. *Other identification methods.* Combinations of personality measures, verbal and quantitative ability tests, and clinical evaluations have been used in early identification programs (Campbell et al., 1970). Biographical data collection is one technique that may be useful in the future (Owens & Schoenfeldt, 1979). The use of biographical data involves scoring an autobiographical form which captures major dimensions of behavior that distinguish different subgroups (e.g., those who achieve middle management by the age of thirty-five versus those who do not). Behaviors that predict managerial success might deal with social leadership and popularity in school, religious involvement, and athletic activity. Research is necessary to determine which biographical items are most predictive of later behavior before such an instrument could be applied to identify high potential managers. Once available, a valid biographical scoring procedure could be used as a screening device, in addition to supervisory potential ratings and assessment centers, to identify those who have a greater likelihood of high potential. For example, suppose nomination to attend an assessment center requires a high supervisory potential rating. Those who did not receive such a rating could be screened using biographical data. Individuals who are predicted to have high potential on the basis of the biographical data could then be given the opportunity to attend the assessment center even though they were not nominated by their supervisor. Used in this way, biographical data would help prevent "false negatives"—that is, the mistake of not including people who would do well if given the opportunity.

Another identification device which should not be overlooked is self-nomination. Individuals who believe they have the ability to advance to higher levels but have not had the opportunity to exhibit that ability could nominate themselves for an assessment center. Assessment is a risky and challenging experience, and when portrayed as such, only those who feel they have a good chance at succeeding would be likely to nominate themselves.

Examples of Identification and Career Planning Programs for High Potential Managers

One program using several of the identification techniques discussed above was outlined by Boehm and Hoyle (1977). Self and supervisory nominations identify employees interested in one of two career directions: supervisory or technical management. Those with supervisory interest attend an assessment center that measures general managerial skills. Those with an interest in technical management jobs are evaluated by their supervisors and/or sent to special assessment centers to evaluate their technical abilities in such areas as sales or engineering. Those who attend the supervisory assessment center, are found to have high potential, and have no interest in technical jobs are considered to be in the pool for placement and development in supervisory management jobs. Those who attend the supervisory assessment center and are found to have limited potential are given the opportunity to be evaluated for a technical management position.

A model we suggest for identification and development of young high potential managers is to have two programs: one for the first year or so in management and another for career planning and accelerated advancement for high potential managers after their first year. These programs are outlined in Fig. 5.1 and Fig. 5.2. The first year (Fig. 5.1) provides the new manager with meaningful work experiences, self-assessment of career ambitions, information regarding opportunities in the company, and general familiarity with one's job and department. New managers should be assigned to supervisors who are good role models and are interested in developing their subordinates. The first year culminates in an evaluation of performance and potential.

This is a "screening in" process by which new managers are selected to follow a standard career route or, in the case of high potential managers, an accelerated advancement program. The majority of new managers will follow the organization's standard career route. This provides opportunities for career planning and development, demonstrating performance and potential, transferring to other positions, and competing for higher level jobs, although at a slower pace than would be appropriate for high potential managers. While it may take an individual seven to ten years to reach middle management on the standard career route, and many on this route will not reach middle management, the accelerated advancement program prepares participants for middle management within three to five years.

Several features of the new manager development process should be noted. For one, it gives the employee a chance to become acclimated to the company before being considered for a high potential program. It also provides a period during which supervisors can observe the manager's on-the-job performance. The program is unlike high-risk, high-reward programs

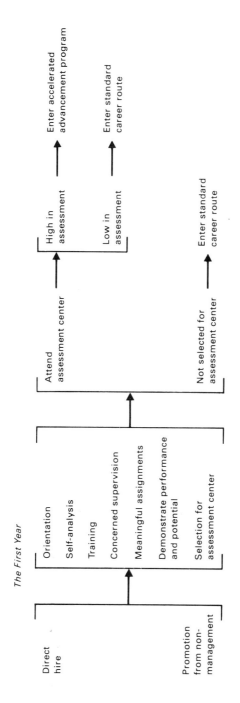

Fig. 5.1 *Exemplary new manager program*

131

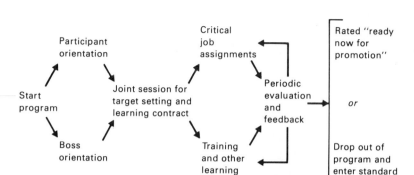

Fig. 5.2 *Exemplary accelerated advancement program for high potential managers*

offered by some companies to recruits immediately after college. While such programs provide early job challenge, their up-or-out nature may result in individuals having difficulty recovering their self-confidence when they fail and will result in the loss of some valuable employees. Also, it is not always possible to judge managerial potential before an individual begins to work for the company. Assessment centers are often too expensive to apply to all applicants who appear to have advancement potential. Some applicants not offered a fast-track position may decide to seek employment elsewhere; however, others may be relieved to have a period to get their feet wet and demonstrate their abilities in a less threatening environment. The program could be modified to accommodate some "super star" applicants who wish to be placed directly into the fast-track program. In general, though, the requirement of at least one year in management before being eligible for the high potential program puts all new managers on an equal footing.

A question arises as to whether or not individuals who did poorly in an assessment center early in their careers should be reassessed for advancement potential several years later. Though assessment results generally do not change much over time (Bray, Campbell, & Grant, 1974), reassessment may be meaningful for individuals who were evaluated positively by their supervisors and nominated for assessment early in their careers but did not do well in the assessment center. We recommend that the results of the early assessment center not be divulged to management for those who did not do well to avoid casting a shadow over their future career progress on the standard career route.

Turning to the accelerated advancement program (Fig. 5.2), this could be directed by a program manager in the company's human resource department. The program might begin with an orientation for the participants and their bosses to prepare them for target setting and the formulation of a "learning contract" with specific training plans. The boss and participant would then meet to set a middle management target job and agree on the learning contract. This would be followed by a sequence of "critical" assignments (those that allow participants to maximally utilize their skills), training experiences, and periodic evaluation and feedback sessions. The program would conclude when the participant is rated "ready now for promotion." Reaching this point should take from three to five years. Completing the program does not guarantee promotion to middle management, since program graduates must compete for positions among themselves and with others who were not in the program. Since only a portion of middle management positions are likely to be filled from the accelerated program (for example, about 30%), exclusion or attrition from the program should not preclude future advancement.

One problem with high potential programs is that labeling employees "high potential" or on the "fast track" can build unrealistic expectations, inflate egos, and cause dissension by creating two groups of new managers. Fast-track programs, nevertheless, provide a way of rewarding capable employees and may be necessary to meet future human resource requirements in middle and top management. Organizations with high potential programs should emphasize that promotional opportunities and career planning programs are available to all managers and that exclusion from one program does not eliminate all other opportunities.

Another problem in high potential programs is that the individual's input to career planning may be lost in the face of human resource planning at higher levels. At Citibank, for example, each of the key business group leaders and major staff area heads meet twice a year with the chairman and president to discuss critical personnel needs (Saklad, 1976). They focus on current staffing and backup candidates for key positions such as senior officers in major overseas countries and corporate lending officers who are in charge of key organization units. There are several hundred key positions in the corporation. The succession planning meetings involve nominating and discussing backup candidates for the incumbents of the new position. Another agenda item is the identification of "corporate property candidates" (those with potential to be promoted to senior vice president within the next three years) and "most promising candidates" (young managers who show promise of moving onto the corporate property list within five years). The group leaders examine personal data sheets for these individuals and discuss their future assignments. Thus, a great deal of planning goes on before the individual is involved or even aware of the career plans.

Exxon holds similar evaluation sessions for their management and professional employees (Career Success at Exxon Corporation, 1980). While they emphasize that the individual's needs or wishes are not lost in the paperwork, some managers find it easier to leave Exxon than to follow the company's recommended plan for their career. This is not perceived as adversely affecting the organization, since Exxon views itself as "heavy on talent and slightly light on opportunity" (p. 2). For this reason, Exxon offers outplacement assistance to good as well as poor performers.

These two examples of executive and management succession planning demonstrate that organizations may initiate career planning for individuals who are viewed as exceptional corporate resources. The result occasionally is individual-organizational conflicts over career direction and developmental experiences. These conflicts are not necessarily resolved by either party "giving in," as in the case of Exxon which has helped valued employees leave the organization when faced with a career conflict.

Programs that emphasize involvement of employees in developmental discussions with their supervisors may run into a different problem: supervisor unwillingness or inability to work with subordinates on career planning. Most programs assume that the supervisor has the motivation and ability to discuss such issues and help set up a meaningful, realistic career plan. Supervisor training and rewards for developing subordinates are essential if joint developmental discussions are to be successful.

A High Potential Promotion Model Versus Slower, Steady Progression

The high potential model of organizational advancement holds that exceptional employees be identified early in their careers so they can receive experiences necessary to function in higher level positions and be rewarded by early promotion. Those not promoted to middle management after several years are not likely to advance to executive levels. In many organizations, early promotion is the only way to the top (Rosenbaum, 1979). Bailyn (1980) describes the early career years as follows:

> *In pursuing a series of new and challenging jobs the young recruit learns to know himself as an organizational employee—to identify his particular areas of competence and interest—and, by learning how his organization works, begins to mesh his capabilities with the available career paths in the organization. The organization, in turn, learns to evaluate the employee—Is he high potential? Is this a candidate who will be able to fill top management roles?—and sets a career track in line with this early evaluation (p. 95).*

Many of those fortunate enough to advance early in their careers, however, may reach an early plateau in middle management. Hierarchical organizations have fewer positions at higher levels. Individuals not selected for top positions may lose their zest for corporate life or seek challenges in other organizations or in other areas of life.

An alternative to the high potential model can be viewed as an *apprenticeship model* (Bailyn, 1980). This model entails "a fairly long period of continued learning and training during the early career, with assignments of only slowly increasing challenge building up to top involvement only at a later period" (Bailyn, 1980, p. 97). Individuals following this process may advance as far if not farther than those following the high potential model, but at a slower pace. The viability of this model has been demonstrated by those who work in paternalistic organizations, those who change occupations in mid-life, married career women, and others who see themselves on a rising career trajectory and anticipate great success.

The apprenticeship model is analogous to the Japanese approach to evaluation and promotion which extends the early career development period for many years. Ouchi (1981) describes this process as follows:

> *Imagine a young man named Sugao, a graduate from the University of Tokyo who has accepted a position at the fictitious Mitsubeni Bank, one of the major banks. For ten years, Sugao will receive exactly the same increases in pay and exactly the same promotions as the other fifteen young men who have entered with him. Only after ten years will anyone make a formal evaluation of Sugao or his peers, not until then will one person receive a larger promotion than another (pp. 25–26).*

In the Japanese system, increased challenge stems from new assignments as the young manager rotates between functions. Rather than movement within a department, the Japanese believe in grooming "nonspecialized experts." The most capable people in the Japanese firm receive more responsible assignments while remaining at lower levels. "Those most able, easily and quickly receive responsibility, but the irreversible step of promotion only comes when they have completely proven themselves" (Ouchi, 1981, p. 28). This suggests that the Japanese promotion model is inflexible when it comes to understanding individual interests and career goals.

If the traditional Western organization were to follow the apprenticeship model, it would require new ways of viewing employee commitment, new standards for judging performance, and a different time span in evaluating organizational employees (Bailyn, 1980). Given the need for such extensive changes, Western organizations are unlikely to move in the direction of the apprenticeship model in the near future, nor is the high potential model necessarily ineffective for Western organizations. In many respects, it is more flexible than the Japanese approach of extended career development and generalist training. Some of the labor turnover that exists in Western organizations may be beneficial to society because it serves an important adjustment function of allowing people to rematch themselves with organizations after more complete job information is obtained. However, some organizations may be more productive and profitable if they adopt a longer-range perspective on careers while maintaining flexible career paths (Bailyn, 1980).

GUIDELINES FOR ORGANIZATIONAL CAREER PLANNING

An organizational career planning system should establish career paths, provide feedback on performance and potential, foster realistic expectations, delineate individual and organizational responsibility, manage information, match jobs and people, maintain program continuity and flexibility, and integrate career planning with other human resource functions. These guidelines are discussed below.

Establish Career Paths

Career planning implies that career paths and developmental experiences by which one can get from one position to another can be identified. Although there are usually no formal paths between all positions, the most salient paths can be identified on an organization-wide or division-wide basis. In a study of several professional samples, Dalton, Thompson, and Price (1977) found that meaningful changes in job assignment, those compatible with one's career stage, were pivotal experiences in helping people develop in their careers.

The development of realistic career paths encompasses three underlying steps: (1) define work activities, (2) identify personal requirements, and (3) establish natural job families (Walker, 1976). The definition of work activities involves job content analysis. This should integrate what employees say they do on the job with what their managers say should be done. Personnel requirements in terms of skills and knowledge are then identified based on the work activities. These requirements are first clustered into positions, and then job families. Job families—groups of jobs with similar requirements—are used to establish the basis for career paths (Walker, 1976; Lopez, Rockmore, & Kesselman, 1980). Selective movement within a job family can be part of a career development process used to prepare individuals for progression into other job families.

Examples of three career path flowcharts for a large insurance company are presented in Fig. 5.3 (systems analyst), 5.4 (sales manager), and 5.5 (group manager). The systems analyst career path is a technical path which begins to assume manager-

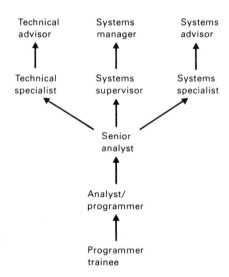

Fig. 5.3 *Systems analyst career path*

Fig. 5.4 *Sales manager career path*

ial responsibility at the third step (senior analyst). The path subsequently forks into two technical career paths and one managerial path. The career path in sales management (Fig. 5.4) is more flexible than that of a systems analyst in that it contains alternative routes to the general manager position. The career path to a group manager (Fig. 5.5) is substantially more complex, involves a greater number of steps and alternatives, and provides two career possibilities for individuals not desiring to reach the top once they have started along the group manager career path (i.e., roles of administrative supervisor and unit supervisor).

Formalized career paths communicate to employees specific step-by-step objectives, and identify the positions of possible role models for them to follow. The goal-setting literature recommends setting specific, not vague or general, goals (Latham & Yukl, 1975). Learning can also take place by observing others (Goldstein & Sorcher, 1974). Consequently supervisors can serve as role models, demonstrating behaviors that are acceptable and valued (Latham & Saari, 1979). The identification of career paths helps individuals pinpoint desirable role models, and it helps middle and higher level managers select protégés (see Chapter

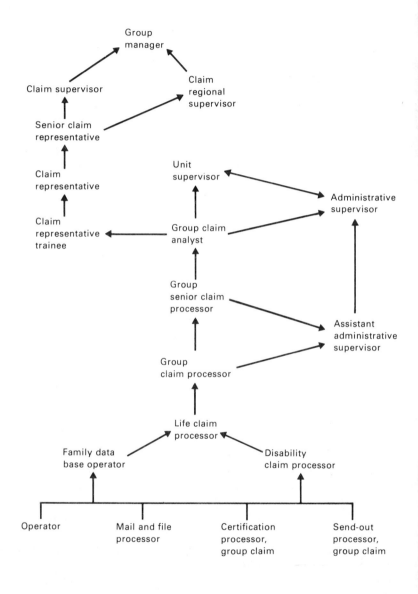

Fig. 5.5 *Group manager career path*

8's discussion of mentor–protégé relationships and career paths as support systems for staffing decisions).

Finally, the identification of career paths is important for the development of the individual. For example, Sears, Roebuck and Company identified a series of job assignment sequences for management development (Wellbank et al., 1978). Their "Job Assignment for Development" system is based on the following principles: (1) many important influences on one's career growth occur on the job, (2) different jobs demand the development of specific skills, (3) development occurs only when the individual has the aptitude and has not already acquired the specific skills, and (4) identifying a rational sequence of job assignments for a person reduces the time required to develop the necessary skills for a chosen job target (Wellbank et al., 1978, p. 55). Hence, general career paths should first be identified, then tailored to the specific developmental needs of the individual.

Provide Feedback on Performance and Potential

Knowing the results of one's behavior (e.g., whether or not goals are met) can enhance learning and result in better performance in the future (Ilgen, Fisher, & Taylor, 1979; Nadler, 1977). Feedback helps individuals determine where they stand. Feedback also serves as a reward. The sense of accomplishment may lead to increased satisfaction—which may be as valuable if not more valuable to some individuals than extrinsic rewards. Feedback can also be used for planning alternative career paths. Negative feedback may convert a person from feeling that "the organization will take care of me" to the notion that "I better begin thinking about myself" (Stumpf & Dawley, 1981).

Feedback helps clarify what types of behaviors will be rewarded. That is, subordinates must know what they have to do in order to attain valued outcomes. Moreover, the desired behaviors should be under the subordinate's control. Path–goal clarity will be weakened when expectati ns from different individuals in the subordinate's work environment conflict, or when the nature of one's task is defined in ambiguous or general terms.

Therefore, an effective career management system should provide concrete explanations of performance in behavioral terms and recognize that some outcomes are not under the subordinate's control.

Foster Realistic Expectations

If employee expectations regarding their careers are unrealistic, their career plans are not so likely to be realized. This could lead to dissatisfaction, feelings of lower self-esteem, lower performance, and turnover. Realistic and moderately difficult career goals are most effective in motivating individuals to perform, particularly for individuals with a high need for achievement (McClelland, 1965).

A second aspect of employees developing realistic career plans involves supervisor–subordinate joint career planning. Participation by both supervisor and subordinate in setting goals generally leads to higher commitment and to a higher rate of goal achievement. Individuals should know what is realistic for them and should be able to set obtainable objectives if coached by a concerned supervisor. Advice from others in goal setting is often helpful in avoiding objectives that are too difficult or too easy.

A joint target-setting session involves the supervisor and subordinate sharing ideas about the subordinate's future. The supervisor's standards for evaluation should be communicated. The supervisor and subordinate should agree on a target job *family,* not a specific target job. This recognizes that changing circumstances make it difficult to predict whether or not any one job will be available when the individual is ready for a new assignment. A tentative target job family should be established as early as possible, recognizing that it should be revised or refined on the basis of new experiences and opportunities. The target job family should depend on: (1) the participant's interests as measured by self-assessment tools such as those described in Chapter 3, (2) skills as measured by supervisory ratings of on-the-job behavior or in an assessment center, and (3) information about future promotional opportunities.

Third, managers and their subordinates must have a realistic understanding of what level of performance will be rewarded and what the rewards are likely to be. Promotion is a reward that should be used as a way to maximally utilize talented individuals. Other rewards should be emphasized: salary increases, bonuses, and stock options; or nonfinancial incentives such as social rewards of increased status (e.g., a "better" office, additional time off, and the opportunity to attend conferences held at an off-site location). Other valued incentives include special leadership assignments, additional responsibility, and being consulted as an expert in a particular area. Supervisors need to: (1) determine which incentives are under their control, (2) identify which incentives are valued by their subordinates (recognizing individual differences), and (3) provide these as rewards for good performance (Lawler, 1971).

A fourth aspect of developing realistic career plans relates to how equitably people believe they are treated. Individuals evaluate the rewards they receive in relation to the rewards they believe others receive. These "comparison others" may be peers, or they may be individuals in other organizations (e.g., friends or relatives). People who feel they received fewer or less valuable outcomes for the same level of work feel underrewarded. Those who feel they received more valuable outcomes for the same level of work feel overrewarded. Methods of resolving such inequity include reinterpreting one's own level of performance or the comparison other's level of performance, changing the amount of one's output (e.g., increasing it when overpaid as long as the total amount of payment remains the same), comparing oneself to someone else, or, as a last resort, leaving the organization (Adams, 1963).

Organizations often attempt to avoid the problem of inequity by maintaining secrecy when administering rewards, particularly salary increases. The problem with this is that individuals may inaccurately perceive how equitably they are treated. One research finding is that people tend to overestimate the pay of individuals at their own organizational level; the greater the overestimation, the greater their dissatisfaction (Lawler, 1971).

Also, people tend to underestimate the differences between their own income and their supervisor's income. While an open pay policy runs the risk of engendering feelings of inequity, it has the potential benefit of communicating the true value of rewards. Managers may be more likely to try for promotions when they have full knowledge of the benefits that can result. Open pay policies clarify the relationship between salary and performance and can be beneficial when there is actually a link between performance and pay. Open pay policies do not necessitate revealing every employee's salary. By releasing information on pay ranges and median salaries for various jobs, individuals can evaluate where they stand in relation to their co-workers (Lawler, 1971).

Delineate Individual and Organizational Responsibility

Clearly defining roles and responsibilities increases the likelihood that action will occur. Specifically, once the organization assumes the responsibility for providing career-related information—and is held accountable for performing this role—the information is likely to be available to the employees. Similarly, once the employee assumes the responsibility for developing a personal career plan, the plan is likely to be enacted. When roles are left undefined or are ill-defined, the role ambiguity that develops tends to inhibit goal-directed behavior (Stumpf, Freedman, & Rabinowitz, 1981; Van Sell, Brief, & Schuler, 1981).

Manage Information

One of the major challenges in an organizational career planning program is the management of information. Information about employees is necessary for human resource planning and training and development; information about the organization needs to be communicated to employees to assist in career planning and developmental activities.

Relevant information about employees includes biographical characteristics, skills, past and current performance (evaluated by a sound and credible method), assessment center results, work experiences, career interests and aspirations, the supervisor's impressions of the employee, and the next assignment recommended for the employee. Information about the company includes opportunities for new hires, target positions, a clear statement of policies and procedures for filling vacancies and obtaining transfers, the number of management positions filled during the past year by job title, and available training programs.

A variety of different methods have been developed by companies to integrate such information. Traditional methods are manager-directed with emphasis on sending the highest potential people through appropriate career paths. Person-centered methods facilitate self-diagnosis and development. The burden on management decreases as individuals gain career management skills (Storey, 1978). However, both the organization and the individual still have an ongoing responsibility for career management.

Career planning programs must be grounded in objective information. The organization's responsibility is to provide this information. Career paths, for example, should consist of descriptions of a logical sequence of work experiences (Walker, 1976). Job requirements should be determined from thorough job analyses. Extensive and frequently updated records should be kept on each individual's skills. Developmental experiences are necessary if individuals are to be prepared to follow defined career paths. Moreover, the career paths must represent logical and rational job changes, including lateral as well as vertical progression (Walker, 1976; Lopez, Rockmore, & Kesselman, 1980).

Match Jobs and People

Computer technology has made career management information systems possible. Personnel data bases or skills inventory systems have the capacity to retain a complete personal profile for each employee. The computer profile can be easily revised as employees acquire additional education, gain new skills, and undertake new work experiences. It is also possible to develop computerized records of job descriptions in terms of requirements necessary to perform each job. Computers can then be used to match job vacancies with available high potential managers. This is especially useful in large, geographically disbursed organizations in which it is difficult to provide equal opportunities to qualified candidates throughout the organization without such devices.

Smaller organizations without the resources or need for a sophisticated computerized system can rely on mechanical means to match individuals and jobs. For example, France's Euroquip Corporation, a firm with about 800 executives geographically disbursed in different plants and offices, uses a card file index (Miret, 1978). The index consists of a card for each manager and a card for each job. Information about job requirements and individual qualifications expressed in common language are coded into about 100 groups. The groupings show the similarity among different jobs, making it possible to identify paths from one job to another. Individuals who occupy two or three groupings in common with a job vacancy would be selected as candidates to fill the vacancy. The person ultimately chosen need not meet all the job requirements since the company recognizes that some skills can be developed on the job.

The subjective element of career planning and career choice should not be ignored. Despite the mechanistic nature of some job matching systems for identifying internal candidates for job vacancies, subjectivity enters into decisions made about people, as well as decisions individuals make about job opportunities. While career paths and realistic information are essential for formulating a meaningful career plan, the individual's goals and interests are also important ingredients. Recognizing this, many companies have instituted person-centered career planning programs. However, the extent of the individual's input into his or her own career plans varies from program to program.

Maintain Program Continuity and Flexibility

Career plans often need to be changed as more information becomes available. This does not invalidate the planning process since the plans serve the purpose of guiding behavior and establishing realistic goals. However, since plans are not facts, they must be kept flexible so that new information can be efficiently incorporated.

Integrate Career Planning with Other Human Resource Functions

The importance of relating career planning to other human resource functions has been emphasized throughout this chapter. Organizational career planning programs need to be closely linked with management training and development to ensure that developmental activities are available and actually used. In some situations, the enactment of the plan will involve new job assignments which are viewed as requisite for subsequent assignments (e.g., Wellbank et al., 1978). Staffing decisions which involve transfers or rotational job assignments should take into account the career plans and developmental needs of the employees. To the extent that career plans lead to development, the use of career planning will generate a larger talent pool to consider when making staffing decisions.

The primary inputs into an organizational career planning program are individual and organizational needs, goals, and abilities. Data on individuals are generated through assessments of performance and potential and self-assessments of career interests and ambitions. Both types of information are necessary to develop realistic career plans. Organizational needs and goals should be established through the human resource planning function and communicated to employees.

Human resource plans should identify future work force needs with respect to specific organizational goals. The organization's forecast of its future staffing requirements should be used to formulate career plans that take into account expected changes in the organization (Burack & Gutteridge, 1978). This should reduce managerial and technical obsolescence, and unrealistic and unfulfilled expectations.

POINTS TO CONSIDER IN DESIGNING AND IMPLEMENTING A CAREER PLANNING PROGRAM

A number of issues should be considered in the development and implementation of a career planning program.

1. *Does everyone need some type of career planning?* In line with a person-centered approach, participation in career planning should be voluntary. While the organization should have relevant career planning information and tools available, not all individuals will want to use them. Differences in abilities and career aspirations will determine who will benefit from a career planning program. Some individuals feel that career planning within the organization is too personal. They may be reluctant to talk about their own abilities and may resist feedback about their performance.

2. *Does career planning raise expectations?* Setting goals for development and advancement may enhance a person's effort to achieve them, but the goals must be attainable. Increasing one's skills in a particular field will result in disappointment if there are few job opportunities in that direction.

3. *Will employees accept job transfers, particularly if the transfer involves relocation?* Employees are more willing to move when the new job promises to be a challenge and a contribution to career development. Younger employees, and those in sales/marketing positions, tend to be more mobile than others (Brett & Werbel, 1980; Veiga, 1981a).

Brett & Werbel (1980) recommend that companies let the employee decide about accepting a job transfer involving relocation rather than preempting the employee's decision by not offering the transfer. They found that many common assumptions about who is willing to accept a job transfer were not true. For example, having teenage children, having a working spouse who was not highly job involved, or being female had little effect on accepting a job transfer. Furthermore, both those who had made a recent job move and those who had rejected a recent transfer opportunity were willing to move in the future.

4. *Can all managerial skills be acquired?* In some cases aptitude may be lacking. In other cases, needed skills may develop only after many years of experience and training (Boehm & Hoyle, 1977). For example, one or more training programs may improve a person's communication skills. Creativity, decision making, and intellectual skills, on the other hand, are factors a person generally brings to the job; they do not change much over time and they are difficult to improve substantially (Bray, Campbell, & Grant, 1974). Therefore, career planning should focus on weaknesses that can be strengthened, and on strengths that can be enhanced.

5. *Will career planning programs, especially those that are person-centered, meet resistance from supervisors?* Some supervisors feel they should plan for their subordinates' careers without involving them. Other supervisors are reluctant to supply subordinates with information they regard as proprietary. Such information may include data on job vacancies or reasons why a subordinate was rejected for a promotion. Moreover, all supervisors are not counselors. Some find it difficult to provide accurate feedback or honestly discuss the subordinate's advancement opportunities.

Another difficulty may arise when the organization depends on supervisors to supply information for a personnel data base for matching individuals to job vacancies. Such information is frequently out of date or inaccurate. Supervisors may avoid submitting complete information on their most valued subordinates for fear of losing them or for fear that the subordinate will receive opportunities that are not in their career plans. These difficulties may be overcome by supervisory training and clearly written, specific policies regarding career planning in the organization.

6. *Do problems arise when giving feedback on potential for advancement?* First, what does one tell a subordinate with low potential? While honesty is desirable, it is difficult to explain to individuals why they are unlikely to go further, especially when there is little they can do to change the situation. However, many managers would appreciate knowing about their prospects in the organization and can use this knowledge to reformulate their expectations or change their career course.

Second, what does one tell a subordinate with high potential when there are limited opportunities in the organization? Some individuals receive high potential ratings year after year with no change in job status. This may occur when there are few opportunities for promotion in a given specialty and there seems to be someone who is better qualified every time a vacancy is filled. Here again the best policy is to explain that while the subordinate's potential is high, the prospects for promotion are limited. This information will allow these subordinates to change their career course or be partially satisfied with the knowledge that they are valued by the organization.

7. *Do person-centered approaches to career planning encourage self-serving biases?* People are likely to overevaluate their own abilities when asked to rate themselves (Larwood & Whittaker, 1977). Mechanisms must be established for helping individuals formulate an accurate self-concept. Several of the methods described above help in this regard by emphasizing the value of feedback.

8. *What is the value of career planning when advancement opportunities are limited by depressed economic times, management surplus, or fewer retirements?* Even when human resource forecasts indicate that managerial talent will be needed in the future at middle and top levels of management, the tendency during low mobility periods is to de-emphasize or discontinue career planning. The fear is that expectations will be raised with little payoff to the individual in the short run. If bad times mean few opportunities for advancement, how can individuals be developed by moving them through the organization? Also, how can the organization justify allocating resources to career planning under such conditions? Career planning should include an examination of opportunities in the short and long run to help the individual understand reality. In such situations, organizations should turn to less traditional methods of development to maintain employee interest and commitment. For instance, job transfers or special short-term assignments may be initiated solely for developmental purposes. Without such opportunities, moves between organizations will become more frequent as a response of young managers in their quest for career advancement.

PERCEIVED EFFECTS OF CAREER PLANNING AND PLANS FOR IMPROVEMENT

Walker and Gutteridge (1979) asked the managers in their sample several questions about the effects of their organizational career planning efforts. The idea that career planning generally disrupts an organization was rejected by 94% of the respondents. The only potentially negative effects were that career planning systems were perceived as straining other personnel systems (27% said "agree" or "strongly agree") and that career planning may increase personal anxiety (39%). On the positive side, 89% of the respondents felt that turnover did *not* increase as a result of career planning efforts, 91% felt that career planning enhanced job performance, 92% felt that it equipped employees to use personnel systems more effectively, and 97% felt it allowed improved utilization of employee talent. However, 63% of the respondents believed that career planning activities increased the amount of work performed by supervisors, and 87% felt that *few* supervisors were currently equipped to do individual career counseling.

Organizational plans for improving their career planning programs included (Walker & Gutteridge, 1979, p. 39):

1. Improving and formalizing current practices.

2. Developing more objective individual assessments and performance appraisals.

3. Training supervisors and managers on career planning functions.

4. Giving more information on job requirements and job availability to employees.

5. Expanding and integrating career planning activities.

6. Increasing program effectiveness by gradual changes and improved linkages to implement personnel actions such as promotions and transfers.

7. Conducting pilot programs on new techniques (e.g., workbooks and workshops).

8. Giving increased attention to the needs of older employees preparing for retirement.

EVALUATING CAREER PLANNING

How do we know when a career planning program is effective? What is the influence of career plans and corresponding developmental activities on career progression? Do those who participate in career planning advance farther, perform better, feel more satisfied with their jobs, and/or have fewer career-family conflicts than those who do not participate? Are career plans used? Do the needed developmental assignments materialize and are the required training programs offered?

Questions such as these demand answers that require rigorous evaluation research. We begin this section by looking at several studies of career planning programs based on a review by Robinson & Glueck (1980). This is followed by a discussion of research problems and recommendations for evaluating career planning programs.

Several studies reviewed by Robinson and Glueck (1980) examine selected aspects of particular career planning programs. For example, Golembiewski (1972) studied the effects of career planning for twenty middle-aged sales managers who were to be demoted and possibly transferred due to budget cuts, not poor performance. The planning technique was an intensive three-phase process designed to prepare the managers for this situation, help them seek and plan a new career opportunity in a sales position, and then work with their new supervisors. Measures of effectiveness (i.e., dependent variables) were obtained at one month, three months, and twelve months after the program. They included self-concept, retention rate (the number of individuals who remained with the company), job satisfaction, productivity (e.g., the number of sales relative to number of calls on customers), and supervisory ratings of performance. The results were that job attitudes improved over time—initially low job satisfaction increased, and only one person left his new position. Performance was rated acceptable for all those who stayed, and productivity was above average or superior for eighteen of the twenty managers.

Crocker National Bank developed a career planning program which treats career counseling as a managerial activity and not a separate personnel function (Miller, 1978). Managers are expected to be aware of their employees' values and career goals as well as their own. A career planning workshop tries to stimulate supervisor-subordinate career discussions. A career planning interview with an employee relations representative aids the process of self-analysis, diagnosis of career opportunities in the organization, and formulation of career plans. Crocker estimates the utility of this overall process by using objective and subjective measures such as personnel replacement costs, number of employees who would have resigned if not for career counseling, job change statistics, and professional growth. The bank estimated it saved approximately $1,950,000 due to career planning based on decreased turnover, increased promotability, and improved performance.

Thornton (1978) evaluated the effects of a six-hour career planning workshop for ninety-seven secretaries. The heart of the program was a career planning activity which encouraged the secretaries to take actions to plan and advance their careers.

> This segment [of the workshop] called for each individual to write down specific actions she would take to: (a) identify current strengths and developmental needs (e.g., ask a peer or supervisor), (b) explore potential career opportunities and goals (e.g., check job posting or call a placement agency), and (c) specify and carry out some means of attaining the goal (e.g., take a course, make application, ask for new responsibility) (p. 473).

At the beginning of the workshop Thornton administered a paper-and-pencil measure of "Internal/External Locus of Control." This construct is a general expectancy for control of one's life. Internals prefer situations that allow them to control outcomes. Moreover, they are more willing to delay gratification and focus on long-term goals, and they are more achievement oriented in unstructured situations (Phares, 1973, cited in Thornton, 1978). In contrast, externals feel they have relatively little control over life events, and that they can do little to affect career outcomes.

Four months after the workshop the secretaries were asked to list specific career planning and advancement actions they had taken since the seminar. The results showed that internals were more likely to have explored potential career goals and to have carried out means of obtaining those goals than externals.

There are several limitations to the study which Thornton (1978) recognizes. There is no evidence that the workshop and the career planning component in particular had any effect at all since there was no control group which did not experience the workshop. (This problem is also true for Golembiewski's study.) Further, no attempt was made to verify the self-report responses about career actions.

Several studies have relied solely on participant reactions as evaluation criteria. Hastings (1978) assessed the reactions of bank officials and selected employees to a career assessment workshop and workbook. Participants' reactions were generally positive. Kotter, Faux, and McArthur (1978) developed a self-guided workbook and course for MBA students. After seven months on their first job, 45% of the graduates rated the course the best or one of the best they had taken. After several years, 80% rated the activity helpful.

These studies, with the exception of the Golembiewski study and the Crocker Bank experience, relied on weak measures of program effectiveness. In general, attitudes about career planning programs or other training devices tend to be highly favorable immediately following the activity, and these positive reactions tend to diminish over time (Goldstein, 1980). The lack of controlled experimental studies with behavioral outcome measures is typical of the training field (Goldstein, 1980; Campbell et al., 1970). One reason for this is the fact that career planning and development programs are designed to meet an organizational need. They do not arise from theories which are subjected to evaluation before or during application. This is not to say that theories have no relevance for career planning. Indeed, many behavioral and psychological principles are involved, as we have seen earlier in this chapter and as will be demonstrated again in the next chapter. But career planning is a case where practice has preceded theoretical development and research.

Another reason for the insufficient amount of research on career planning is that there are many different career planning programs, each with its own way of defining and interpreting career changes and program effectiveness (Robinson & Glueck, 1980). Longitudinal research is difficult and expensive to conduct particularly with adequate controls. Career plans may not be followed because organizational needs take precedence.

Table 5.4 depicts a model for an ideal evaluation research study. This is a standard Solomon four-group design intended to

TABLE 5.4
Solomon Four-Group Design for Evaluation Research

RANDOM AS-SIGNMENT OF 100 OR MORE PARTICIPANTS TO EXPERI-MENTAL AND CONTROL GROUPS	PRETEST IS GIVEN TO GROUPS 1 AND 2 ON SEVERAL EFFEC-TIVENESS MEASURES	GROUPS 1 AND 3 RECEIVE TRAINING	POSTTEST OF EFFECTIVENESS MEASURES GIVEN TO ALL GROUPS
Group 1	Pretest	Training	Effectiveness measures
Group 2	Pretest	No training (control group)	Effectiveness measures
Group 3	No pretest	Training	Effectiveness measures
Group 4	No pretest	No training (control group)	Effectiveness measures

separate the effects of career planning from measurement effects and normal changes over time. Participants are randomly selected for the study and randomly assigned to groups. Multiple indices of effectiveness should be used depending on the goals the program was designed to attain. Outcome measures include objective indices such as the quality and quantity of work, turnover, absenteeism, participation in developmental activities, rate of advancement, transfers and other job changes, and evidence that career plans are actually used in making career decisions. Subjective measures include job satisfaction, career satisfaction, career expectations, and reactions to the program.

Two control groups in the design do not experience career planning, although they may experience it sometime after the evaluation. More favorable outcomes should result for those who had career planning than for those who did not. To determine if the passage of time affects the outcome measures regardless of career planning, the Solomon four-group design compares the group that was measured at both points in time and *did not* have career planning with the group that was measured at both points in time and *did* have career planning. To evaluate the effects of being measured, the design compares the groups measured at both points in time with those measured only at the second point in time.

The time interval between measures presents some difficulty for career planning evaluation. Career planning should be part of a continuous cycle of planning, development, assessment of progress, and further planning. Therefore, career planning should not be a one-time event. Moreover, the effective enactment of career plans may have long-term effects.

Ideally, measurements should be taken at several points in time. But for how long? This should depend on the purpose of the program. If the intention is to plan for the next year, then one year would be a suitable time interval. Shorter time spans may be used if the desired effect is more immediate, as it was in the case of the sales manager and secretary career planning studies. If the intended effect is more than a year, it may be impossible or impractical to withhold career planning from the control groups until the evaluation is concluded. In such cases, "quasi-experiments" will be necessary. One type is a time series analysis which measures a group at several points in time before and after career planning. There may be several comparison groups differing in when they receive the career planning activity. (Chapter 6's discussion of evaluation methods for training and development can also be applied to career planning.)

SUMMARY

Organizational career planning practices include communicating career-related information, providing materials and support for self-assessment and planning, and offering career counseling and training programs. Career planning activities can be classified as individual, counselor–client, boss as counselor or coach, and group and other activities. Organizational career planning programs usually integrate several methods. Some programs are universal, meaning they are intended for anyone in the organization who chooses to use them. Others are designed for specific groups, such as managers with high advancement potential.

Potential ratings and assessment centers are methods for identifying high potential managers. Several identification techniques can be used as a screening-in process which separates those who should follow a standard career route from those who should be in an accelerated advancement program. This process should occur early in one's managerial career after one has had an opportunity to receive necessary orientation and other training, demonstrate performance and potential, and reflect on career goals. Individuals placed in an accelerated advancement program should experience a structured sequence of career planning and development activities.

An alternative approach to the establishment of an accelerated advancement program is to develop nonspecialized managers through extensive job rotation and slow progression. While job responsibilities are increased for those who are most able, promotions occur only when individuals have completely proven themselves.

Guidelines for a career planning system suggest that the organization establish flexible career paths, provide feedback on performance and potential, foster realistic expectations, delineate individual and organizational responsibility, manage information, match jobs and people, maintain program continuity and flexibility, and integrate career planning with other human resource functions.

Designing and implementing a career planning system requires determining the need for career planning, dealing with raised expectations, addressing job transfer and relocation issues, realizing that some performance dimensions are more easily developed than others, facing resistance from supervisors, being honest about opportunities in the organization, discouraging individuals from overevaluating their abilities, and recognizing the value of career planning in depressed economic times or conditions of management surplus and fewer retirements. Although career planning programs are generally perceived to be effective by those using them, evaluation research using multiple effectiveness measures and rigorous research designs is necessary to evaluate career planning programs.

Training and Development

6

The last chapter viewed career planning as an individual responsibility facilitated by organizational resources. Examples of
career planning programs were presented along with issues in
designing and evaluating such programs. This chapter describes
organizationally sponsored training and development programs.
The types of development needed by different individuals are
considered. Examples of organizational approaches to career
development are presented along with suggestions for implementing a career development program. Next, a method for
conducting training needs analysis is described. Training
methods are reviewed and types of training programs which may
be part of a career development effort are discussed. The chapter
concludes with suggestions for choosing and evaluating a training program.

ORGANIZATIONAL CAREER DEVELOPMENT

From the organization's perspective, career development consists of "those actions and circumstances leading to having the
needed number, and no more than the needed number, of fully
effective managers at all levels of the organization" (Bray, 1975).
Development helps the organization ensure that it will meet, but
not exceed, its human resource needs. It allows the organization
to promote high potential individuals from within rather than

having to rely on outside sources. To do this, the organization should continually monitor the availability of its human resource talent, evaluate individuals' strengths and weaknesses, and institute procedures for meeting future human resource needs.

These procedures cover more than isolated training programs. They involve the integration of human resource planning, individual career planning, and staffing decisions. Recruitment, selection, performance appraisal, and career planning all have developmental components—as do job assignments, supervisor—subordinate relations, and training in technical and supervisory skills. Who receives developmental experiences and the nature of these experiences will depend on the needs of the organization (identified through human resource planning), the desires and abilities of the individual (established through career planning), and job opportunities (arising through changes in technology, changes in personnel, changes in organizational objectives, etc.). Career development, therefore, should be viewed broadly as a sequence of training courses, job assignments, and other activities aimed at achieving career goals.

FACTORS AFFECTING CAREER DEVELOPMENT

Career Orientation

People differ in their views of what is acceptable career progress. Some people are concerned primarily with developing technical skills in their functional areas. They see themselves as professionals and have little desire to move into general management positions or other functions. They may be content to remain in the organization or they may "advance" by finding similar higher paying technical jobs in other organizations.

Some individuals want to improve both their technical and supervisory skills. They find it possible to maintain a strong identification with their profession while exhibiting loyalty to their employer. They may leave their technical specialty for a general management position, but they continue their involvement in the activities of professional societies.

Still others are interested in general management without a

specific area of expertise. Progression for them often means moving up the hierarchy even if it requires becoming knowledgeable in several technical areas.

Level in the Organization

Most organizations target training and development programs to employees at different hierarchical levels. While some organizations offer generic programs suitable to individuals at many levels, it is usually recognized that individuals at lower levels have different training needs from those at higher levels. The goal of training for career development is to provide experiences that are not normally available in the employee's job to prepare him or her for positions at the next organizational level. A training needs analysis is generally necessary to identify deficiencies between competent individuals at one level and the skills generally mastered at lower levels.

Career Stages

In Chapters 4 and 5 we noted that the nature of career planning differs in different career stages. A similar analysis can be made of development requirements at each career stage.

Stage 1: Exploration and trial.   The early career period should be a time for acclimation, learning, and becoming proficient on the job. A new hire's first year or two should provide ample opportunity to learn the first job and demonstrate performance and potential.

A developmental program for new hires should:

1. Provide opportunity to learn the first job and demonstrate performance on that job, and potential for other jobs.

2. Acclimate the employee to the organization and generate realistic expectations.

3. Provide time for self-analysis and initial career planning.

4. Facilitate learning about the organization, department, and career paths.

5. Offer needed supervisory and technical training.

6. Recognize individual differences in career interests and need for advancement.

7. Begin to screen employees into high potential programs.

The last point deserves explanation. The first few years should involve a screening-in process (see Chapter 5). Screening-in implies that all employees are initially on a standard career route. Those individuals who demonstrate high potential for advancement may be offered an accelerated advancement program, whereas others progress along the standard career route. Individuals performing inadequately are offered developmental experiences, transferred, or terminated.

This scenario differs from how some organizations train individuals in their early career years. Some provide no explicit training; others offer high potential applicants a strenuous "make-it or break-it" program as their first assignment. The latter two alternatives are not as desirable as the first, in our opinion. The rationale for screening people into a high potential program during the first or second year rather than immediately after entry into the organization is to help them become familiar with available opportunities and career alternatives while proving their worth. This should reduce the anxiety generated by a high risk–high reward program while still attracting ambitious applicants to the organization.

Stage 2: Establishment and advancement. During the next several years, individuals progress along a variety of career paths. Those in high potential programs will have training experiences which prepare them for higher levels. Those on a standard career route may have the opportunity to participate in similar training programs, but not in close succession. The pace may be slower and participation in training may be voluntary.

Training during establishment and advancement should be more general than during the early career stage when the emphasis is on learning a specific job. During establishment and advancement, job rotations may be used to give individuals new experiences and acquaint them with different areas of the organization. Leadership training may be important as individuals take on supervisory responsibilities. Training in other management skills may be implemented during this stage as well.

Stage 3: Mid-career.   Mid-career involves continued growth for some, maintenance for others, and decline for still others. Training for those in a "growth" mode during mid-career is likely to be similar to training during the establishment and advancement stage. That is, it will be a continuation of experiences that broaden and strengthen skills and prepare the individual for higher level positions. Training for those in a "maintenance" mode is likely to be self-initiated. These individuals seek out training for continued intellectual stimulation, to keep up with technical advances, or to learn new ways to manage younger employees. The organization may provide policy seminars for mid-career individuals, particularly those at higher levels, to enhance awareness of the environment and ways to manage change. Training for those in a "decline" mode may be aimed at reversing this descending career direction by acquiring new skills. Alternatively, it may prepare individuals for early retirement or for a second career outside the organization.

Stage 4: Disengagement.   Leaving one's formal work-role calls for financial planning and becoming more involved in nonwork activities. Training during this stage may help the individual prepare for termination or retirement. Some organizations have developed programs specifically for this purpose.

In summary, we view career development as a sequence of goal-directed training courses, job assignments, and other activities that should be varied depending on an individual's career orientation, level in the organization, and career stage. The next section suggests a framework for career development which links the above factors to development activities. It also demonstrates the tie between organizational career planning programs and employee development programs.

Fig. 6.1 *A career development framework*

A CAREER DEVELOPMENT FRAMEWORK

Before discussing specific training programs in the latter part of the chapter, we review what an overall targeted career development effort might look like. A model for such an effort is depicted in Fig. 6.1. The model outlines a process similar to the one used in the accelerated advancement program in Chapter 5 and suggests a cyclical relationship between career planning and training and development.

After initial target setting and career planning, development should consist of a series of critical job assignments and training experiences building toward a career target, with periodic evaluation, feedback, and reconsideration of the target and learning contract. In the following sections we discuss the notion of targeted development, the meaning of critical assignments, and different types of training experiences. A discussion of performance evaluation and feedback methods is beyond the scope of this book. For a review, see Latham and Wexley (1981).

Targeted Development

A career development program should link the results of individual assessment and career planning activities to training experiences. Development goes beyond courses to include positions, special projects, short-term assignments, and observing and modeling higher level personnel. The development experiences a person has should be based on *targeted development*— that is, matching the experiences to skills needed for target jobs. Experiences should be chosen based on the individual's strengths and weaknesses and the type of job the individual hopes to attain. The focus should be on skills that can be developed and on providing experiences that use and enhance current strengths.

Guidelines for Targeted Development

Behavioral science knowledge and practical experience provide a set of guidelines organizations may follow for employee development. The guidelines represent an ideal toward which organizations should strive. While the guidelines do not exhaust all desirable actions for development, they cover a range of actions from assessment of skills and abilities to setting targets and actions to achieve them. The guidelines are as follows:

1. Have an accurate and thorough understanding of skills and abilities required for each target position.

2. Provide development activities that reflect individual strengths, weaknesses, preferences, and goals.

3. Set target jobs and specific time frames for reaching those jobs.

4. Provide challenging job assignments as early as possible.

5. Assign the individual to effective role models who can provide enabling resources.

6. Provide job performance feedback.

7. Ensure accuracy and realism of expectations.

8. Expose the individual to a variety of functional areas within a department or in different departments.

9. Encourage a high level of commitment and involvement on the part of top management and participants.

10. Allow periodic evaluation and redirection of career plans.[1]

---

[1]We thank Joel Moses for his contribution to these guidelines.

Examples of activities for following these guidelines are listed in Table 6.1. Understanding required skills and abilities can be aided by well-documented job descriptions and clear communication of the job requirements. Supervisors who are effective role models should be identified and assigned to individuals on a targeted development program. Training may help supervisors provide meaningful feedback and communicate accurate and realistic expectations to subordinates. Commitment and involvement of supervisors and subordinates in targeted development can be enhanced by involving them in the design of the process as well as carrying it out. Also, subordinates' development should be part of the supervisor's objectives and contribute to the supervisor's performance evaluation and pay.

The targeted development model outlined in Fig. 6.1 specifies that individuals in the program receive critical job assignments, a variety of job experiences, and a sequence of courses and other training experiences directed to enhance skills needed for target jobs. These elements of the program are discussed below.

Job Assignments

Development should include a variety of job assignments, especially for high potential managers with some experience in their initial management position. Job variety helps maintain challenge and interest and ensures that the individual has experience in the areas important to the organization. The number and length of the positions held is an individual matter. Jobs vary along such dimensions as line and staff, technical and nontechnical, and working with others and working alone. Participants should have experience in jobs with various combinations of relevant dimensions (although not necessarily all possible combinations of dimensions). Since some departments like to develop their lower level managers within the department, it may be necessary to take advantage of the variability within departments in making job transfers for developmental purposes.

Critical lower level assignments are those that require knowledge and abilities typically used by middle managers but

TABLE 6.1
Activities for Following Guidelines for Targeted Development

GUIDELINES	ACTIVITIES
Ensure understanding of target job skills and abilities.	Prepare well-documented job descriptions.
	Supervisors clearly communicate job requirements.
Provide developmental activities.	Use learning contracts that specify a logical sequence of training experiences.
Set target jobs and time frames.	Discuss and establish as part of career planning.
Provide challenging job assignments.	Identify jobs and projects with components critical to the individual and the organization.
	Redesign jobs and projects along critical dimensions.
Assign effective role models.	Assign individuals to supervisors who are known to be good role models.
Provide feedback.	Train supervisors to give meaningful feedback.
Ensure accurate and realistic expectations.	Clearly communicate expectations. Encourage job visits.
Ensure a variety of experiences.	Vary assignments along such dimensions as line-staff, technical-nontechnical, working with others and alone.
	Take advantage of variation between jobs within departments for easy transfers.
Encourage commitment and involvement.	Involve supervisors and subordinates in designing and carrying out the program.
	Reward supervisors for developing subordinates.
Allow evaluation and redirection.	Annual examination of career progress. Rewrite learning contract and reset targets.

not lower level managers. Characteristics of critical assignments include working constructively with subordinates, working with peers, recommending and/or developing policies, working under pressure, making oral presentations, developing specialized skills, coping with rapid change and ambiguity, making important judgmental decisions, and having an opportunity to take risks.

A checklist might be formulated and applied to each job possibility to determine the extent to which it possesses critical elements. An example of such a checklist is presented in Table 6.2. The first part of the checklist could have been developed by an individual prior to a career planning meeting with his supervisors. The individual selected job elements he believed were critical to his career development. The supervisor selected items she believed were critical to the individual's development. These are listed on the second part of the form. The supervisor and subordinate then discuss their lists, revise them, and check items that apply to each target job considered during the career planning discussion. Since a custom-designed checklist such as the one in Table 6.2 might not include important items, and time may not be available to generate and revise such a list, a standard instrument might be used, such as the Job Diagnostic Survey (Hackman & Oldham, 1980) or the Position Description Questionnaire (Page & Gomez, 1979; Colarelli, Stumpf, & Wall, 1981). Such devices would help evaluate the contribution of each targeted job to the individual's career development. They could also be applied to the individual's current assignment or project, to identify areas that might be redesigned to enhance the position's developmental value (Dunnette, Hough, & Rosse, 1979).

Courses and Other Training Experiences

Training should follow a planned sequence of experiential and nonexperiential activities. These might be specified in a "learning contract" written by the participant during career planning. Examples of relevant training programs are discussed later in this chapter. In addition to formal training, individuals should take advantage of experiences available in the organization but

TABLE 6.2
Example of a Job Description Checklist

Potential Target Job: _____   Date: _____

Part I. Job elements critical to my career development.

_____ Making decisions.
_____ Supervising project work
_____ Working with peers
_____ Recommending and/or developing programs
_____ Giving oral presentations
_____ Analyzing market research reports
_____ Defining problem areas for supervisor attention
_____ Using different skills
_____ Monitoring key business indicators
_____ Being creative
_____ Receiving feedback
_____ Having clear objectives
_____ Chairing a committee or task force

Part II. My supervisor's list of job elements critical to my career development.

_____ Dealing with uncertainty
_____ Delegating
_____ Coordinating
_____ Giving feedback
_____ Having responsibility for entire projects
_____ Taking calculated risks
_____ Learning a different part of the department's operation
_____ Working under pressure
_____ Periodic reassignment to different projects
_____ Having to meet target dates

which are not usually thought of as training. Examples include making public presentations, recruiting job applicants for professional positions, and working on special assignments such as a task force.

Examples of Career Development Programs

Several of the career planning programs described in Chapter 5 have development components. As noted above, the processes of career planning and career development are integrally related. For instance, Bell of Pennsylvania's career program helps individuals establish a realistic schedule for meeting their career goals. This includes a five-year personal development plan and a work preference document to help obtain developmental assignments. The insurance company's career paths designate job assignments which would be part of a developmental program. Polaroid's career development activities consist of workshops geared to developing self-assessment and career planning skills. Our accelerated advancement program, as already noted, prescribes a cyclical process of planning and development.

IMPLEMENTING A CAREER DEVELOPMENT PROGRAM

Linking career planning with development implies a long-term comprehensive program tailored to individual needs. For instance, a program may consist of a job orientation, joint boss-subordinate target setting, critical job assignments, courses, and other experiences to prepare high potential individuals for middle management. Making this happen requires an operating structure. The first step in creating this structure is to delineate responsibility for different elements of the program.

The Program Manager's Role

Since the employee's unit is ultimately responsible for effectively utilizing its human talent, program managers may be needed to help generate cooperation and commitment. The organization's human resource department can assist by providing career planning resources, monitoring each individual's progress, and evaluating the program as a whole. In organizations where each department maintains prime responsibility for personnel management, this function may be assigned to a departmental personnel coordinator.

While a program manager is not a necessary component to all career planning and development programs, the program manager can be critical to a development program's success. We have observed several cases of programs that failed because of the lack of program managers or because program managers are disinterested. In one case, a program was greatly improved when a new manager was assigned to the position. The manager had many contacts within the organization, was respected, and took the position's responsibilities seriously.

The program manager's role would typically include many of the following tasks:

- Conducting orientation programs
- Providing participants with self-development and career planning aids
- Helping determine target jobs, career plans, and a learning contract detailing planned training experiences
- Monitoring progress toward career objectives
- Acting as an interface with bosses and participants
- Helping negotiate transfers and promotions
- Providing career counseling
- Holding group meetings to share experiences
- Arranging for training courses and other activities (e.g., job visits)
- Holding subordinate-boss meetings to discuss the subordinate's career plans and progress

The success of many career development programs depends on the selection, training, and evaluation of the program manager. The program manager should be an individual with high potential for advancement and with experience in a variety of positions and functions. The program manager should be adept in data gathering and possess analytical, evaluative, feedback, and interpersonal skills. The company should support the program manager by viewing the position as an important developmental assignment. Training and support staff should be provided, good performance should be rewarded, and the manager's role in relationship to bosses and program participants should be clearly specified.

Program Evaluation

Evaluating a large-scale career development program is similar to the evaluation of career planning programs and is more complex than evaluating a single course (which is discussed later in this chapter). Program managers should maintain data for monitoring the program, including a record of how many participants are completing the program and how long it is taking. They should compare participants in the program with those not in the program on their career progress, quality of work, career satisfaction, and turnover. Moreover, program managers should be sure that job assignments and training experiences are consistent with job targets and learning contracts.

Summary

The previous two sections consider career development as a broad range of activities integrated with individual assessment and career planning. Targeted development links individual needs to development activities. These activities consist of critical assignments and a variety of training experiences. Implementing a career development program can be facilitated by a program manager. Finally, program evaluation is an important part of a program's operation.

The rest of the chapter focuses on the content of various training programs and evaluation criteria. We begin by discussing a training needs analysis—a method for determining what types of training programs should be offered by the organization. We recognize that new training programs cannot be developed to meet each individual's needs. While targeted development directs individuals to one program or another, training needs analysis identifies where major deficiencies lie for various groups of employees in the organization and what skills and abilities training programs should focus on. Next we examine different training methods and types of training programs. Examples of training programs are then given, including programs offered by corporations, management training firms, and universities. In the last sections, we cover issues in selecting a training program and methods for evaluation.

TRAINING NEEDS ANALYSIS

Developing and operating a training program can involve considerable time and expense. Consequently, there should be a specific need for the program. Sometimes the need is obvious— for example, new employees may require specific job knowledge in order to perform well. In other situations the need is less obvious. In general, training for career development should arise from the needs of individuals to have certain experiences which they feel, or the organization believes, will foster their career progression. More specifically, "a developmental need . . . deals with the total growth and effectiveness of the individual, particularly as the person expands realized abilities toward the potential that he or she seems capable of achieving. . . . Developmental activities are pointed toward future, higher-order responsibilities than those held by the individual at present" (Morrison, 1976, p. 9–2).

Each individual's development needs should be identified during the career planning process. The development program can then be varied to fit the individual depending on the person's career orientation, organizational level, and career stage. Organizations, however, must determine what training programs they will offer and what outside programs they will support. Organizational training policies and program investment decisions should be made on the basis of an aggregate needs analysis—one that encompasses the needs of the organization or major subunits of the organization. For instance, an analysis may be conducted for all third level managers regardless of job function, or more specifically for all third level marketing managers.

There are two primary elements to a needs analysis: (1) development of a "mastery model" detailing characteristics of highly competent individuals, and (2) diagnosis of deficiencies in individuals who have not yet reached that level of competency (e.g., new employees) (Barr, 1980).

Generating a Mastery Model

A mastery model should consist of a definition of the tasks carried out by those who are competent performers, and a detailed description of the knowledge and skills that allow them to maintain a level of mastery (Barr, 1980). The steps involved in developing such a model are: (1) identifying the most competent performers, (2) analyzing their job behaviors and personal characteristics, and (3) synthesizing the material to generate a description of the various tasks, resources used, and skills and knowledge required to perform each task.

Identifying highly competent performers.   A highly competent performer is someone who excels in the job, performs at the highest levels, and exhibits mastery of the most important tasks.

Nominations of highly competent performers may be obtained from supervisors, resource review committees (i.e., groups of supervisors who periodically discuss human resource requirements and make staffing decisions), or top executives. Departmental promotion lists or performance appraisal data are other sources that can be used to identify competent performers.

Analyzing job behaviors and personal characteristics.   A comprehensive job analysis is the foundation of a training needs analysis. The elements of behavior and individual characteristics under investigation will depend on the group of individuals being analyzed. If the competency model is based on a single job in one functional area, then elements may be highly specific. If the model is to apply to all those at a certain organizational level across job functions, then elements will have to be more general. The advantage of the general approach is that the mastery model can be applied broadly to many jobs in the organization. The disadvantage is that specific task elements may be missed. Training requirements for such specific tasks would have to be identified and addressed at the department level.

There are many job analysis methods from which to select. These include checklists, frequency counts, questionnaires, interviews, and observations (Cascio, 1978). The checklist method requires the job incumbent to check from a long list of those behaviors required by the job. A checklist may be augmented by noting the frequency of each behavior and its importance to the job. Questionnaires have also been designed to assess both the amount and importance of job activities along previously defined dimensions.

Another method involves interviews during which the job analyst asks highly competent performers to describe their jobs. The job analyst collects examples of particularly effective behavior and may also observe the individual and record the frequency of various behaviors. One study of this sort was conducted by Mintzberg (1973) who observed the presidents of several organizations for one week each. Mintzberg also had the presidents maintain a diary, a schedule of meetings, and records of telephone conversations.

Checklists, questionnaires, interviews, and observations focus on job behaviors. Another aspect of the development of a mastery model is the assessment of personal characteristics that distinguish better from poorer performers. This focuses on basic abilities, personality attributes, and other individual characteristics. For instance, a test battery may assess elements of intelligence, interpersonal ability, needs, attitudes, expectations, and ambitions relevant to highly competent performance.

Probably the best approach to job analysis and individual assessment is to use a variety of methods (Cascio, 1978). The most relevant information is that which is corroborated by several different techniques.

Synthesizing results into a mastery model.   The above process results in the components of a mastery model—a description of what highly competent performers do, how they do it, and what knowledge and skills are required. These components need to be integrated for subsequent use in decision making. Variation in the job behaviors of highly competent performers should be expected since there are different ways to perform well in the same job. Variation might also occur when the individuals have somewhat different job functions even though they are at the same organizational level. A mastery model that covers many jobs has a wide "bandwidth." The tasks and behaviors are organized into general categories, such as leadership or planning. In cases where the mastery model applies to only specific jobs, the tasks and behaviors need not be grouped.

Example of a Mastery Model

A growing national fast food restaurant chain was concerned about preparing its new franchise owner-operators for management responsibilities. Many of the new owners had little prior supervisory experience. The headquarters training group offered courses in accounting, marketing, and technical aspects of franchise operation, but there were no courses in managing people. Several franchise owners had serious problems with turnover, tardiness, and absenteeism. The headquarters staff decided that a training needs analysis was necessary before embarking on a training program, if indeed this was the appropriate solution.

The study began by identifying thirty of the most competent franchise owners—those with high profits and few personnel problems. Interview questions were prepared and twenty of the thirty franchise owners were interviewed. Three critical performance dimensions associated with managing people were identified: (1) motivating employees, (2) giving directions, and (3) coordinating work activities. In addition, four relevant individual characteristics (skill dimensions) were identified: (1) planning and organizing skills, (2) interpersonal skills, (3) leadership—the ability to direct others to accomplish tasks, and (4) flexibility.

The researchers then observed each of the ten remaining managers in the highly competent group. Observations recording the frequency of various behaviors were made on two eight-hour days two weeks apart. The owners were interviewed after the observations so the researchers would thoroughly understand the reasons for different actions.

Next, the mastery model was written. The document had a separate section for each performance dimension with several examples of critical incidents for each dimension. Each critical incident description contained a summary of the resources used, the behaviors involved, the outcomes, and the primary skills applied. A portion of the mastery model is shown in Table 6.3. Additional sections (not included in the table) described the fre-

TABLE 6.3
Excerpt from the Franchise Owner's Mastery Model for Managing People

---

Performance dimension: Motivating employees

Critical incident: Designed a lottery for personnel who were present and on time each day for a week. The lottery, held every Saturday night, offered a chance to win record albums. Later instituted a second lottery for clerks with correct cash register accounts.

Resources: Employee's desire to participate; cost of albums.

Behaviors: Maintaining records to determine eligibility for the lotteries; determining what albums were valued.

Outcomes: Lower absenteeism and tardiness; lower dollar losses due to errors.

Skills: Organizing and planning; interpersonal skills; flexibility.

Performance dimension: Coordinating work activities

Critical incident: Instituted a monthly "round table" discussion on ways to improve service quality.

Resources: Cooperation among employees; taking the time.

Behaviors: Scheduling meetings; preparing agendas; willingness to implement suggestions.

Outcomes: Better understanding of what customers want; increased business; increased employee cooperation.

Skills: Interpersonal skills; flexibility; organizing and planning.

Performance dimension: Giving direction

Critical incident: Developed a system for employees' self-monitoring of inventory and waste during a recent supplier's strike.

Resources: Inventory data; employees' cooperation.

Behavior: Holding employees accountable.

Outcomes: More effective use of ingredients and supplies; a system that could be used after the strike.

Skills: Leadership; interpersonal skills.

---

quency and importance of the different resource behaviors, outcomes, and skills, and provided flow charts of work activities.

Deficiency Diagnosis

A mastery model lists critical elements of highly competent performance. It does not describe average performance or minimum performance requirements. Training needs are evident when the knowledge and skills typical of highly competent performance are compared to the knowledge and skills of those who have not yet achieved that level of mastery. Therefore, a diagnostic analysis is necessary to (1) support the mastery model, (2) determine the target population's skills and knowledge, and (3) identify deficiencies in the target population compared with the mastery performers (Barr, 1980). This can be made explicit by returning to our example.

A diagnostic test was conducted on all the franchise owners in the company. These people were divided into four subgroups for purposes of analysis: (1) new franchise owners—the target population, (2) owners with two or more years experience who had the most personnel problems and who might also need training, (3) experienced owners with a few personnel problems, (4) owners in the highly competent group. If the diagnosis revealed differences between the highly competent owners and the others, the mastery model would be supported and deficiencies could be identified.

Several assessment procedures were considered for the deficiency diagnosis including multiple-choice questions, observation of on-the-job behavior, and business simulations. The procedures chosen were an essay test and an in-basket which asked the franchise owners how they would handle several critical situations. Different situations were presented for each of the three performance dimensions. The scoring evaluated the quality of the solutions and the frequency with which each skill dimension was exhibited.

The results indicated that planning and organizing skills were strong for all owners but that leadership and interpersonal skills were weaknesses for new owners and the least competent experienced owners. Flexibility seemed to increase somewhat with experience but was still lowest for the least competent owners. Regarding the performance dimensions, greatest weaknesses were identified in motivating employees and giving direction.

"Developability"

After a needs analysis has been conducted and deficiencies have been identified, it is necessary to tie these deficiencies to training experiences in an effort to alleviate the deficiencies, and in some cases, turn them into strengths. Some management skills cannot be developed. By the time a person begins working, certain individual characteristics have been established. These include intelligence, decision-making ability, and perhaps the ability to work with others. While it may be possible to make some changes in such dimensions, the cost to the organization and the time involved may make training infeasible. Nevertheless, developmental job assignments and courses may be valuable to individuals who are already fairly strong on these dimensions so they can enhance their abilities and prepare for higher level positions. Some skills, such as communication ability, can be changed more easily, and an effective training program may lead to considerable improvement. In cases where training and development may not be fruitful, the solution may be to select people who already have the needed skills.

Once it has been decided what skills and knowledge dimensions are important and can be developed, it is necessary to identify training methods. This is the topic of the next section.

To continue the example of the training needs analysis conducted for the franchise owners, the results of the analysis led to the development of a sequence of two three-day courses covering incentive systems, behavior modification applied to business, team building, and participative management. It was recognized that some of the elements of leadership may not improve since some individuals would find it difficult to implement the principles discussed in the courses. In hopes of improving the program's success, a trainer visited each owner several weeks after the program to reinforce desired behaviors and make suggestions for change.

TRAINING METHODS

Training generally involves several different ways to communicate information (Campbell et al., 1970). One is *information presentation.* Lectures, films, and reading material are all examples of this approach. The participant tends to be a passive recipient and there is no opportunity to vary the training to suit the needs of different individuals. *Group discussions* and *self-paced learning,* on the other hand, require that the individuals participate in the process by demonstrating what is learned or asking for new information. *Cases* and *simulations* such as role playing involve the trainee in a vicarious and/or experiential learning process. *On-the-job training,* however, is most common. Unfortunately, this is seldom formalized. Managers often have little incentive to provide special training for subordinates. Moreover, all managers are not suitable trainers since effective training requires patience, knowledge of reinforcement techniques, and ability to serve as a successful role model. Managers who are marginal performers cannot be expected to inculcate inner work standards in their subordinates.

Another type of training is *self-instruction.* The trainee purchases (or is given) training materials and learns without the aid of an instructor or guide. Many organizations offer short courses, stemming from correspondence courses, to those motivated to participate in self-instruction.

Sabbaticals are another form of training. Borrowing the idea from academic institutions, some companies such as Xerox, Polaroid, and IBM offer executives time off with pay to participate in community action projects, research, special scientific endeavors, and government or professional activities not directly related to their function in the organization. Such programs benefit the community as well as the company's reputation. They tend to provide the participant with new experiences and a feeling of self-renewal.

The desire to design more effective training methods has led to the development of a sophisticated training technology. Audio cassettes, videotapes, films, workbooks, and computer programs are examples of techniques used alone or in combination with others. The goal in all cases is to present the material clearly and in a manner that will maintain interest.

Behavior Modeling

The early works of Watson, Thorndike, Skinner, and others in behavioral modification contributed substantially to the training field. The essential notion of behavior modification is that individuals repeat behaviors that lead to desirable consequences (i.e., reinforcements) (Hamner, 1974). While some training programs rely solely on behavior modification, others combine behavior modification with other procedures.

Behavior modeling applies certain behavior modification principles to training. Assume a class is being trained in leadership skills. A videotape is used to demonstrate conditions requiring that the supervisor structure the subordinate's task. Managers in the class are given an opportunity to role-play the situation while being observed by the instructor. The instructor rewards appropriate behavior with verbal praise and corrects inappropriate behavior. The trainees' supervisors are also trained to reward appropriate behavior so that classroom learning transfers to the job setting.

The principles involved in behavior modeling are as follows (after Goldstein & Sorcher, 1974):

- *Modeling*—Trainees are taught learning points and are provided with examples via videotape.
- *Role-playing*—Trainees play the role of supervisors and subordinates engaged in an interaction similar to the one on the videotape.

- *Reinforcement*—The instructor uses social reinforcement (e.g., praise) to encourage trainees to apply the behavior demonstrated.
- *Transfer of training*—Supervisors are trained to reinforce their subordinates when they exhibit the behavior taught in the training program.

Behavior modeling uses behavior modification by demonstrating to the trainee the nature of the situation (stimulus) and the desired behavior (response). Trainees are reinforced with praise (consequence) when they demonstrate the behavior during the practice session and on the job. This process requires (1) clearly specifying the behaviors that are to be trained, (2) observing behaviors and measuring their occurrence, (3) rewarding the desired behavior, and (4) observing appropriate changes in behavior (Miller, 1978).

Several studies report the effectiveness of behavior modeling training (Byham, Adams, & Kiggins, 1976; Decker, 1980; Latham & Saari, 1979; Moses & Ritchie, 1976). While more evaluation research is needed (McGhee & Tullar, 1978), behavior modeling is one training method that has a strong theoretical foundation and that may be applied in training general managerial skills such as elements of supervision.

TYPES OF TRAINING PROGRAMS

Three types of training may be distinguished: *orientation training, technical skills training,* and *managerial skills training.* Orientation training is used at all levels to indoctrinate newcomers (Wanous, 1980). New recruits, for example, are frequently given an orientation to the organization, covering its objectives and the benefits it offers as well as formal rules employees are expected to follow. Orientation sessions may also be held for newly promoted individuals to help them get acquainted with their new peers, introduce them to top executives, and explain procedures and behaviors expected of them. In addition to the content of orientation programs, the fact that they are offered suggests to the new employees the importance of their roles.

Technical skills training focuses on acquainting employees with new technology, recent advances in the field, or instruction in a new or outside field. The goals are to broaden perspectives and guard against professional obsolescence. Such training may be short-term and offered "in-house" by the company staff—as would be likely for refresher courses—or it may be long-term and given "off-site" at a university or company-sponsored training institute.

The third type of training focuses on general managerial skills. This training takes on different forms at different organizational levels. Lower level managers may be given an opportunity to participate in workshops lasting several hours to several days. These workshops may be offered by trainers employed by the company, consultants, or local university faculty. Examples of subjects include time management, budget planning, leadership, decision making, conflict management, and career planning. Workshops for higher level managers may focus on corporate strategy, organization design, productivity, and economic and political trends and their impact on the organization. Experts may be asked to present different views. Many universities offer executive development programs ranging from several weeks to a year. Participants may cover material on the arts, humanities, and social sciences in addition to management. The assumption in these cases is that managers with an eclectic education will be better able to cope with the changing business environment.

To summarize, there are a variety of training methods and different types of training that might be adopted in response to a training needs analysis. We now discuss examples of management training programs offered by different organizations.

EXAMPLES OF MANAGEMENT TRAINING PROGRAMS

Some organizations offer sequences of training courses. Individuals may take part in different training at different stages of their careers. One course or workshop builds on what was learned in previous training experiences. Other organizations institute training on an as-needed basis with little or no concern for the link between the training programs and their contribution to overall career development. Technical and managerial skills training represents a useful investment only if those trained spend much of their careers in the organization. Thus, the most extensive training programs are likely to be offered by long-term employers rather than employers who experience rapid turnover.

The following examples describe one or more management training programs offered by different organizations as of this writing. Some of the programs may no longer exist in the forms described since training programs are frequently refined, and new programs are added in response to changing needs. Nevertheless, the examples are valuable in demonstrating the types of programs offered.

The Bell System

The American Telephone and Telegraph Company (AT&T) emphasizes the selection and identification of management potential using assessment centers and supervisory potential ratings (Digman, 1978). Assessment center ratings are also used as criteria for advancement and transfers. Training programs are used to enhance managerial skills. Examples of a number of different management training programs at AT&T are reviewed below (after Luxenberg, 1978/79).

Supervisory relationships training. The goal of this course is to help first level managers deal more effectively with their subordinates. Situations covered include work performance, absenteeism, and discrimination. The course meets one half day per week for five, consecutive weeks. Following a behavior modeling approach, the course is instructor-led with videotape demonstrations, behavior rehearsals, and group feedback. Trainees utilize what they have learned and share experiences at the next class session. The objectives are to maintain open communications between subordinates and supervisors, enhance subordinates' self-esteem, and solve interpersonal problems with a minimum of destructive conflict.

Bell advanced management program.   This program arose from the need to prepare high potential managers for officer level positions. An analysis of mandatory retirements and other attrition yielded an expected turnover of over 50% of those at presidential and officer levels between 1976 and 1983. While the company realized that challenging job assignments would be necessary to develop high potential managers, additional experience would also be necessary if the future executives were to be able to bring about the needed changes in the business due to decreased government regulation, the growing emphasis on marketing, and the importance of human resource planning and utilization. A month-long program was designed, focusing on the skills needed to evaluate and respond to vested interest groups, how to identify key concerns from ambiguous situations, and how to maintain a flexible posture. Participants are high potential upper-middle managers (those at fourth and fifth level in a seven level hierarchy) identified by company presidents and vice presidents. The philosophy in selecting participants is, "select your best so they can do their best." A steering committee determines program content. The program, held at a major university, draws instructors from a number of universities, selecting them on the basis of their teaching ability and consulting experience. Each class, consisting of about thirty-six managers, is directed by a Bell System vice president. The methods used include cases, group discussions, films, and lectures to cover such topics as the business environment, the management of change, leadership, and patterns of conflict escalation and resolution.

Corporate policy seminars.   This is a year-round program held at a conference center. When in operation, approximately sixty fifth and sixth level managers participate during each one-week session. After all managers at these levels have experienced the program, a new seminar is designed and the process begins again. The aim is to increase top managers' understanding of critical outside forces. Issues covered are political, social, and economic. Human resources and technological advances are emphasized. Outside experts and AT&T professionals make presentations and moderate group discussions. Topics covered change periodically depending on changes in issues facing the company.

Some of the Bell System operating telephone companies have instituted policy seminars for middle level managers. These seminars allow dialogue on the critical issues facing particular operating units. The seminars vary in length and may include problem solving and progress reports on emerging issues.

Other Bell System programs. Many other training programs exist in the Bell System. A directory compiled in 1977 listed 286 management training modules. Many of these were developed by the operating telephone companies to meet specific needs. Courses are available in such areas as counseling skills, affirmative action, finance, group development, management communications, reading skills, safety, and time management. Also, executive development courses and MBA programs offered at local universities often complement Bell System programs. The philosophy is that university courses and programs should directly prepare employees for operating the telecommunications business (Luxenberg, 1978/79). An effort is made to consolidate and centralize training programs to avoid duplication and ensure high quality.

IBM

Other organizations such as IBM have similar types of management training directed toward their needs. IBM managers at many levels, for example, participate in developmental seminars and other training courses covering functionally oriented topics (Digman, 1978).

New first level managers attend a one-week "New Managers School" within thirty days of their appointment. Self-study courses and other management training are used as managers gain more experience. Experienced managers attend a one-week management school every few years. Topics covered with lower level managers include techniques of management; higher level managers focus on decision-making skills. High potential middle managers—those on an "executive resource list"—attend a three-week advanced management school focusing on the external forces affecting the company. A three-week program for executives (including one week at the Brookings Institution) provides key functional managers with a broader perspective on the external environment. In addition, executive level seminars are held at several major universities to expose managers to current and future oriented business philosophies.

Xerox

Xerox has established minimum, mandatory management training requirements similar to the IBM approach. Xerox's programs start with individuals who have not yet held a management job and extend to those in senior management positions. The management preparatory course, lasting one week, covers fundamentals of management and provides participants with an opportunity to think about whether or not they want a management position. A one-week course for newly appointed managers covers company values, important personnel policies and procedures, and general managerial skills. A two-week middle management course deals with managing people. It covers interpersonal skills, observation methods, and feedback techniques and concludes with a one-and-a-half-day planning process. A course lasting two weeks for upper middle managers and another one-week course for executives cover business strategy and planning and are run by business school professors.

Lockheed

The need to react quickly and effectively to an often turbulent business environment led Lockheed to develop executive level courses similar to AT&T's corporate policy seminars and the programs offered by IBM to its executives. Lockheed's Executive Institute accommodates twenty high potential executives one level below the corporate officer level. Forty percent of the training time involves making persuasive oral communications, using videotape feedback, and coaching. Unlike some programs, Lockheed's approach is highly "results oriented." Immediate improvement in personal effectiveness is expected.

Union Carbide Corporation

Union Carbide offers several series of developmental programs tailored to specific classes of employees including: "Programs for Supervisors," "Programs for Managers," and "Programs for Executives." Participation in each series is voluntary; however, attendance is based on a job-related need and requires departmental sponsorship. Program goals are to help individuals already doing an effective job do an even better job and prepare individuals for future career growth within the company. All programs are designed to complement other forms of skill development such as on-the-job training and attendance at university or other external programs.

Union Carbide's Corporate Management Development Unit offers a "Needs Analysis Guide" for each series of programs. Potential participants are instructed to discuss with their managers the areas that need development and their career plans, reflect on their strengths and weaknesses, and seek feedback from peers that might clarify the areas needing work. Once the areas to be improved are identified, individuals are directed to the Needs Analysis Guide to select the specific program(s) designed to fulfill their needs. There are a variety of programs including Finance and Accounting, Time Management, and Productive Conflict Management (Wall, Awal, & Stumpf, 1981). A special program—Analyzing Managerial Skills—is also available to help individuals diagnose their managerial strengths and weaknesses (Colarelli, Stumpf, & Wall, 1981).

ARCO

Arco offers its managers a series of three five-day "Management Continuum" courses. The first is for those who do not yet have supervisory responsibilities to train them in basic supervisory skills. Leadership skills are covered in the second course. The third course is for higher level managers. The company also offers a two-week executive seminar which includes speakers from inside and outside the company. Aimed at executives, the course covers corporate strategies and changes in, and responses to, the external environment. The goal is to broaden the perspective of executives who often are highly specialized and have a tendency to lose sight of the many factors facing the business.

Consulting Firms and Nonprofit Associations

Consulting firms and management associations offer a wide variety of management development programs. These may be useful to organizations that are just starting a training program or do not choose to operate their own training department. The American Management Association, the National Training Laboratories, and many universities offer workshops in cities nationwide. Typical programs offered by these and other organizations are reviewed below. They are mentioned not as endorsements but as illustrations of available courses and workshops. In most cases, the following information was obtained from brochures advertising the course; data regarding their effectiveness were not presented.

The Center for Creative Leadership, headquartered in Greensboro, North Carolina, is an example of an organization that offers a spectrum of management courses. Topics covered include decision making, creativity, performance appraisal, and leadership. A series of programs entitled "By Women—For Women" consists of short courses in career development, management effectiveness, public speaking, coalition building, and interview effectiveness. The Center specializes in a leadership development program which features extensive individual assessment and feedback. The course material is also available in manual form to aid companies in instituting their own programs. Center for Creative Leadership courses typically feature multimedia presentations, realistic simulations, and group discussions.

The American Management Association (AMA) offers a variety of standardized programs for managers at all levels. Their Executive Effectiveness Course consists of two units; unstructured group sessions to help "see yourself as others see you" and more structured group sessions covering conflict resolution, team management, and role playing. Each unit is one week long and is given two to six months apart from the other unit. Another AMA course is entitled "For Men and Women Moving Up in Management." Four separate one-week units cover managerial dynamics (e.g., forecasting, setting objectives, organizing, communicating, and decision making), analytical tools of management (focusing on the planning process and financial management), human resource management (including performance measurement, appraisal, motivation, and stress management), and a leadership laboratory (with experiences in team building, job enrichment, and management by objectives). A special course addresses "Management Skills for New First-Line Women Supervisors and Administrative Assistants." "Action Tools for the Middle Manager" is a course on career management, communications, problem solving/decision making, and coaching for staff development. Instructors for these courses are often affiliated with business or consulting firms and/or universities. AMA courses are offered in their own facilities and in hotels around the country. In addition to numerous management courses and workshops, AMA publishes books, self-study manuals, and audio cassettes in most areas of business.

The National Training Laboratories (NTL) Institute for Applied Behavioral Science began in 1947 with the development of human relations laboratories called T (for training)-groups. T-groups utilize small unstructured groups to help trainees develop insights about themselves and others. While T-groups tend to be stressful, they have been found to lead to valuable self-insight. NTL has considerably expanded its offerings to include experience-based learning aimed at developing many areas of individual potential. Titles of courses on management and executive development include "Managing Change for Managers," "Men and Women in Organizations: Issues, Feelings, Actions," and "Professional and Personal Skills for Women Managers."

Special programs are offered for senior executives; one workshop is entitled "Presidents' and Spouses' Conference on Human Behavior." Similar to other training organizations, NTL's seminars are given at the Institute's own facilities and in hotel conference centers in many cities.

University Programs

Many business schools offer extension courses on their campuses or at other convenient locations. Examples include two-day seminars on "Improving White Collar Productivity" and "Setting and Implementing Management Goals" presented by the Wharton School of the University of Pennsylvania. The Harvard Business School offers two- and three-week courses in "Managing Corporate Control and Planning," "Marketing Management," and a "Program for Senior Managers in Government."

New York University offers a week-long "Management Effectiveness Program" for high potential middle managers. This program is designed to: (1) assist managers in diagnosing their interpersonal, judgmental, and analytical skills as they relate to executive level positions; (2) update technical skills in finance, marketing, and organizational behavior; and (3) facilitate career management.

Pennsylvania State University designed a two-week "Human Resources Management Program" for senior corporate directors of human resources or other line and staff executives responsible for human resource functions. The program content covers managerial career planning and development, managing organizational change, quality of work life, trends in union– management relations, strategies for behavior management, and the expanded role of the human resource professional.

CHOOSING A TRAINING PROGRAM

Choosing a training program requires substantial judgment since course brochures rarely provide objective information on course effectiveness. Testimonials from satisfied customers abound, but data on dollars saved, increases in productivity, or decreases in turnover are not usually available. This is not surprising since many companies do not evaluate their in-house courses. In the case of outside courses, the trainees in any one class typically represent many different organizations in different industries, making it difficult to collect information on changes in job behavior resulting from the training.

The high cost of programs and the lack of evaluation research suggests caution before enrolling in a course. The reputation of the sponsoring firm and the instructors should be considered. Personal communications with past participants should be sought. A company representative should try the program before others register. In addition, the American Society for Training and Development headquartered in Madison, Wisconsin is a source for learning about management training and consulting firms.

The large number of management development programs suggests that there is no one best way to develop managers. Digman (1978) believes that companies use what has worked for them in the past and what they feel will work for them in the future. Starting out with highly capable, motivated managers is an important step in developing a high quality management team (Bray, 1975). This means that management selection and development should be integrated efforts. Moreover, organizations should rely on many forms of instruction (e.g., simulations, video feedback, cases, group discussions) rather than on one type. Further, on-the-job training is a crucial component of management development in most organizations, and supervisors must be aware of, and rewarded for, this function.

Morgan, Hall, and Martier (1979) raise several issues and problems related to management development. They emphasize the importance of matching developmental opportunities with expectations. Too often managers participate in programs expecting immediate career advancement. Trainees should recognize the inherent value of a course or workshop for its content. They should be aware that the number of advancement opportunities in an organization is limited. Too much training may lead to overdevelopment just as advanced degrees may lead to overqualification for many jobs. Organizations must also guard against the "crown prince effect" such that participation in a particular program becomes a "rite of passage" for advancement to higher levels. Development programs should not be instituted for cosmetic reasons. Programs should be based on specific needs, and organizations should not hesitate to eliminate programs once the needs are met (Morgan, Hall, & Martier, 1979).

TRAINING EVALUATION METHODS

The extent to which evaluation is important will depend on the benefits expected from the training program and the cost of the program. If a major investment in training is expected to increase productivity or sales, then it is important to measure the impact of the training program on these outcomes. If training is inexpensive and intended only to improve morale, evaluation may be less important. In most cases, however, training is costly and substantial benefits are anticipated. Yet rigorous training evaluation is rare (Goldstein, 1980). Some reasons for this are that evaluation adds to the training cost, it is time consuming, it may mean a delay in obtaining the full benefits of the program, and some of those who design and implement training programs claim that they know the value of the programs and do not have to conduct studies to prove it. Alternatively, individuals who advocate programs without empirical support for the program's benefits may not want to risk discovering negative results.

Overcoming resistance to training evaluation is essential. Training should be viewed as an investment, not an expense. As such, organizations need to know the return on their training investment just as they would on other investments. Training evaluation need not be expensive, time consuming, or complex. Fairly simple, practical research designs can provide sufficient data for a meaningful evaluation.

Steps in the evaluation process include determining what criteria should be measured and what research design should be adopted. Typically, rigor is sacrificed to some extent because of limited resources. The goal in designing most evaluation research projects is to identify methods that provide the most accurate and meaningful information with the least amount of resources.

Establishing Criteria

Criteria are the variables the training is expected to affect. Selecting criteria and identifying ways to measure them is a first step in training evaluation. Which criteria to use generally depends on their relevance. Appropriate criteria often stem directly from the purpose of the training. For example, supervisory training that emerges from the need to increase employee morale would generally use measures of subordinate satisfaction as criteria. In some cases, criteria can be identified only after some exploration and judgment. A workshop on managerial skills such as organizing and planning and decision making might use future advancement as a criterion. Another criterion might be whether the behavior taught is exhibited on the job. This suggests that criteria differ along a number of dimensions, and that these dimensions in addition to relevance should be considered when selecting criteria. Five such dimensions are described in Table 6.4: close versus distant, objective versus subjective, criterion-referenced versus norm-referenced, obtrusive versus unobtrusive, and behavior versus results oriented.

Table 6.5 lists several criteria and characterizes them along the dimensions described in Table 6.4. For example, absenteeism in a manager's work group six months after a management seminar on reward systems would be distant, objective, norm-referenced (if compared to organization- or industry-wide standards), unobtrusive, and behavioral. The number of course participants who developed a new incentive system on the basis of course material would be distant, objective, criterion-referenced, unobtrusive or obtrusive depending on how it was determined, and behavioral.

Perhaps the best training evaluation will result from criteria that are a combination of the above. Both close and distant criteria that focus on behavior and results should be collected. Objective measures that are obtrusive and others that are unobtrusive should also be used. By using multiple criteria, it will be

TABLE 6.4
Dimensions of Criteria for Training Evaluation

Close versus distant criteria

- Criteria measured soon after training are called close or prox-imal; and those measured later, distant. The more distant the criterion from the time of training, the more external factors are likely to diminish the effects of training.
- Criteria measured soon after training may include paper-and-pencil tests or behavioral simulations. Measures of the trainees' satisfaction with the training are frequently used. However, they generally explain little about the effects of the training program. On-the-job behaviors measured a short time after training demonstrate the extent of training transfer to the job setting.
- Distant criteria include indices of goal accomplishment as well as measures of behaviors that contribute to goal accomplish-ment. Relevant criteria are likely to change over time. For example, effective communication, organizing, and goal-setting may be relevant criteria for the new manager who has just completed orientation training, while decision making, subordinate morale, and goal accomplishment may be more relevant criteria several months later. While the training pro-gram may be geared toward all these dimensions, some di-mensions of performance may not be observable until later. In general, the more distant the criterion, the more it is possible to assess the lasting effects of the training.

Objective versus subjective criteria

- Objective criteria are based on clearly observable behaviors or outcomes (e.g., number of units produced). Subjective criteria, which are more likely to be applied to managers, are impres-sions or judgments made by others (e.g., supervisors' ratings of the trainees' behavior or the trainees' satisfaction with the program). Subjective criteria are susceptible to perceptual biases and random errors limiting their reliability and validity. (Reliability refers to the consistency of the measures over time or the agreement between measures at one point in time; validity refers to the relevance of the measures and whether they are measuring what they are supposed to measure).
- The reliability and validity of subjective criteria can be im-proved by training raters to observe relevant behaviors (i.e., behaviors found in research to be associated with key dimen-sions of effectiveness) and averaging the judgments of multi-ple raters. This strategy is followed for assessors' ratings in

assessment centers, and in fact such ratings are often referred to as objective.

Criterion-referenced versus norm-referenced criteria

- Criterion-referenced measures are based on an absolute standard (Goldstein, 1974). Frequencies of behaviors, number of units produced, number of errors, and work time are examples.

- Norm-referenced measures depend on relative standards. A test score that is compared to the scores obtained by a comparable group is an example. Finding that a trainee is in the 90th percentile on a post-training test, for instance, means that 89% of those in the norm sample received a lower score.

- Norm-referenced measures explain how well a person did in comparison to others; criterion-referenced measures provide specific information about the level of a person's performance.

Obtrusive versus unobtrusive measures

- Obtrusive measures are those collected with the knowledge of the individual being evaluated. Observation of behavior in a simulation or on the job is obtrusive when the observer is visible or the trainee knows he or she is being observed and measured.

- Unobtrusive measurement does not inform the individual when the data are collected. The individual's consent should be obtained prior to collecting unobtrusive measures, but he/she need not be aware of exactly when the measurement takes place (Webb et al., 1981). The advantage of unobtrusive data is that the individual's behavior is not affected by being observed.

Behavior versus results oriented criteria

- Behavioral criteria are measures of actual behavior on the job.

- Results criteria are indices of organizational outcomes—e.g., cost reductions, grievances, increases in production quality and quantity, profits, and work group morale (Cascio, 1978).

- Determining if changes in results are due to a training program or other organizational events is often difficult since so many factors affect work outcomes and many of these factors are beyond the control of the individual. Consequently, changes in on-the-job behaviors that are closely associated with those that are taught in a training program may be more meaningful criteria in training evaluation. A training program that is shown to affect on-the-job behavior does not mean that it also affects organizational outcomes.

possible to achieve a greater understanding of the effects of training.

Evaluating Training: An Example

An example should help convey the value of multiple criteria and the application of a simple research design to training evaluation. A training program in sales management was evaluated in one geographical region of a national insurance company. Resulting from a needs analysis, the week-long program was to improve the efficiency with which sales managers organize their work, conduct sales meetings with the insurance agents on their staff, set sales targets with the agents, and provide per-

TABLE 6.5
Examples of Criteria for Training Evaluation

CRITERIA	CHARACTERISTICS
Participants' ratings of satisfaction immediately following training.	Close, subjective, criterion-referenced, obtrusive
Absenteeism and turnover in participants' work group six months after training.	Distant, objective, norm-referenced if compared to organization or industry standards, unobtrusive, behavior-oriented
Number of participants who developed an incentive system one month after attending a course on that topic.	Close, objective, criterion-referenced, unobtrusive or obtrusive depending on how it is determined, and behavior-oriented
Performance ratings of participants.	Distant, subjective, criterion-referenced, obtrusive, results-oriented
Advancement of participant three years after training.	Distant, objective, norm-referenced if compared with others' advancement, unobtrusive, results-oriented

formance feedback. The course cost $2,500 per manager including travel to the company headquarters training facility where the course was conducted. Criteria included indices of insurance office effectiveness (e.g., dollar value of sales, number of sales, targets met, contacts made). Behaviors observed included whether or not sales meetings were held, targets were set, and feedback was given. Sales managers' subordinates rated their effectiveness. These data were obtained from records, interviews, and researchers' observations. Half the sales managers in the region were randomly selected to attend the course. The other half served as a comparison group. Measures of office effectiveness and subordinate ratings of sales managers' effectiveness were gathered six months before and six months after the course.

The results are summarized in Table 6.6. On average, all measures were approximately equal for the two groups before training. The follow-up measures revealed that the managers in the training group conducted more sales meetings and were more likely to set sales targets with insurance agents. There was a positive difference in frequency of feedback. Subordinates' ratings of sales managers' effectiveness were higher in the training group than in the comparison group. Number of sales was about equal in both groups, but the dollar volume of sales was higher in the training group. Apparently the insurance agents working for the managers who were trained sold more expensive policies than those in the other group. Headquarters estimated that this would mean an increase in profits of about $3,000 per trained sales manager for the first year and additional profits during subsequent years. The number of contacts with potential customers was also higher in the training group. Also, targets were more likely to be met in the training group. Just how much of this was due to the new methods implemented by the sales managers and how much was due to the expectations of the agents who knew whether or not their managers attended the course was uncertain. The effects of the training beyond six months were not yet known. Nevertheless, the company decided to offer the course to other sales managers across the country

TABLE 6.6
Evaluation of Sales Managers' Training: Summary Measures

Criteria	TRAINING GROUP		COMPARISON GROUP	
	Before	After	Before	After
Dollar volume of sales per agent	$14,400	$21,700	$14,900	$15,600
Number of sales	28	30	27	29
Proportion of targets met	70	95	72	75
Contacts	110	170	105	110
Number of sales meetings held per manager	4	14	4	5
Number of managers setting targets	3	21	2	7
Frequency of feedback per agent during 6 months	3	17	4	5
Subordinates' ratings of managers on 7-point scale	5.7	6.7	5.4	5.2

and to have the training group managers determine how long the behaviors resulting from the training continued.

GUIDELINES FOR TRAINING EVALUATION

Campbell et al. (1970, pp. 284–285) summarize the essential elements for measuring the outcomes of training:

1. Use multiple criteria to reflect multiple contributions of managers to organizational goals.

2. Study the criteria themselves to determine the degree to which they are interrelated.

3. Use a research design that will allow the inference that the training program caused changes in the criteria.

4. Discuss the practical and theoretical significance of the results—not just the statistical significance.

5. Conduct a thorough, logical analysis of the process and content of the training itself.

6. Consider how the training affects, and is affected by, other organizational factors such as the organization's compensation system, whether the skills learned can be used on the job, and the relationship between these skills and other job functions.

Readers interested in a detailed description of training evaluation research designs should see Campbell et al. (1970), Goldstein (1974), Campbell and Stanley (1966), and Cook and Campbell (1976). Also, the evaluation methods for career planning programs discussed in the last chapter apply to training evaluation.

SUMMARY

Career development helps meet organizational goals by having the required human resource talent ready when it is needed. Defined broadly, career development refers to training courses, job assignments, and other activities aimed at achieving career goals. Individual training requirements vary depending on career orientation, organizational level, and career stage. A program for targeted development should match individual needs to development in a cycle of target setting, critical assignments, training experiences, and periodic evaluation, feedback, and reconsideration of targets. Operating such a program can be facilitated by program managers and routine program evaluation.

While a targeted development program directs individuals to developmental activities that are best for them, a training needs analysis determines what courses and other development experiences an organization should offer based on the skills and abilities of all employees or a group of employees. One way to perform a training needs analysis is to first generate a mastery model and then conduct a deficiency diagnosis. Some management skills and abilities cannot be developed easily through organizational training programs. Management training generally enhances strengths and, when possible, corrects weaknesses.

Once skills for training have been identified, it is necessary to choose one or more training methods, such as behavior modeling. Types of training programs include orientation training, technical training, and managerial skills training. Many different management training programs are offered by corporations, management training and consulting firms, and universities. Training programs must be chosen with care. Evaluating training programs requires establishing multiple criteria and using a practical research design.

Section IV
The Career Management Process

Organizational Staffing: Promotion and Transfer Decisions

7

Previous chapters focused on how individuals plan their careers and make career decisions, and how organizations provide resources to assist in this process. Chapter 7 considers how organizations make decisions about their employees; specifically, how managers fill job vacancies with candidates from within the organization. These are called *internal* staffing decisions, as opposed to external staffing decisions which involve filling a position by hiring someone from outside the organization.

Organizations vary in the extent to which positions are filled from within. In many organizations, the majority of vacant management positions are filled through internal staffing decisions. One common exception to internal staffing, however, is the selection of some outsiders for entry level jobs such as management trainee positions. Other exceptions include filling some technical and professional positions at higher levels with outsiders because the jobs require individuals who meet specific degree or experience requirements. Rapidly growing organizations and organizations that have entered new markets may lack qualified personnel at several levels, hence the need to look outside the organization. Even chief executive officers may be recruited from outside.

Selection methods for such external staffing decisions were addressed briefly in Chapter 3 when we discussed the screening processes job seekers are likely to face. Here we concentrate on internal management staffing decisions. Unlike external selection decisions which have been researched in depth, much less is known about internal staffing. Yet these decisions are critical to the organization and to the careers of those involved. We focus on promotion decisions since they are central to organizational effectiveness and individual career progression. Much of what we discuss, however, applies to other management staffing decisions such as transfers. A reason for concentrating on *management* staffing decisions is that, unlike promotions and transfers within nonmanagement, staffing within management is less likely to be guided by rules, standard procedures, and objective criteria such as seniority.

This chapter differs from several earlier chapters in that the guidelines suggested are more tentative because we apply knowledge about decision making in general to staffing decisions in particular. In so doing, we identify many factors that may influence the decision process. Additional research is necessary before the most important factors can be clearly specified.

PROMOTION DECISIONS

Promotions affect the quality of leadership and management in most organizations. A promotion usually means a new job with increased responsibilities and the possibility for further advancement.

The need to make a staffing decision typically arises from another staffing decision made at a higher organizational level or in a different department. A vacancy may be created when an individual is promoted or transferred. Alternatively, a vacancy may result from the retirement, resignation, termination, or death of the incumbent. A vacancy may also arise from the creation of a new job or from organizational growth. Company policy may specify that job rotations occur every several years to avoid stagnation and ensure employee development. This would necessitate several staffing decisions which may involve promotions. Changes in corporate or departmental objectives may require reorganization which could also result in staffing decisions.

Responsibility for filling a vacancy generally falls to the immediate supervisor of the vacant position, a higher level boss, or a group of managers. Consequently, promotion decisions are periodically made by managers at most levels and in most departments. Since promotions are judgmental decisions, they are often based on ambiguous criteria and numerous sources of information, many of which are subjective.

The importance of the systematic consideration of promotion decisions stems from three concerns: organizational effectiveness, equal employment opportunity, and career planning and development. Organizational effectiveness is enhanced by selecting the most qualified individual available, not just someone who will perform at an acceptable level. Selecting an individual with high potential for future assignments may be as important as selecting someone who can perform well in the vacant position. Decision effectiveness also depends on the candidate's willingness to accept the promotion and the candidate's availability. Understanding how candidates are identified, what selection standards are used, and the relationship between the decision process and outcomes is necessary before guidelines for better promotion decisions can be prescribed.

Equal Employment Opportunity— Affirmative Action programs are an important factor in promotion decisions (Hammer, 1979; Gruenfeld, 1975; Hall & Albrecht, 1979; Kleinman & Durham, 1981). While the Equal Employment Opportunity Commission guidelines on employee selection procedures have been applied primarily to entry level positions, the guidelines are equally applicable to the treatment of individuals once they are members of the organization. Hence, systematic promotion and transfer policies and procedures that do not discriminate are necessary.

Career planning and development programs create pressures for employers to take a more systematic view of advancement policies. If internal staffing decisions are to be a part of a career management system, then these decisions should be made with career plans in mind. Also, career plans should reflect the realities of the organization's staffing policies and procedures.

Promotion from Within

Many companies fill middle and upper level management vacancies by promotion from within the ranks of current employees rather than from outside (London, 1978; Campbell et al., 1970). Veiga (1981a) studied three major U.S. corporations and found that only 10% of all job moves involved moving between corporations. Investigations of other organizations also indicate that organizations create labor markets within themselves through a process of wage differentials, transfers, and promotions (Doeringer & Piore, 1971).

Promotion from within occurs in several ways. A vacancy may be filled by promoting someone from a lower level position in the same department. Assuming a high performer is promoted, promotion from within the department provides a visible reward for good performance and suggests a model for other individuals if they wish to advance. However, there is a disadvantage in promoting a person to a supervisory position over former peers. Both the new supervisor and the subordinates must adjust to the role change.

Promotions may also involve job moves between departments and functions. Such promotions often assume that the new position requires general management skills and that specific aspects of the job can be learned over time. A lateral transfer between departments or functions may also be viewed as a promotion when the new job entails a significant raise in pay and an increase in responsibility. Such transfers for high potential middle managers can be profitable for both the individual and the organization (Pitts, 1977).

Promotion from within has a number of advantages. It demonstrates that opportunities for advancement are available in the organization. This has a positive effect on morale when the decisions are perceived as equitable and based on meaningful performance standards (Latham & Wexley, 1981). It also utilizes the existing talents of individuals who are already familiar with the organization. Training time is considerably shorter when individuals are selected from inside the organization. Companies who use expensive training procedures are justifiably reluctant to look elsewhere for high level managers. In addition, more information is available about internal candidates than external applicants, thereby decreasing the risk of making an ineffective decision when filling a vacancy from within.

Does promotion from within lead to stagnation by selecting individuals who "fit the mold"? Some people have an image of the ideal person who attains advancement to higher levels. In some organizations there is an unwritten set of assumptions regarding essential qualifications for advancement. Fortunately, equal employment opportunity laws and corporate policies have helped minorities, females, and others make substantial inroads within the ranks of management during the past decade. Yet managers may still be reluctant to recommend people for promotion who are unlike those they believe should be promoted. The extent to which subjectivity enters into the promotion decision will depend on whether organizational standards for promotion are delineated. Thorough job analyses, job function codes, and the use of behaviorally anchored rating scales to document performance can increase objectivity in promotion decisions in many organizations.

DETERMINANTS OF INTERNAL STAFFING DECISIONS[1]

In order to better understand how organizations affect career progressions, we examine individual and organizational factors which influence promotion and other staffing decisions. Since we view staffing decisions as similar to other types of strategic decisions (e.g., budget allocations or capital expenditures), we draw upon the judgmental decision-making literature to examine the staffing decision process.

---

[1]The remainder of this chapter is based on Stumpf and London (1981b).

The following sections should benefit managers who have made many effective promotion and transfer decisions by helping them see the systematic processes underlying their decisions. Others should benefit by learning how to make more effective decisions and how to apply decision mechanisms which help maintain objectivity and equity. Individuals who are, or will be, the subjects of these decisions should benefit from a better understanding of the many factors affecting internal staffing decisions and from knowledge of what behaviors are likely to lead to desirable career outcomes.

Internal Staffing as a Systematic Process

An underlying assumption regarding internal staffing decisions is that the development and movement of personnel through an organization is a deliberate process which can benefit the individual and the organization. Yet some suggest that individual mobility is a nearly random process—that individuals follow opportunities which are seldom planned (March & March, 1977; Rothstein, 1980). Even if opportunities are not planned, the offer of a job to an individual is still likely to be a rational, organizational decision (Stumpf & London, 1981b; Stumpf & Colarelli, 1981).

Studies of intraorganizational movement suggest that identifiable patterns of vertical and horizontal movement evolve (Anderson, Milkovich, & Tsui, 1981; Martin & Strauss, 1956; Vardi, 1980). Such mobility patterns (or career paths) have generalizable lengths, heights, directions, and overlap. It is therefore possible to plan career movement by taking into account natural patterns as well as designing career paths for specific developmental purposes.

Research on which career moves lead to managerial success, as externally indexed by status attainment or salary, suggests that there are many routes to senior management positions (March & March, 1977; Helmich, 1977; Kanter, 1977). While many individuals believe promotions are the only way to progress, research suggests that lateral moves across divisional or busi-

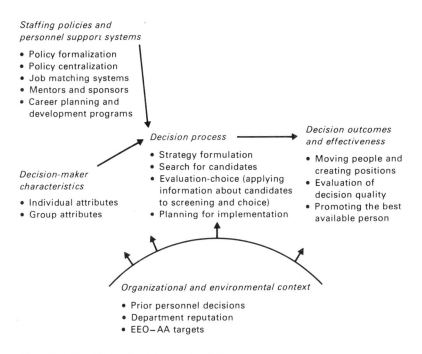

Fig. 7.1 *Staffing decisions model*

ness unit lines often have positive effects on a person's career and can also be viewed as progression (Veiga, 1981a).

Fig. 7.1 presents a framework for relating the different contextual, antecedent, process, and outcome variables involved in staffing decisions. Four components are examined in this chapter: (1) decision outcomes and effectiveness, (2) the decision process (including strategy formulation, search for candidates, evaluation-choice, and planning for implementation), (3) characteristics of the individual or group responsible for the decision, and (4) the organizational and environmental context. Staffing policies and personnel support systems are discussed in Chapter 8.

The extent to which the processes we discuss are applicable in a given situation depends on the demands placed on the decision maker. These vary from decision to decision. For instance, in some cases there is only one suitable candidate for a vacancy and the "decision" involves only obtaining approval. In other cases, a few viable candidates are readily identifiable and the decision is primarily a choice process. In still other cases, a search is necessary to uncover viable candidates. Perhaps the most common case is one in which a couple of candidates are easily identified, one of whom may be initially preferred by the decision maker, and organizational policy prescribes searching for other candidates via formal search mechanisms (London & Stumpf, 1979). The individual promoted may or may not be one of those initially identified. Most of the components in the model shown in Fig. 7.1 are applicable to this latter situation.

A potential dysfunction of analyzing the internal staffing decision process in a detailed way is that one may lose track of what actually happens and conclude that staffing decisions are unnecessarily complicated. However, outlining the components of a staffing decision, examining research relevant to each component, and suggesting practical guidelines on the basis of that research, can lead to a better understanding of decisions which are often taken for granted and occasionally misinterpreted.

DECISION OUTCOMES AND EFFECTIVENESS

Since decision processes will be discussed in relation to their potential effectiveness, we begin by delineating the outcomes and effectiveness of a staffing decision. Two outcomes are a career move for one or more individuals and the creation of additional vacancies down the organizational hierarchy requiring a chain of staffing decisions. The chain of decisions may be made sequentially or simultaneously.

Determining the effectiveness of a staffing decision (or a set of decisions) involves defining the appropriate criteria and collecting suitable measures. Staffing decision effectiveness criteria include the eventual performance of the candidate selected to fill the vacancy and the organizational unit's success along such dimensions as goal accomplishment, growth, technological leadership, and return on investment. These criteria summarize what we mean when we refer to decision effectiveness. Unfortunately, such criteria are difficult to measure in a time frame which permits altering a staffing decision before substantial costs have been incurred, if indeed the decision can be altered at all. It is not easy to remove someone from a job, particularly if the individual has recently been promoted. Performance appraisals are not available until several months after an individual has started a new position. Therefore, as in most selection decisions, the decision maker must predict each candidate's effectiveness before making a decision. These judgments, however, typically exhibit little agreement with objective indices of effectiveness or independent ratings by experts (Stumpf & Zand, 1981). Decision makers tend to overestimate their decision's anticipated effectiveness. The questionable accuracy of individual judgments suggests the importance of the decision process in making an effective decision.

THE DECISION PROCESS

The process of filling a position vacancy consists of four stages: strategy formulation, candidate search, evaluation-choice, and planning for implementation.[2] While the stages often occur in the sequence listed, they may be iterative. They may also vary depending on how quickly the decision must be made, how many qualified candidates are available, who is making the decision, and contextual factors such as prior staffing decisions and Equal Employment Opportunity— Affirmative Action targets (London & Stumpf, 1979; Payne, 1976).

---

[2]Evidence that these stages occur in a number of different judgmental decisions may be found in the work of Beach and Mitchell (1978), Mintzberg, Raisinghani, and Théorêt (1976), and Lang, Dittrich, and White (1978).

Formulating a Strategy

Strategy formulation is the extent to which the decision maker formulates a strategy for making the decision before identifying or reviewing candidates. Strategy formulation may occur before a vacancy arises or immediately after it arises but before action has been taken.

The importance of designing a strategy to fit the situation has been examined by Stumpf, Freedman, and Zand (1979). They found that the effectiveness of strategies used to make a decision were contingent upon the expertise available, the nature of the decision, and the conflict associated with the situation. Strategies formulated prior to embarking on the decision-making task influenced the decision's effectiveness.

We found several a priori strategies for filling management vacancies in an interview study of eighty-two managers at five different levels in an organization (London & Stumpf, 1979). Some of the strategies included the development of a detailed human resource plan in advance of vacancies, a specification of promotion standards, and the identification of "promotable now" candidates before a vacancy arose. One manager in our sample reported maintaining a diary of high potential managers at lower levels. A manager of a training group described tracking particularly capable trainees as possible candidates for later vacancies. Another manager stated she routinely discussed high potential subordinates with her peers. These managers were all trying to formulate up-to-date lists of promotable individuals. However, many of the managers interviewed either had no clear decision-making strategy or evolved a strategy while making the decision.

Managers who have to search outside their departments for candidates are frequently at a disadvantage. Fellow supervisors are sometimes reluctant to provide names of qualified subordinates for fear of losing good people who could develop in their own departments. Some supervisors may give positive recommendations to subordinates they would rather lose. Consequently, knowing where to turn for names of qualified candidates may be difficult for the manager who does not plan ahead.

Strategy formulation also refers to establishing standards for evaluating candidates, deciding what information should be sought and how it should be weighted, planning how much time should be spent reviewing candidates, and deciding who else should be involved in the decision. Many times a strategy will evolve as the decision is made. For example, selection standards may be set after discovering what types of information are available. The number of candidates may determine how carefully the decision maker can review each one. Discussions with higher level supervisors may reveal information not previously considered. Certain uncontrollable constraints may influence the decision, such as how soon the individual selected must be on the department's payroll. The manager who formulates a strategy must be flexible enough to alter the strategy when such constraints arise or when the initial strategy does not yield the desired results. On the other hand, not formulating a strategy may lead to disappointment in finding qualified candidates, having the recommended candidate rejected, or not being able to obtain the release of the most qualified person.

Guidelines for effective strategy formulation. It is important to design a strategy that reflects the salient situational and organizational factors associated with a particular staffing decision. One's strategy guides the decision-making process. Strategy formulation is most fruitful when personnel changes are frequent. However, a strategy may unnecessarily limit the decision maker. The manager who spends time following the careers of several talented people, for example, may inadvertently miss new talent. In general, when decision situations are uncertain, the strategy followed should allow sufficient flexibility to accommodate unforeseen factors.

Searching for Candidates

The extent to which one searches for alternative candidates is a function of the decision maker and the situation (Ebert & Mitchell, 1975; Stumpf, Colarelli, & Hartman, 1981). Decision makers vary in the breadth and thoroughness of their search for alternatives (March & Simon, 1958; Mintzberg, Raisinghani, & Théorêt, 1976). Situations vary in the demands placed on the decision maker, in the number of easily identifiable candidates, and in the perceived or actual constraints placed on the decision. While search behavior is motivated, it is often simple-minded, biased, and sequential (Cyert & March, 1963; March & Simon, 1958). Lindblom (1959) suggests that search is limited to alternatives near existing problems. Mintzberg, Raisinghani, and Théorêt (1976) found support for these views by studying strategic decision processes. They found that the search process began simply and proceeded step by step covering various information sources starting with those most likely to yield relevant information.

Individuals making staffing decisions vary in the extent to which they must search for candidates. In some cases, there are a number of promotable subordinates in the department. In fact, the department may groom high potential subordinates for this purpose. In other cases, no qualified candidates are apparent.

Organizational procedures sometimes help in obtaining candidates (Gruenfeld, 1975). For example, some companies maintain promotion lists of managers who are designated "ready now" for promotion or developmental transfer. Or, formalized career plans may indicate who is targeted for a particular position. A procedure used in some organizations is to circulate a "Notice of Position Vacancy" to middle managers asking for recommendations. Another procedure is to publish or post a notice of the vacancy, thereby informing all individuals of the opportunity. Those who believe they are qualified may nominate themselves. Self-nominations, however, may not create the desired impression. A decision maker may wonder why the candidate's supervisor did not recommend the individual. If this is a problem in the organization, interested managers may be required to ask their supervisors for a recommendation and/or to nominate them for the position.

Formal mechanisms of this sort do not always identify a suitable number of high quality candidates. Identifying candidates who are willing to accept the position may be difficult when the position requires relocating a family to an undesirable geographical area. Occasionally positions in large corporations are rotational. The position is offered for two or three years, then the individual is expected to return to his or her home office. This temporary nature may be unattractive to some highly qualified candidates.

We examined the outcomes of the search process for managers making simulated management promotion decisions (London & Stumpf, 1980a, b). In two separate studies, candidates currently in positions structurally closer to the vacancy were preferred to more distant candidates; for example, candidates in the department experiencing the vacancy were viewed more favorably than those in other departments.

Pedigo and Meyer (1979) surveyed management promotion practices to determine the extent to which various sources of information on candidates were used. In their survey of 250 managers who had made a promotion decision during the previous year, they found that several formal and informal procedures were consistently applied. Sixty-eight percent reported asking the personnel staff for a list of candidates, 42% circulated a job profile, 12% posted a formal job notice or published a notice in the company bulletin. For the informal procedures, 73% identified qualified candidates in their own departments, 60% asked peers to suggest candidates, 36% asked subordinates for candidate suggestions, and 48% indicated having one candidate in mind who was likely to receive first consideration for the promotion. While these results are specific to the companies studied, they reflect the procedures used in other business organizations (Gruenfeld, 1975).

Guidelines for candidate search. Decision makers should be as thorough as possible in searching for candidates. A thorough candidate search will often extend promotional opportunities to more people and result in identifying more qualified candidates. In some cases, however, candidate search should be limited to avoid needlessly raising employee expectations and generating nominations of many unqualified hopefuls. Furthermore, a structured search process (e.g., circulating a notice of position vacancy form) may be unnecessary when exceptional candidates are already identified.

Evaluation and Choice

Once candidates have been identified, the decision maker must evaluate the candidates and make a decision. The choice may involve recommending top candidates to higher level managers, selecting a candidate, and/or justifying one's recommendation or decision. Possible evaluation-choice processes include: (1) evaluating *all* candidates as thoroughly as possible to identify the optimal candidate, (2) continuing the search and evaluation process until a satisfactory candidate has been identified, (3) screening all candidates and then thoroughly evaluating only the top candidates, and (4) identifying a favorite candidate, then comparing other candidates to the favorite. These and other possible evaluation-choice models are discussed in general terms by Simon (1957), Tversky (1969), Payne (1976), and Beach and Mitchell (1978).

The evaluation-choice process used is likely to depend on how the promotion decision is perceived by the decision maker (e.g., its familiarity, ambiguity, complexity), how the decision environment is perceived (e.g., is the decision reversible, is it significant, are there time constraints?), and the personal characteristics of the decision maker (e.g., knowledge, ability, motivation) (Beach & Mitchell, 1978). Beach and Mitchell (1978) developed propositions specifying when more demanding and complex evaluation-choice processes will be used as a function of these variables. The evaluation-choice process selected "is viewed as a compromise between the press for more decision accuracy as the demands of the decision task increase and the decision maker's resistance to the expenditure of his or her personal resources" (Beach & Mitchell, 1978, p. 447).

The demands of a staffing decision are likely to increase as the number of candidates increases, as the quantity and variety of information increases, and as one staffing decision becomes contingent upon others. The process is also likely to be affected by the importance of the decision to the decision maker and the organization, as well as the ability and motivation of the decision maker to use diverse information in making a choice.

Information used to evaluate candidates is reviewed below. This is followed by a discussion of what information employees and decision makers believe is used to evaluate candidates. We then discuss strategies used to make a choice.

Collecting candidate information. The information used to evaluate and choose candidates is likely to depend on the nature of the decision and the preferences of the decision maker (Pedigo & Meyer, 1979; Stumpf & London, 1981a; Taylor, 1975). Several possible sources of information about candidates are listed in Table 7.1. Each source has some limitations. For instance, the low accuracy of interviewer judgments greatly affects their usefulness in making decisions (Arvey, 1979; Schmitt, 1976). Fortunately, the interview is probably not as important an information gathering device for making internal promotion and transfer decisions as it is for sharing information or evaluating candidates from outside the organization. Substantial information is generally available about internal candidates, and decision makers often screen out candidates before interviewing those who remain. Hence, only the top candidates are generally interviewed.

TABLE 7.1
Sources of Information about Candidates

Performance appraisals
Job histories
Educational records
Managerial potential ratings
Assessment center results
Opinions of others
Personal knowledge
Oral and written recommendations
Interviews with candidates

We know of several companies in which it is considered inappropriate to interview all candidates for a vacancy. The feeling is that interviewing informs everyone that there is a vacancy and lets them know who is being considered. Interviewees' hopes are raised, generating discontent among those not selected. These companies encourage managers to collect extensive information from personnel records and supervisors. The decision maker may "visit" the prime candidates without revealing the purpose of the visit. Once a decision is about to be made, the chosen candidate is formally interviewed. If the interview goes well, the candidate is offered the job. If not, the search continues.

The interview may be a particularly valuable tool in matching individual interests with position requirements. While statements of interests, willingness to relocate, and other career concerns may be available in writing on a career planning form, the interview can be used to describe an opportunity to a candidate and discuss the candidate's career goals in relation to the opportunity.

Types of candidate information. Common candidate characteristics used as standards for management promotion include current membership in the organization, a college degree, and supervisory work experience (Gruenfeld, 1975; Helmich, 1977; Rosenbaum, 1979). Past performance is also used to make promotion decisions (Gemmill & DeSalvia, 1977; Pedigo & Meyer, 1979; Rosen, Billings, & Turney, 1976). However, many organizations do not have systematic performance appraisal systems, and when someone is recommended for promotion, it is unclear which measure of past performance is actually used (Taylor, 1975). Performance appraisals are also likely to be confounded with other factors; for example, sex, race, friendship, and appearance (Bigoness, 1976; Quinn, Tabor, & Gordon, 1968; Rosen & Jerdee, 1973). We found that managers making promotion decisions had little confidence in performance appraisals and recommendations unless they personally knew the evaluator (London & Stumpf, 1979).

Equally if not more important than past performance is one's potential to perform at the next higher level. Assessment centers and supervisor ratings of potential have been designed to identify managerial potential in several firms (Bray, Campbell, & Grant, 1973; Finkle, 1976; Rosen, Billings, & Turney, 1976), and potential ratings have been used in making promotion decisions (London & Stumpf, 1979, 1980b; Pedigo & Meyer, 1979; Rosen, Billings, & Turney, 1976; Stumpf & London, 1981a).

Other factors found to influence promotion decisions include political influence through acquaintance with the decision maker or through one's mentor (Kothari, 1974; Roche, 1979), seniority, affirmative action programs, and the match between the individual and the job in terms of both abilities and career interests. While these factors are viewed as important, their relative importance in a particular promotion decision or across decisions has received little attention. When promotion decisions have been studied in controlled settings, a manager's stated preference for different types of information and his/her recollection of the information used has only partially coincided with observer records or statistical analyses indicating the information actually used (London & Stumpf, 1980b; Taylor, 1975).

While many types of information may affect staffing decisions, some types are likely to be used only during the candidate identification process. Such initial screening reduces the complexity of the task and has been shown to be typical of decision-making behavior with a complex task (Payne, 1976). For example, the decision to promote from within is often company policy and not generally part of a decision maker's span of discretion. This policy eliminates external candidates from consideration until it is clear that no internal candidates are suitable for the position. Similarly, not having a college degree, insufficient work experience, and less than outstanding past performance are factors often used to screen out candidates quickly.

Staffing decisions are affected by a candidate's job experiences and current standing. Rosenbaum (1979), who described staffing as a "tournament mobility model," conceptualized career movement as a sequence of competitions, each of which has implications for an individual's mobility in subsequent promotions and transfers. Such a model is shown in Fig. 7.2. Individuals selected for advancement have the opportunity to compete for higher level job opportunities with no assurance of attaining them. Those promoted continue competing, and early experiences have consequences for losers. Rosenbaum found evidence for a tournament model for managers in a large corporation over a 13-year period.

An obvious implication of the tournament model is that a manager filling a job vacancy does not select from all people the organization. Not only are there fewer individuals available at higher levels, but also job experiences and specific requirements are more crucial, and specific managerial skills are more impor-

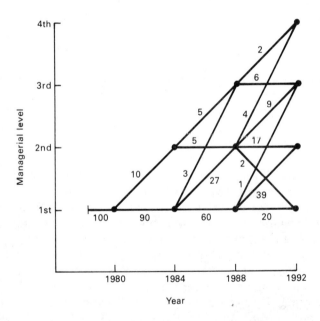

Fig 7.2 *Career tree for tournament mobility model* (Note: *The numbers on the tree indicate the number of individuals out of 100 entry level manager following a particular path.*)

tant. At higher organizational levels, prior job experiences pre-select candidates so that small numbers of people compete for even a smaller number of vacancies. The standards are more specific and often more subjective (e.g., recommendations and personal knowledge of the candidates) than at lower levels where more people compete on the basis of more objective information (e.g., output produced by the candidate). Nevertheless, standard-ized methods can be developed to make promotion decisions about higher level managers. For example, an assessment center was recently developed to evaluate the potential of middle man-agers for officer level in the Bell System.

Technology and organizational controls also influence whether selection standards are objective or subjective (Halaby, 1978). The more complex and specialized the job requirements, the more subjective the standards for promotion are likely to be. The more routine, less specialized, and less complex the job, the more objective standards such as test scores and units produced can be applied. In addition, more subjective standards are likely to be used when less central control exists over filling job vacan-cies. Decentralized decisions are likely when the diversity of jobs is great, or when the organization or personnel department is directed by someone who is not sufficiently familiar with the employees and the jobs to make centralized decisions.

In Chapter 8 we discuss mechanisms for centralized policies and decentralized decision making. Since the existence of standard procedures may counter a force toward individual dis-cretion and increased subjectivity in filling vacancies, uniform guidelines for candidate search, information selection, and weighting information can provide wider opportunities for more people and ensure that the decision will be made adequately. For instance, requiring that notices of all job vacancies be sent to all middle managers and above may result in identifying some can-didates who would not otherwise have been brought to the deci-sion maker's attention. Requiring that all individuals considered for promotion to a particular organizational level be evaluated in an assessment center may help standardize the information available on each candidate. Having to justify the promotion or transfer decision to a higher level manager may increase the weight the decision maker gives to objective, easily justifiable information.

To summarize, decision makers may use a variety of information sources and types of information to make promotion and transfer decisions. The tournament model of mobility emphasizes that background and prior experiences often predetermine eligibility for a given position. The higher the organizational level the more competition for a position is concentrated in a preselected group of candidates. The extent to which judgment or individual discretion affects a staffing decision is likely to increase with organizational level, complexity of the job vacancy, and amount of organizational change currently taking place. Policies and standard procedures, however, can reduce the subjectivity and increase decision objectivity.

Guidelines for collecting candidate information.   Collect information from multiple sources. Redundancy can help determine reliable information. Information from multiple sources also facilitates comparisons between candidates when different types of information are available about each candidate.

Use standard types of information and standard collection procedures. Require that the decision be justified by such information. These steps should increase the objectivity of the decision process.

Beliefs about promotion decisions.   What information do individuals *believe* is used to make staffing decisions? Results of studies addressing this question are described in Table 7.2 from the standpoint of the employee affected by promotion decisions, and in Table 7.3 from the standpoint of the decision maker.

To summarize these results, individuals who are not upwardly mobile are likely to have a different view of the promotion process than those who have been promoted a number of times. Those who have not received many promotions are likely to view the process as involving politics and image; others do not view these as important factors. When managers are asked to make simulated promotion decisions, they tend to use what personnel experts consider to be low quality information (e.g., interviews and recommendations), although they state that they give more

TABLE 7.2

Studies of Employees' Beliefs About How Promotion Decisions
Are Made About Them

Beehr, Taber, and Walsh (1980)

- 957 employees at all levels of a manufacturing plant were
  surveyed. Overall, they perceived 3 means for obtaining a
  better job in the plant: performance, race/sex, and luck/
  favoritism.
- Employees with higher career satisfaction, greater intrinsic
  motivation, more effort, and more education tended to perceive performance as the primary means of achieving mobility; those lower on these variables perceived the externally
  controlled factors (race/sex, luck/favoritism) as leading to
  greater mobility.

Beyer, Stevens, and Trice (1980)

- 634 managers in 9 executive departments of the U.S. government were surveyed. In general, the managers expected performance criteria to be more important for their promotion
  than either technical skills or seniority.
- Lower status managers expected seniority and technical skills
  to be more highly rewarded than other managers, while higher
  status and more mobile managers expected performance to be
  more important than other managers.
- Older managers and those supervising lower-skilled workers
  saw seniority as more important than did other workers.

Gemmill and DeSalvia (1977)

- 209 managers in 2 manufacturing firms were surveyed. They
  believed 3 factors influenced promotions: managerial proficiency, public image, and political proficiency.
- Upwardly mobile managers were more likely to believe that
  ability-related factors (managerial proficiency) are determinants of promotions; whereas less successful managers were
  likely to believe that nonability factors affect promotions.

Kothari (1976)

- Interviews and questionnaires were administered to 26 managers, 13 union representatives, and 99 employees in 3 Cana-
  dian businesses. Past experience, job performance, and training were perceived to be the most important determinants of
  promotions. Union officials rated seniority as most important.
- Less than 25% of the employees were completely aware of
  what information was used by management to make promotion decisions.

TABLE 7.3

Studies of Managers' Beliefs about How They Make Promotion Decisions

Kothari (1976)

- Most managers believed they objectively and fairly applied standards, basing their promotion decisions on merit and seniority.
- More than half the managers reported using subjective judgments of personal characteristics as a partial basis for their decision.

Taylor (1975)

- 75 male line managers at all levels of factory management in a large manufacturing firm participated in a promotion decision simulation. The managers' stated preferences for different types of candidate information did not coincide with the information they actually used more frequently.
- Performance appraisals were used least often and interviews and application forms were used most often, although the managers stated preferences were the reverse.

Pedigo and Meyer (1979)

- A survey of 250 managers at all but the top levels of management in 6 companies revealed that both objective and subjective information was deemed important in making management promotion decisions.
- Commonly cited objective information included the candidate's technical knowledge, past performance, career interests, and availability. Few managers stated they used seniority.
- Commonly cited subjective information included ratings of candidates' managerial skills, advancement potential, and dependability. Many managers admitted the importance of personal contact with the candidate.

Quinn, Tabor, and Gordon (1968)

- Interviews with 139 managers in 3 companies revealed the expressed importance of ability and nonability related candidate information.
- Ability information included job experience, job knowledge, training, and managerial skills.
- Nonability information included social credentials, image of responsibility, and appearance.

TABLE 7.3 (continued)

London and Stumpf (1980b)

- 72 managers representing 3 organizational levels in 3 companies expressed little or no preference for nonability factors, and they behaved consistently with their preferences in a simulated staffing decision.
- The most important candidate characteristics were supervisory ratings of the candidate's potential for advancement, assessment center judgments of performance, and the person's current position.

Stumpf and London (1981a)

- 43 managers from different companies and 51 business students participated in a simulated promotion decision. The analyses grouped the subjects into clusters of similar decision-making policies. More than half the subjects made their decisions on the basis of a single type of candidate information such as potential, position, or weakness. Slightly less than half the subjects used more complex decision processes involving multiple criteria.
- The results suggest that training and clear promotion policies are necessary if all decision makers are to weight criteria for promotion similarly.

---

weight to performance information. They also tend to use less information than is available and relevant. Surveys of managers in several companies support the finding that managers use both objective and subjective information to make staffing decisions. Further, some of the subjective information used often has little to do with the candidate's ability to do the job.

Guidelines for increasing the accuracy of perceptions of the promotion process.   Formulate and communicate standard policies and procedures for making promotion decisions. This will help employees affected by the decisions understand how the decisions are made and will increase the uniformity with which candidate information is applied to make the decisions. It should also increase the fairness of the decision process by encouraging the use of more objective information and provide documentation on how promotion decisions are made.

Next we turn to how information is used to evaluate candidates and make a final choice.

Decision strategies. A decision strategy includes when and how the decision maker determines what information to use, how this information is initially applied to evaluate and screen candidates, and the final decision. Each of these stages of the decision-making process is described below.

A. *Selecting a strategy.* Formulating a strategy, as discussed earlier, deals with developing methods for identifying and evaluating candidates. Often this occurs before a vacancy arises as a manager grooms subordinates and explores possible sources of candidates. These managers have in mind general qualities their staff members should possess. When a vacancy occurs, specific job requirements are considered together with general managerial skills. These requirements comprise a set of desired characteristics describing the ideal candidate. This information may be evident as soon as the job opening arises, or it may evolve as the availability of candidates becomes known. Occasionally, the job description may be altered to fit a candidate's particular qualifications. The candidate's characteristics may suggest new or different skills which should be part of the job. The existence of candidates who meet some job requirements but not others may require applying less stringent standards in order to fill the vacancy. In addition, the company's affirmative action policies may suggest, and sometimes dictate, restrictions on who may be considered for the job.

Another type of strategy involves first applying preformulated cutoffs to screen out candidates, and then examining the remaining candidates to identify additional pertinent information. This would occur when, for example, the decision maker chooses not to search for candidates outside the department involved or to consider only those individuals who have done well in an assessment center. Such early decisions narrow the field of candidates and necessitate fine discrimination among candidates who survive the initial cutoff.

B. *Screening candidates.* Once the decision maker selects variables which are relevant and which distinguish among candidates, this information is usually applied to arrive at a final set of candidates. This stage is particularly important when there are a fair number of initial candidates (say five or more). The application of the standards will depend on the information (e.g., whether or not it describes a candidate's strengths or weaknesses), the quality of candidates available, and the cognitive processes the decision maker follows.

Our study of management staffing decisions indicated that initial screening strategies vary in a number of respects (London & Stumpf, 1979). They vary depending on whether the process is one of elimination based on weaknesses or selection based on strengths; whether candidates are compared to each other or judged on an absolute standard; and whether candidates are evaluated on the basis of each variable separately or on the basis of an overall image. Screening candidates is usually a sequential process. This occurs when, for instance, the decision maker first eliminates all those with an unacceptable weakness and then re-evaluates the remaining candidates, selecting those who are highest or above a minimum on other characteristics. The result is usually a small number of top candidates.

The time it takes to conduct the initial screening may vary considerably from decision to decision. A decision maker may sequentially apply several of the screening strategies in an hour. Alternatively, screening may take many hours or may be spread out over a number of days or weeks. Screening typically takes more time when more people are involved in the decision and as the job requirements become more complex.

How candidates should be screened will depend on whether candidate information is relevant, reliably measured, and equitably applied. Using information simply because it makes the decision easier (e.g., because it is quantified and results in quickly reducing the number of candidates) may not be effective if it eliminates candidates who are more highly qualified in some respects than those who remain. Which information can or should be used is often a matter of company policy, as when the company discourages or prevents the use of performance appraisals that are more than three years old. The best strategy for screening candidates will depend on the decision-maker's objective. The goal in filling a vacancy may be to select the best person in the company, the best available person, the first acceptable candidate, or perhaps a person who is weak in some areas but can benefit from the job assignment as a developmental experience. Therefore, it is essential to articulate the objectives clearly and to choose relevant information accordingly.

Guidelines for screening candidates. The following guidelines for *screening* candidates demonstrate the importance of the decision maker's objectives and the job requirements.[3] At least two candidates would generally remain after the screening process is complete.

1. Screen by eliminating candidates on the basis of weaknesses when the nature of the job specifies minimum requirements or unacceptable weaknesses.

2. Screen by selecting on the basis of candidates' strengths when many highly qualified candidates are available and when certain individual characteristics would be highly desirable to perform the job well.

3. Screen by comparing candidates one variable at a time (e.g., first eliminate candidates who are weak on the most important variable, then on the second most important variable, and so on) when the same types of information are available on all candidates and when it is necessary to justify why certain candidates were eliminated.

4. Form a composite or overall image of each candidate when the information about candidates is fairly ambiguous and/or subjective, and when there are a large number of variables. Eliminate weak candidates and/or select the best candidates on the basis of the composite.

C. *Choice.* Once most of the candidates have been eliminated, several may remain who are similar in many respects. Indeed,

---

[3]We thank Mark Kurman for contributing to these guidelines.

any one of them may be able to do the job well. Research on information processing suggests that a relatively small amount of information is likely to be used in choosing from several viable candidates (Taylor, 1975). Individuals tend to focus on a few variables and to categorize or aggregate large amounts of data to reduce the information load (Newell & Simon, 1972). Hence, judgment is important in the choice process.

Guidelines for final choice. The final decision may be one that maximizes strengths, minimizes weaknesses, or both. Candidates may be compared to each other or to an ideal, and this comparison may be done separately on individual characteristics or on the basis of a composite of each candidate. The final selection is usually a short process following one of the guidelines presented below.

1. Eliminate candidates on the basis of weaknesses when the goal is to minimize risks. This implies that it is better to select someone who can definitely do the job well than to select someone who may do an even better job but who has other drawbacks (such as difficulty getting along with peers).

2. Select on the basis of strengths when individuals can be compared on one or more important and relevant characteristics.

3. Form a composite image of the final candidates when each candidate has a number of different characteristics which are not directly comparable, especially when these characteristics are based on the decision maker's impressions rather than on objective data.

Planning for Implementation

Most staffing decisions are actually recommendations until they are approved at a higher organizational level. A plan to obtain that approval can be crucial in the process of getting a decision implemented. The importance of obtaining decision acceptance in problem solving has been actively discussed, researched, and supported (e.g., Stumpf, Zand, & Freedman, 1979; Vroom & Yetton, 1973).

A second aspect of planning for implementation is ensuring that the chosen candidate will be available. It may be necessary to negotiate the release of an individual from his or her current unit if the promotion or transfer involves a move to another department. If relocation is necessary, the candidate's nonwork needs and interests should be considered. Although some people may resist relocation and refuse a promotion that necessitates disrupting family life (Hall & Hall, 1978), it is important that organizations offer the promotion or transfer to the preferred individual. Assuming that someone will not relocate without asking the individual is often a faulty assumption (Brett & Werbel, 1980).

Guideline for planning for implementation.   Involve others in making the decision when they are likely to share important information and when their involvement is likely to generate confidence in and acceptance of the decision.

CHARACTERISTICS OF DECISION MAKERS

Individual Decisions

A promotion decision can be made by a personnel specialist, the supervisor of the position to be filled, or a promotion committee (permanent or ad hoc). The more ambiguous the situation and the more specific requirements that must be met, the more promotion decisions are likely to be made by the persons or group closest to the position (London, 1978). This likelihood implies that promotion decisions are frequently made by individuals who are not highly trained in interviewing techniques or personnel matters. Personnel specialists can improve the process by providing training and establishing decision-making policies and procedures.

Several attributes of the decision maker may influence the decision process, such as one's information handling capacity, risk-taking tendency, and motivation to spend time and resources to fill the vacancy (Ebert & Mitchell, 1975). We propose that decision-maker characteristics are more likely to affect the promotion decision when personnel policies and procedures do not delineate what process should be followed to identify and evaluate candidates. The effect of decision-maker characteristics may be minimized through the use of a group or committee consisting of individuals with diverse and relevant information.

Group Decisions

A decision made by a group of supervisors may have an advantage over an individual's decision when different viewpoints or types of expertise are needed. Group decisions are more likely to encourage fair treatment of all employees because they generally require members to justify their opinions. However, group decisions involve more organizational resources and frequently more time. Group decisions are likely to be superior when information is dispersed, the decision task is complex and judgmental, and the group members share the organization's goals (Vroom & Yetton, 1973). Promotion committees allow managers to contribute information about subordinates who are unknown to other committee members. When several members have firsthand knowledge of the same candidate, they often provide more information than is available from a candidate's personnel file alone. Also, the vested interests of the department or unit with the vacancy are more likely to be in balance with the interests of the organization when the decision is made by a group.

When a decision is made by a committee, a number of group process variables may influence the outcome (Hackman & Morris, 1975). Group process depends on the task demands (e.g., the number of candidates available, amount of information available on each candidate, and how quickly the decision must be reached). The task difficulty may be compounded when group members have different goals or different beliefs about what information should be examined and how heavily it should be weighted (London, 1977). The larger the group, the more difficult it may be to reach a consensus, although there is no clear rule about optimal group size (Shaw, 1975).

One typical problem with groups is difficulty in formulating and implementing a decision strategy (Stumpf, Zand, & Freedman, 1979). One way to establish the direction for the group is to have a leader whose objectives and suggestions are clear and likely to be accepted. Another way is to hold a pre-decision planning discussion to set goals and timetables. A third way is through clear personnel policies and practices that are enforced. Once members agree on what must be done to accomplish the task, the group is likely to make an effective decision sooner. Group characteristics are likely to affect the promotion decision process and outcomes negatively when the group's structure and goals are *not* clarified and accepted by its members, or when personnel policies and procedures do *not* delineate what process should be followed to identify and evaluate candidates.

THE ORGANIZATIONAL AND ENVIRONMENTAL CONTEXT

Contextual factors that affect judgmental decisions range from the immediate work environment of the decision maker to the labor market, social forces, and government (Gladwin & Walter, 1980). Intermediate environments include the technical, managerial, and institutional levels of organizational activity (Thompson, 1967). Each "environment" partially defines a decision problem, affects the selection of a decision maker, influences future organizational policies regarding similar decision situations, and partially determines the subsequent decision process.

The contextual factors relevant to a judgmental decision vary based on who the decision maker is and what policies govern the situation. For example, the task and social environment of the decision maker can affect the decision. Job demands may affect the decision maker by establishing a perceptual frame of reference and determining the time available for making the decision. Organizational level and departmental functions further define the context. Blankenship and Miles (1968) found that decision makers near the top of their hierarchies had more influence, responsibility, and autonomy, and relied more on subordinates than managers at lower levels. Shrode and Brown (1970) reported that people-oriented decisions were made more often by higher level managers and managers in an administrative services department.

Kanter's (1977) study of one large organization suggests that management staffing decisions often extend over long periods of time, involve many career development activities, and encompass many implicit choices prior to the formal decision. Research on managerial succession provides some support for such a longitudinal process with respect to the selection of corporate presidents (Helmich, 1977). The feasible set of candidates for promotion, as we mentioned earlier, is often greatly reduced based on previous decisions which effectively eliminate individuals from consideration. Prior promotions, job assignments, and work experiences often determine who are viable candidates.

The location of the vacancy in the organization influences the staffing decision process. Some departments or positions are stepping stones to higher levels. They are part of pre-existing career paths (Anderson, Milkovich, & Tsui, 1981; Martin & Strauss, 1956). When vacancies arise in these departments or positions, there are many candidates to select from and it is easy to obtain the release of a valued employee from other departments. In contrast, vacancies in departments with poor reputations, or positions that are isolated or viewed as dead ends, are difficult to fill with an acceptable candidate.

Equal Employment Opportunity—Affirmative Action objectives also influence promotion decisions both directly and indirectly. In some cases, the organization may want to fill a vacancy with a woman or minority member. The search process centers on identifying someone who meets the affirmative action objective. In other instances the EEO plan influences the career development activities offered to employees to prepare them for future promotion.

EXAMPLES OF PROMOTION DECISIONS

Although it is impossible to demonstrate all the processes described above, two case examples of promotion decisions will help clarify how candidates are identified and evaluated in the process of filling a vacancy and what factors influence the process. Both cases are examples of individual decisions; one person is primarily responsible for filling the vacancy. Also, the cases are examples of decentralized decisions in that the decision maker is selecting his of her future subordinate. Examples of other types of decisions—e.g., group and centralized decisions—are presented in Chapter 8.

An Engineering Department Vacancy

Frank Harper had been with the company for twenty-five years and had just been transferred to his current fifth-level position when he needed to fill a vacancy in his unit. Prior to assuming this job, he was a plant supervisor for the West Coast operation. Now he has responsibility for the engineering department in the East Coast division. This involves construction of new facilities and testing and maintaining older facilities. Six people report directly to him: two fourth-level managers, three third-level managers, and one secretary. Frank was appointed to his present position as a result of a company-wide reorganization. His immediate supervisor, James Morrison, is the director of operations. He was Frank's boss for four years before the reorganization. Morrison became director of operations several months before Frank was promoted to his job.

Frank's first task in his new position was to fill a fourth-level vacancy. This was a top priority, and it took two weeks of almost full-time work. The reorganization would formally take effect on April 1st, one month after he assumed his new job. While it was not essential that the position be filled by April 1st, it was strongly desired. Frank wanted the person selected to have input in making the third-level appointments required by the reorganization.

The job requirements of the fourth-level position were established by the committee working on the reorganization. Frank began his search by considering the people he felt could do the job well. A candidate who immediately came to mind, Ralph Clawson, had been in the West Coast division and had been transferred recently to a third-level job at company headquarters several months earlier. Clawson had done a remarkable job of improving unit performance in his former job, and Frank was certain that Clawson's background and managerial skills were right for the fourth-level vacancy. But there were several factors that led him to finally select another candidate. First, Frank wanted to consider people from the East Coast division if at all possible. The reorganization had resulted in "importing" a number of people including Frank and Jim Morrison. Jim wanted Frank to be certain that a qualified candidate from the East Coast division could not be found before recommending a candidate from outside. Second, Clawson had just moved to headquarters and he was not anxious to relocate again.

Frank had made a number of promotion decisions in the past at lower levels where he knew candidates personally. His dilemma now was that he knew very few people connected with the East Coast division. Consequently, he decided to make an extensive search by collecting information from a number of different sources. Following routine procedures, he asked the headquarters personnel department to submit names of qualified candidates from all divisions. He also talked to many East Coast people, especially the local personnel manager who had been there for many years. This enabled Frank to corroborate opinions and resolve conflicting recommendations.

Five candidates were identified, including Frank's initial favorite from the West Coast division, Ralph Clawson. The others were from the East Coast. Two East Coast people were eliminated since they only had engineering experience, and Frank wanted someone with a construction background to complement the other fourth-level manager whose background was engineering. A third East Coast division candidate was eliminated for lack of technical experience. The director of operations in another division recommended Clawson. Clawson's boss also recommended him, although another supervisor did not. Frank did not weight this negative information heavily since the supervisor happened to be fairly new on his job. This left two candidates: Clawson and an East Coast candidate, Norma Wilson.

The next step was to meet Norma Wilson. Frank arranged a trip to Wilson's district for this purpose. Nothing was said to her about the position vacancy, but Wilson was probably aware that this was at least one reason for Frank's visit. Frank found Wilson to be similar to Clawson in that they both had a good technical background and commanded respect from their co-workers. Nevertheless, Wilson did not seem to be as "strong a personality" as Clawson.

This single visit did not convince Frank. Since Wilson had been a third-level manager in the district for the last three years, she had been in her position long enough to have had a significant impact on the district's performance. Frank decided to compare this district with three others in the East Coast division on seventeen different indices. He obtained the data for the previous fourteen months. Wilson's was best a number of times, although not always. Even her lowest indices, however, were generally better than most of the other units. Frank's conclusion was that Wilson seemed to have the most consistently favorable operation.

The final decision was a matter of judgment. Both candidates' results were good, although not directly comparable. Frank's decision was to choose Norma Wilson because "this was the most feasible option." Wilson was well known and would not have to establish her credibility in the area. Moreover, her promotion would demonstrate to others in the East Coast division that senior management was concerned with recognizing the abilities of personnel in that area.

Frank's decision followed a sequential decision process. Most job requirements were predefined for Frank whose initial strategy was to identify someone he knew could do the job well. Clawson had some drawbacks, however, and the situation demanded that Frank search within his new territory. Identifying candidates from formal and informal sources and securing corroborating information yielded five top candidates. Recommendations from others and an analysis of the candidates resulted in two final alternatives: Clawson, the initial favorite, and Wilson who was previously unknown to Frank. Frank interviewed Wilson and collected data about her performance, but could not collect similar information for Clawson. The final decision turned on the political feasibility of who would be most acceptable to Frank's boss and to others in the division.

As Frank reflected on the decision process, he seemed somewhat surprised. He admitted that he initially thought he knew the person he wanted and was just doing his duty by searching in the East Coast area. As he collected information, he began to wonder if Clawson was the best candidate after all. The task was no longer a matter of duty, but rather an effort to identify and select the best candidate.

Reactions to the decision to choose Wilson were positive. Several weeks after the appointment, an equipment breakdown occurred in Wilson's old unit, and she was able to rush in with the needed direction to repair the damage. Frank noted with satisfaction that Clawson might not have been as effective in an emergency so soon after assuming the job.

A Market Research Vacancy

Ann Miles had been with the company for eleven years and had been in her present position for one year when a vacancy arose in her unit. She is responsible for making price and quantity forecasts for input to the engineering and sales departments. She has eight immediate subordinates, all at the highest band of second level.

The vacant position was a three-year rotational assignment. When Ann assumed her present job, there was a need to fill a number of openings to meet the increasing demand placed on the department. She wanted someone with import-export experience to conduct research on this market since she predicted that international sales would become more important over time.

To initiate the candidate search process, Ann prepared a vacancy announcement to circulate to the sales departments throughout the company. This announcement was distributed with others which were sent out quarterly. No candidates were nominated in response. Ann reasoned that the lack of response occurred because the departments in the company want to keep their best sales people even when they are promotable. Over four months passed and no viable candidates were identified.

Ann then contacted her department's personnel coordinator to obtain names of promotable candidates who had been submitted in the recent past in response to other position vacancies but had been rejected. She was able to identify several suitable candidates. One candidate, Bill Campbell, was a low band second level with import sales experience. Campbell was Ann's first choice. Ann called Campbell's supervisor to determine if he could be released. This necessitated justifying her selection and what the rotation would do for Campbell's career. When the supervisor agreed to Campbell's release (it took about a week to obtain this decision), Ann contacted her personnel coordinator to prepare the necessary paperwork for approving the promotion.

After written approval was obtained from Campbell's home office, Ann telephoned Campbell to arrange a visit to headquarters. Ann did not offer Campbell the job when she arranged this meeting, but she felt he would not have come if he were not interested in moving. Ann and her boss interviewed Campbell, and offered him the job that day. Ann estimated that she was 90% responsible for the decision and that her supervisor was 10% responsible. Ann was not pressured for time, and the selection process took about six months.

Ann began the process by setting standards based on her expectations of a new demand on her department. Her next step was to follow formal procedures to identify candidates. When this did not work, she looked to other sources. Only one individual surfaced who had the necessary experience. Implementing her decision required convincing the candidate's current department as well as her boss. If Campbell had not been interested in the job, Ann might have delayed filling the vacancy until a suitable candidate could be found. Alternatively, she might have eliminated the international marketing experience requirement in hopes of finding more candidates sooner.

SUMMARY

The process of filling a job vacancy is crucial to organizational effectiveness, equal employment opportunity, and individual career planning and development. Internal staffing decisions, including promotions and transfers, can be examined with respect to the relationships among decision outcomes and effectiveness, decision process, decision-maker characteristics, and the organizational and environmental context. The difficulty in determining the effectiveness of a staffing decision makes it hard to alter such a decision before substantial costs are incurred. Consequently, how a promotion or transfer decision is made is important to its ultimate effectiveness. Understanding the staffing decision process can be valuable to decision makers in reaching more objective and equitable decisions and to those affected by staffing decisions in determining what behaviors lead to desired career outcomes.

The decision process consists of strategy formulation, candidate search, evaluation-choice (which covers applying information about candidates to screening and final choice), and planning for implementation. Tentative guidelines were offered for each of these decision process elements, often noting conditions under which each guideline is most likely to be applicable or most effective. The guidelines can be summarized as follows:

1. Formulate strategies that reflect salient situational factors while allowing flexibility to accommodate unforeseen events.

2. Search for candidates as thoroughly as possible, but realize that the need for a thorough search may be limited by situational factors.

3. Collect information from multiple standardized sources, and require decision makers to justify their decisions, thereby encouraging the use of objective information.

4. Formulate and communicate standard policies and procedures for making promotion decisions.

5. Screen candidates and make the final choice on the basis of candidates' strengths, weaknesses, or both, depending on the decision maker's objectives, the job requirements, and the type and amount of information available.

6. Involve others in making the decision when they are likely to reveal important information and when their confidence in and acceptance of the decision is important.

More research on promotion and transfer decisions will be necessary to refine and extend these guidelines.

Individual characteristics such as the decision maker's motivation, information capacity, and risk-taking tendency may affect staffing decisions. Group characteristics may also influence the outcome of committee decisions. Finally, contextual factors, such as location of the vacancy and organizational policies, influence the staffing decision process and outcomes. Organizations should be aware of these variables when establishing staffing decision policies and procedures. Two cases illustrated how the decision processes and factors affecting them operate in individual, decentralized decisions.

Career Management Support Systems

8

The last chapter examined elements of the internal staffing decision process. Here we focus on formal and informal mechanisms which exist in organizations for making staffing decisions and in the processes used for managing careers. Formal support systems include promotion and transfer policies, standard operating procedures, human resource forecasting and planning, succession planning, job matching, and job posting. Informal support systems include role modeling, sponsorship, and mentoring. Each of these mechanisms is reviewed and exemplified below. The chapter concludes with suggestions for developing staffing support systems.

FORMAL SUPPORT SYSTEMS

Promotion and Transfer Policies

Promotion and transfer policies vary in their degree of formalization and centralization (Bureau of National Affairs, 1978). The degree of formalization is a function of the content and explicitness of the organization's personnel policies (Dimick, 1978). Centralization refers to the locus of decision making, which ranges from decisions made completely by the organization's headquarters personnel department (centralized) to those made by the manager filling a job vacancy.

Formal policies are often articulated in written guidelines and other documents delineating personnel practices. In contrast, informal policies are seldom put in writing and must be inferred from past practices and/or observation of managers' behavior (Yoder & Heneman, 1974).

There are both advantages and disadvantages to formal staffing policies. Formal policies can increase the opportunities for and ensure fairer treatment of employees, as well as inform managers about how candidates for promotion and transfer should be identified. They also can specify the standards that should be used in the selection process. However, formalization may limit the decision maker's discretion and increase the time required to fill a vacancy.

While formal policies establish and clarify procedures for making promotions, a centralized promotion and transfer system focuses on the needs of the entire company or unit, not just a particular vacancy. Centralized personnel departments can standardize forms and methods of collecting information about candidates. Such uniformity can facilitate equal treatment of candidates and provide documents to support decisions. Staffing decisions made in personnel systems that are formalized and centralized are more likely to achieve organizational compliance with EEO-Affirmative Action targets and other legal aspects associated with the fair treatment of employees (Stumpf, Greller, & Freedman, 1980).

Documents that express a company's promotion and transfer philosophy aid managers in making staffing decisions. Statements can range from broad generalities to very specific suggestions. Consider the following examples of explicit policies as they relate to different phases of the staffing decision process:

Policies for Candidate Search

- Our company's policy is to provide equal employment opportunity to all personnel without discriminating because of race, color, religion, national origin, gender, age, or physical handicaps. This applies to recruiting, hiring, working conditions, benefits, promotions, compensation, training, transfers, and terminations.

- Management vacancies above first level should be filled

from the ranks of current managers. Hiring from outside the company except for special technical positions requires approval at the highest level in the division.

- Due to an employee surplus, vacancies should be filled by transfers whenever possible. Promotions require formal approval.

- Promotability is determined by evaluating current performance and potential for advancement ratings, each weighted equally.

- All departments should maintain a list of individuals who are "ready-now" for promotion. Only individuals designated promotable may be considered for promotion.

- A company-wide search should be conducted for each management vacancy.

- A notice of each position vacancy must be circulated to all middle managers and above. Managers should use their judgment in sharing these notices with their subordinates.

- A notice of each position vacancy should be published in the company bulletin. Supervisors are encouraged to nominate interested subordinates. Subordinates who wish to be nominated may request that the personnel department submit their names without going through their immediate supervisor.

Policies for Evaluation and Choice

- Entry level managers comprise a human resource talent pool. They are to be selected for their potential to the company, not solely for their ability to perform a particular job.

- No individual shall be promoted without having been rated high in potential at an assessment center unless an override is approved at the vice-presidential level.

- No job assignment shall be designated permanent. All individuals should have the capability to move to other jobs at the same level or at higher levels. Moreover, such movement should be encouraged after three years in the same position.

- Seniority is not adequate justification for promotion or transfer.

Policies for Decision Approval

- An individual who declines a promotion or transfer for personal reasons shall not be penalized in any way and should be considered eligible for other opportunities as they arise.
- All promotion decisions must be documented in writing with a statement describing who was selected and why, and who was rejected and why.
- Approval for a staffing decision is required by management one or more levels above that of the decision maker.
- The selected candidate's previous department must agree to take back the individual within six months if he or she is unsuccessful or unhappy with the change.

The above statements are not necessarily representative or ideal policies; they are examples from different organizations. Often such policies are not made explicit. They are assumed by virtue of tradition ("That's how we've always done things around here.") or unwritten fiat of corporate officials. Discovering and understanding implicit policies is important for successful management. To avoid such a necessity, organizations should generally formulate and communicate explicit promotion policies and procedures.

Communicating policies.   There are several ways to communicate staffing policies to the decision makers and to the individuals affected by staffing decisions. Memos or pamphlets explaining policies can be distributed by the personnel department to employees. Policies might also be printed in the company newsletter. Staffing issues can be covered in orientation meetings for entry level employees, and in supervisory training programs for recently promoted individuals. The company's personnel handbook should also contain such policies so that they can be reviewed periodically as vacancies occur.

Studies cited in Chapter 7 suggest that a surprising proportion of employees are unclear about what factors lead to promotion. Those at lower levels believe that nonability factors often control the process (e.g., who you know, appearance, sex).

Clarifying the path to promotion—that is, detailing what information and standards are used to select promotees—will help employees better manage their careers. Clear policy communication also helps to standardize staffing procedures and ensure equal employment opportunity.

Standard Operating Procedures

Standard operating procedures (SOPs) regarding staffing decisions are more specific than staffing policies and are often published in corporate personnel handbooks. Such SOPs describe staffing procedures for the company's employees and serve as a source of information for prospective employees and newcomers about salary and benefit administration, promotion and transfer policies, performance appraisals, and career planning opportunities. An excerpt from a personnel handbook detailing the SOP for filling a vacancy is shown in Table 8.1. Two forms mentioned in this document are presented as Tables 8.2 and 8.3. These examples should not be considered representative or ideal since SOPs by their very nature reflect the internal systems of an organization, and organizations differ widely in their personnel practices.

The first section of the handbook excerpt describes forms that must be completed by the supervisor with the vacancy to obtain information on EEO requirements, announce the vacancy, receive nominations, and obtain approval for the decision. In this example, the manager first seeks budget approval for filling the position before making the decision (even when a person is being replaced). A "Notice of Position Vacancy" (Table 8.2) is sent through departmental channels to the Management Careers Office where it is assigned a vacancy number and affirmative action deficiencies are noted. The notice is posted in a "Monthly Management Changes" bulletin which is distributed to all managers. The supervisor with the vacancy also brings the notice to the attention of other supervisors who might have suitable candidates. Finally, a "Management Selection Documentation" form (Table 8.3) is completed describing who was selected.

TABLE 8.1
Metrobank Personnel Handbook (Excerpt 1)

How to fill a management job

1. When a position vacancy arises, whether due to a force loss, increase in the workload, or a force reorganization, a "Notice of Position Vacancy" form (see Table 8.2) must be completed by the supervisor.
2. Before filing this form, budget clearance should be checked through the appropriate channels.
3. The form should be sent for approval to the department's Vice President or Assistant Vice President. Once signed, the form should be returned to the supervisor who then forwards it to the Management Careers Office.
4. In the Management Careers Office, it is assigned a vacancy number, and any affirmative action deficiencies for that job class are indicated. Arrangements are made for the vacancy to be posted in the "Monthly Management Changes" notice. This notice is distributed monthly to all managers at first level and above. Managers are encouraged to nominate qualified subordinates by sending a memo to the supervisor.
5. The supervisor distributes the "Notice of Position Vacancy" to other supervisors in departments that might have qualified candidates for the position. This procedure combined with the above encourages the nomination of candidates from different departments.
6. Candidates are evaluated by the supervisor who makes a decision. The supervisor records this decision on the "Management Selection Documentation" form (see Table 8.3). This form describes the individual selected and must be approved by the next level supervisor and the departmental Vice President.
7. A "Management Selection Documentation" form must be completed for all reassignments including promotions, temporary promotions, and transfers between or within departments at the same level (i.e., lateral transfers). Lateral transfers within departments for purposes of reorganization do not require submitting a "Notice of Position Vacancy" for each change, but each change does require a "Management Selection Documentation" form.

TABLE 8.2
Notice of Position Vacancy

DEPARTMENT: Business Customer Services
TITLE: Business Office District Manager
LOCATION: Central Division, Monroeville District (District C)
COMPENSATION LEVEL: 3
IMMEDIATE SUPERVISOR: Central Division Manager
_____ New Position   __X__ Replacement for: Fran Jones
_____ Permanent   _____ Rotational for _____ months.

JOB DUTIES

This position is responsible for operations in Monroeville District.

A. Supervises 6 office managers and directs the operations of 6 offices.
   1. Analyzes weekly and monthly reports and indices for individual offices.
   2. Determines weak spots, plans, and takes corrective actions, i.e., visits office to discuss, assist, and correct deficiencies, solves problems with office manager and subordinate force.
   3. Conducts service reviews with office managers, determines strong and weak areas, and formulates plans to improve performance.
   4. Conducts appraisals and recommends salary classifications of subordinates.
   5. With the aid of the Division Manager, identifies potential of office managers, plans personnel changes and transfers for personnel growth and service improvements.
B. Develops short and long range service plans and objectives, analyzes results, and determines future force requirements.
C. Participates in community relations activities, and supervises involvement of office managers in community relations work.
D. This position acts as the focal point for customer reactions. Consequently, the decisions, responsibility, and risk for office performance results is inherent in the job. The incumbent is guided by practices, experience, and the supervisor.

TABLE 8.2 (continued)

QUALIFICATIONS REQUIRED FOR POSITION

Candidate must have:
1. High inner work standards
2. Good organization and planning
3. Good decision making
4. Impact well on others: customers and interdepartmental
5. Excellent facility for oral and written expression
6. Good stability with resistance to pressure
7. Ability to work under minimum supervision
8. Ability to lead others

NAMES OF DEPARTMENTAL CANDIDATES

District A: Thomas L. Zimmer

District B: Donna S. Walsh

District C: Susan Michaels, William P. Berg

District D: Martin L. Franklin, Bradley Taylor, Linda Parker,
Marilyn Clarke

AVP Signature _____   Management Careers Office
                                        Vacancy Number: 82-3624

TABLE 8.3
Management Selection Documentation

JOB TITLE _____ LEVEL _____

NATURE OF APPOINTMENT: (Circle)

PROMOTION   TEMPORARY PROMOTION
TEMPORARY PROMOTION MADE PERMANENT
NEW HIRE   TRANSFER FROM A SUBSIDIARY
REASSIGNMENT (LATERAL TRANSFER)

CANDIDATE SELECTED

NAME   PRESENT TITLE   SEX   PRESENT WORK UNIT/DEPARTMENT

TABLE 8.2   (continued)

SELECTED BECAUSE _____

_____

_____

OTHER CANDIDATES IN ORDER OF PREFERENCE

NAME   PRESENT TITLE   SEX   PRESENT WORK UNIT/DEPARTMENT

_____

REJECTED BECAUSE _____

_____

_____

_____

NAME   PRESENT TITLE   SEX   PRESENT WORK UNIT/DEPARTMENT

_____

REJECTED BECAUSE _____

_____

_____

_____

USE ANOTHER PAGE TO LIST MORE CANDIDATES OR IF ADDITIONAL INFORMATION IS NECESSARY

SELECTOR: _____ DATE: _____

_____

FINAL APPROVAL:

_____ DATE: _____

_____

This procedure does not mention what should be done if candidates do not readily emerge from circulation of the notice of position vacancy, nor what standards should be used to select candidates. The handbook does describe the types of information that may be available about candidates (see Table 8.4). Com-

TABLE 8.4
Metrobank Personnel Handbook (Excerpt 2)

The personnel profile

The vehicle used to input information from the supervisor on each management candidate is the "Personnel Profile." This Profile is comprised of two sections, a history or background section and an evaluative section. The form is completed annually by the employee's supervisor as a summary of items covered in supervisor/subordinate discussions throughout the year. The components of the form are described below.

A. Background Information—this section covers the factual background of an employee's work, training, and educational experience both from inside and outside the company. It includes the following:

1. Educational background.
2. Other training: Experiences useful for a career in this company.
3. Previous work history: Significant work experience prior to joining the company.
4. Company work history: Significant work experience after joining the company.

B. Performance Appraisal Summary—this includes the following:

1. Strong areas: A few of the individual's outstanding qualities.
2. Areas needing improvement: Those most affecting one's potential.
3. Evaluation: This includes 4 distinctly different elements—
   a. *Performance appraisal rating*—a judgment of the individual's output is made on a 5 point scale ranging from 1 = poor, 2 = needs immediate improvement, 3 = satisfactory, 4 = very good, 5 = outstanding.
   b. *Potential rating*—this is defined as an evaluation of the quality of the process used to produce the output by looking at 8 skills (leadership, decision making, organizing and planning, written communication, flexibility, oral communication, performance stability, and inner work standards). These skills are used by the supervisor to describe an individual's strengths on the Personnel Profile. Potential ratings fall into 5

TABLE 8.4   (continued)

categories: 1 = very little, 2 = questionable, 3 = satisfactory, 4 = good, 5 = a great deal.

c. *Promotability rating*—this judgment is made by the individual's supervisor together with other supervisors in the department. The individual is placed into 1 of 6 categories: 1 = promotable now, 2 = promotable now but additional development is desirable, 3 = promotable at some future date, 4 = mixed reports, 5 = is not ready but may be promotable if performance and potential improve, 6 = not promotable.

d. *Assessment center statement*—this is the outcome of a standardized program consisting of a series of individual and group exercises administered over a 2-day period to aid management in the selection of candidates for third-level supervisory positions. The assessment staff, consisting of other managers, observes the individual and writes a formal report which often accompanies the Personnel Profile. Also, the staff makes an overall judgment of the individual's potential. "More than acceptable," "Acceptable," "Questionable," or "Low level of supervisory ability." Not all managers attend assessment centers, so this information is not available for everyone.

Equal Employment Opportunity policy

It is the policy of the company to provide Equal Employment Opportunity to all personnel, without discrimination because of race, color, religion, national origin, sex, age, mental or physical handicap. This policy applies to recruiting, hiring, working conditions, benefits, promotions, compensation, training, transfers, and termination. The company has an irrevocable commitment to implementing this policy and observing the "spirit" as well as the "letter" of the law.

---

ponents of the personnel profile are described with attention given to the meaning of performance appraisal, potential, and promotability ratings as well as assessment center statements. This SOP excerpt states the company's affirmative action policy in general terms.

Human Resource Forecasting and Planning

Human resource forecasting and planning are processes concerned with providing the right number and kinds of people, at the right place and time to do the activities that help fulfill organizational as well as individual objectives (Burack & Gutteridge, 1978). It involves predicting the number and kinds of people who will be necessary in the future and formulating action plans for securing the required labor force (Clark & Thurston, 1977). The former function involves forecasting while the latter function is programming (Burack & Smith, 1977). Programming activities encompass selection, development, promotion, and other aspects of succession. The present focus is on methods used to predict the number, type, and quality of personnel needed (Cashel, 1978).

The need for planning. Organizations develop plans to assist managers in making decisions. Predicting the future allows an organization to be both reactive and proactive (Cascio, 1978). By anticipating changes, the organization may be able to respond more effectively.

In addition, the organization can establish policies that help make the changes. For example, a manufacturing company predicting changes in product demand or new technology can redesign its processes or structure to accommodate a new marketing strategy. Competition, marketing approaches, relationships with labor unions, growth, and legislation are just some of the changing external factors impinging on organizations. General societal trends that also affect organizations include the recent knowledge and information explosion (Zand, 1981), the need for more effective training and development programs, and the accelerated pace of change itself (Cascio, 1978).

In addition to planned change, many changes are a reaction to unanticipated occurrences. These occurrences can precipitate the need to use past and current information to take immediate action as well as predict the future. For example, a consumer package goods company which is suddenly confronted with a competitor's innovation may have to make product changes while it is conducting studies to estimate the impact of the innovation on the market.

A similar need to predict future events and estimate environmental changes applies to human resource planning. External changes, such as the passage of legislation affecting the mandatory retirement age or equal employment opportunity, may force an organization to effect immediate changes in policy and formulate new plans for meeting future human resource requirements. Slow trends in population growth or education levels may suggest the need to create new recruitment, selection, and training programs. Long-term forecasts allow ample time to design new policies and adjust procedures as new data emerge.

The need to coordinate plans.   Changes in one organizational function affect planning in other areas. Budgeting, product design, production schedules, introducing technological developments, capital expenditures, and other activities are interrelated with human resource planning. Population changes, the age of the work force, and competition for talented individuals in the labor market are examples of human resource factors that affect other functional areas.

Decisions affecting the organization's product line, capital expenditures, or expansion plans will influence labor force requirements. The decision to be capital intensive may lead to technological developments and equipment purchases which eliminate the need for lower level personnel and place more emphasis on middle and upper management to operate the business (Cashel, 1978).

The organization's career development philosophy will also influence human resource planning. The decision to promote from within, to rely on college hires for entry level positions, and/or to provide developmental opportunities to those who demonstrate high potential early in their careers will have different implications from a decision to rely primarily on external resources to meet human resource needs. Decisions about organizational design such as the optimal span of control, and decisions about career development such as whether to rotate individuals between functions or promote only within functional lines, will also have implications for planning. Therefore, management philosophies must be clearly communicated to human resource planners (Cashel, 1978).

Human resource planning is integrally related to other human resource functions. Components of career progression (movement between and within levels, retirements, voluntary and involuntary terminations, etc.) will determine the number of vacancies available at each level. Predictions of personnel movement can be made from analysis of past trends and current characteristics of the work force (e.g., age, retirement plans). This information, coupled with how the organization selects, assesses, and develops talent, will influence intake of new personnel. Organizations relying on promotion from within will have to plan ahead to fill vacancies in middle management and above. Sudden changes in vacancies may necessitate changing career development processes—e.g., accelerating rotation in job assignments or hiring from outside the organization to meet demands for certain expertise.

Planning for managerial progression. The previous section indicates that planning and implementing human resource plans is a fluid, systematic process which depends on career development programs, anticipated changes in the work force, plans and changes in other organizational functions, and several external forces. Human resource planning is particularly important within management. A competent management force is critical to the long-range success of the organization. Managers are often highly skilled personnel, and they require substantial time to develop expertise. Moreover, they are usually highly paid, and their loss—particularly to competitors—can have severe impact on the organization (Hoffman & Wyatt, 1977).

Technological advancement and increasing organizational complexity result in greater reliance on managers. The greater the diversity of skills required, the more interdependence will occur between different functions (Schein, 1978). Interdependence leads to a greater need for effective integration of specialties. General managers need to rely on their technically trained subordinates for decision making in such instances. Rather than making the decisions, the general manager manages the decision-making process. This involves identifying and formulating the problem, defining standards for an effective decision, bringing the right people together, determining a mode of group functioning, and facilitating an effective group process (Stumpf, Zand, & Freedman, 1979; Vroom & Yetton, 1973).

Thus, planning for managerial progression is essential to ensure that the organization will have sufficient talent to cope with the human error and inadequacies which tend to emerge in complex organizations. Interpersonal conflict, turnover, low morale, and reliance on managers to train and develop their subordinates to meet future needs are some of the reasons for the organization's increasing reliance on the management function.

Another reason for the importance of planning for managerial progression, in addition to the increase in functional interdependence, is that changing social values regarding the role of work have made it more complicated to manage people (Schein, 1978). Individuals vary in their career goals. Some aim toward senior management positions, others wish to maintain their professional role with minimal managerial responsibilities, and still others prefer security at low levels of the organizational hierarchy. This has made it necessary for some organizations to develop multiple career ladders and to identify and plan for the career progression of employees based on their career goals.

Personal crises at every career stage have required that organizations become more responsive to the interaction between the work and nonwork domains of an individual's life. Rising economic affluence has lessened the extent to which work is a central life interest for some people. Dual-career families and increased opportunities for women in management and other professional role with minimal managerial responsibilities, and still others prefer security at low levels of the organizational hierardecisions in staffing management positions. Relocations and changes in job assignments cannot be made easily without consulting the individuals involved and often their families as well (Hall & Hall, 1976).

Planning functions.   Clark and Thurston (1977), of the U.S. Civil Service System, suggest functions for developing specific planning efforts. They include the following:

1. *Information collection and transfer.* This is the routine collection of information describing the current work force structure. This should include an inventory of individuals' skills and potential in relationship to the demands of their present jobs. An information system is necessary for routinely collecting and recording data. Provisions should be made for regularly transmitting the information to personnel officials and managers in other functions who contribute to staffing decisions.

2. *Information analysis.* Data on human resources and staffing changes should be routinely analyzed. This would include analysis of the following: (a) levels and changes in skills and pay distributions in different functions or occupations, (b) levels and changes in work force composition in different functions or occupations according to age, gender, minority status, and length of service, and (c) levels and changes in new hires, promotions, transfers, and losses due to voluntary and involuntary terminations.

3. *Forecasting.* This is the systematic estimation of current and future staffing needs. The output should be a projection of human resource requirements in terms of the number of people and skills needed. This is derived from an analysis of job vacancies likely to arise from turnover, transfers, promotions, and other staffing moves. The kinds of personnel actions which will be required should also be specified.

4. *Work force planning.* Management should be apprised of the human resource forecasts and their implications for management staffing. The feasibility of meeting the human resource needs forecasted should be assessed based on an analysis of the labor market, the number of managers currently in training, attrition rates, and so forth. Means to provide this manpower staff, including recruiting, training, promotions, and compensation, should be evaluated along with the costs of new or changed personnel procedures and adjustments in salaries and benefits. Planning should also account for the impact of proposed programs on current employees and the organization's obligations to meet government standards (e.g., EEO requirements) and self-imposed policies (e.g., promotion from within). Forecasts should be used to establish operational goals for all personnel functions.

5. *Evaluation.* This is the assessment of the extent to which human resource goals and objectives are met. Evaluation requires reliable data and research designs which allow estimating the causal impact of various factors in the environment on the accuracy of forecasts and human resource plans. The information should be used to continuously calibrate forecasting procedures to improve the accuracy of future predictions.

Taking responsibility for human resource planning and forecasting. Human resource planning is generally thought to be a staff function conducted by the personnel department. This is true insofar as personnel experts collect information about current human resource assets, maintain records, and establish procedures for hiring and developing the work force (i.e., recruitment, selection testing, performance appraisal, and career planning). Forecasting human resource needs can be a complex process requiring knowledge of statistics, mathematical modeling, computer programming, economics, and other specialized skills (Walker, 1980). The sophisticated predictions which emerge provide a macro-level snapshot of future trends. They estimate what will happen at different functional, divisional, and organizational levels.

On the micro-level, these predictions must be translated into plans or programs for specific departments and individuals. The personnel department may develop policies to guide the management process in line with forecasts, but managers are usually responsible for anticipating changes in their own departments and taking actions to meet these changes. Both line and staff managers use human resource forecasts to help subordinates plan their careers, decide who should receive developmental opportunities, and structure the nature of these opportunities. Coordinating personnel changes with managers in other units is often necessary.

The fact that most managers in an organization are involved in identifying and allocating human resources means that procedures and supporting information provided by the personnel department must be clearly communicated and perceived as contributing to the achievement of the organization's objectives. Both personnel experts and the managers they serve are jointly responsible for the development and implementation of human resource plans, and it is essential that both groups understand the elements of human resource planning and how they are applied.

Matching planning techniques to the organization.   Before presenting an example of how human resource planning can be applied, it should be emphasized that the planning techniques adopted by an organization depend on the organization's needs and capabilities. Attempting sophistication greater than that which an organization is capable of using is unnecessary. Large and complex planning systems may fail even in large profitable organizations with exceptional computer facilities and support personnel. The critical point is that the methods used and the output produced must be within the bounds of the willingness and capability of organizational members to understand and implement (Drandell, 1975).

In general, one should be wary of complicated and excessively mechanistic human resource planning systems. The interpretation of the output of such models and subsequent policy decisions will always depend on factors not included in the models. Informed judgment is required to translate statistical findings into practical policies. If forecasting becomes habitual year after year, the value of the exercise for evaluating and improving policies and formulating new policies should be questioned.

Armstrong (1978) believes that one rule to follow in long-term forecasting is KISS—Keep it simple, stupid! He places emphasis on simple methods to reach forecasting objectives. In addition, he suggests that it is good practice to be suspicious when people tell you they need more information. Additional information becomes redundant quickly in making predictions.

Guidelines for an effective human resource planning policy.   The above discussion suggests five guidelines which should be considered when establishing policies for human resource planning:

1. Recognize the relationships between human resource planning and planning in other functions of the organization. A forecast in one function may have an impact on forecasts in other functions. This impact should be estimated and forecasts for different functions should be coordinated.

2. Identify external factors affecting the staffing process for use in developing forecasts. This may entail obtaining information from outside the organization (e.g., from the U.S. Department of Labor or the Census Bureau) as well as closely observing other organizations in the industry.

3. Involve individuals from relevant levels and departments in the planning process. They are necessary to provide information and formulate their own plans based on centrally developed forecasts. They are also necessary to implement general organizational policies and procedures.

4. Consider individuals' career and life goals as input to human resource forecasting. Plans based solely on quantitative data may fail if social and cultural trends are ignored. Such trends involve not only individual attitudes and behaviors but also legislation and court decisions.

5. Use forecasts to take a proactive stance in meeting future human resource needs. This requires designing personnel procedures, such as recruiting and training, which reflect the skills required in the future.

How to Apply Human Resource Planning Data to Career Development Programs: An Illustration

Chapter 5 described a career management program for the accelerated development of high potential managers. The accelerated advancement program prepares first-level managers for middle management. The number of individuals selected into the program depends on projections of the number and type of middle and upper level managers needed in the future. The number of new entrants may fluctuate from year to year depending on anticipated demand. The following example indicates how human resource forecasts will affect such a program, and whether or not organizations using the program will be able to select the required number of participants.

Projecting force requirements. Table 8.5 provides an example of the estimated number of third-level managers required during the next three years. For every 100 third-level managers, thirty losses are expected. This figure is based on an attrition estimate of 9 to 11% per year which includes retirements, terminations, and promotions. Ten new positions are also expected due to growth in the organization. In total, forty third-level vacancies for every 100 current third-level positions are projected during the next three years. Assume that 30% of these, or twelve, will be filled from the accelerated advancement program. In *each* of the next three years, approximately ten losses and three gains are expected. Of these thirteen vacancies each year, four are expected to be filled from the accelerated advancement program.

Meeting third-level force requirements. The development process begins with all new first-level managers with a minimum of one year in management (see Table 8.6). This could include management hires in general management jobs, management hires in specialty areas, and promotees from nonmanagement. However, not all first-level managers will have high performance and high potential ratings from their supervisors. Assume that forty out of 100 have high performance and high potential; they would be invited to an assessment center for first- and second-level

TABLE 8.5
Force Projection Example

FOR EVERY 100 THIRD-LEVEL MANAGERS

	Replacements	+	Additions	=	Force Requirements	× .30	=	From Accelerated Advancement Program
Each year	10	+	3	=	13	× .30	=	4
Over next 3 years	30	+	10	=	40	× .30	=	12

TABLE 8.6
Meeting Third-Level Force Requirements

All new 1st-level managers (1 year minimum experience)	For every 100 eligible 1st-level managers
Estimated as having potential for 3rd level—should go to the assessment center as soon as possible (40%).	40
Passing assessment and entering accelerated advancement program (25%).	10
Completing program—in promotable pool for 3rd level in 3 years (loss rate estimated at 10%/yr.) Depends on progress in program.	up to 7
Ultimately promoted to 3rd level.	?

managers to assess their potential for third level. Past assessment center success rates indicate that about 25% of the first-level managers attending a center receive high ratings. Thus, entry to the accelerated advancement program is a multiple hurdle procedure requiring high supervisory performance and potential ratings, and a high rating in an assessment center designed to assess third-level management potential. Those who fail assessment early in their careers would enter the standard career route and have an opportunity for reassessment and promotion later in their careers.

These projections mean that about ten out of every 100 new managers will enter the accelerated program. Given an estimated loss rate of 10% per year (due to voluntary and involuntary terminations from the program), a maximum of seven out of ten participants will complete the program within three years. Four of the seven program graduates could be expected to be promoted to third level immediately after finishing the program. Just who is promoted, and whether the others are promoted and how soon, will depend on the opportunities available and competition with other managers who, although not graduates of the program, are also viable candidates for promotion to third level.

Since it takes time for such a program to become operational, it would not begin to meet the company's human resource requirements for several years. Adjustments may be necessary, such as initially having more experienced managers participate in the program for a shorter period of time to prepare them for promotion in the next year or two. Furthermore, annual updates in forecasts will be needed to adjust the program to meet changes in staffing requirements. If this is not done, the organization increases the risk of preparing too many or too few candidates for early promotion.

In summary, human resource forecasting and planning should be used to make personnel changes and provide development programs that will meet future force requirements. Guidelines for effective human resource planning encourage recognizing the relationships between human resource planning and other organizational functions, incorporating external factors in developing forecasts, involving individuals from different departments and levels in the planning process, considering individual career and life goals as input to human resource forecasts, and taking a proactive stance in meeting human resource needs. The example demonstrated how projected force requirements can be matched with the organization's capability of meeting these requirements.

Succession Planning

Succession planning involves defining the requirements of future positions and determining the availability of candidates and their readiness to move into various jobs (Walker, 1980). Replacement charts are often used to record possible successors for key positions. Chapter 5 described the succession planning process in several corporations as examples of how organizations plan the careers of their employees. We noted that this is often done by supervisors with little input from subordinates. Ideally, succession planning and career planning should be united so that individuals understand the relationship between their career objectives and the organization's goals. Realistically, however, the organization often determines an employee's career destiny. This section examines how organizations formulate and use replacement charts as a staffing support system.

Developing replacement charts. Maintaining organizational continuity requires being able to replace employees who retire or receive promotions or transfers with individuals who have similar qualifications or who will meet the job requirements when a vacancy arises (Kellogg, 1979). Some executives believe that a manager's first responsibility is to identify and prepare his or her successor (Walker, 1980). Replacement planning facilitates the staffing decision process by identifying capable individuals before vacancies arise. This is often accomplished in annual review meetings during which department managers review prospective candidates for key positions (or in some cases all positions), and determine whether or not the positions are likely to be vacated during the next year. The candidates best suited for the job are listed on an organizational chart under the name of the person currently occupying the position.

Fig. 8.1 provides an example of a replacement chart used by a major oil company. The chart indicates the current status of the position (e.g., whether it will become vacant), and lists as many as four possible replacements. Each individual's current performance and advancement potential are given along with when he or she will be qualified for advancement.

Walker (1980) notes that while replacement planning is a valuable tool for management development in the absence of a formalized program, it suffers from several shortcomings:

- There is little consideration of the actual requirements of the positions, or of the prospective changes that will occur in the jobs when the incumbents are succeeded.
- Identification of backups or replacement candidates is largely subjective, based on personal knowledge of the nominating managers.
- There are rarely objective indicators of performance, individual capabilities, or past achievements. Even basic biographical data are often not considered.

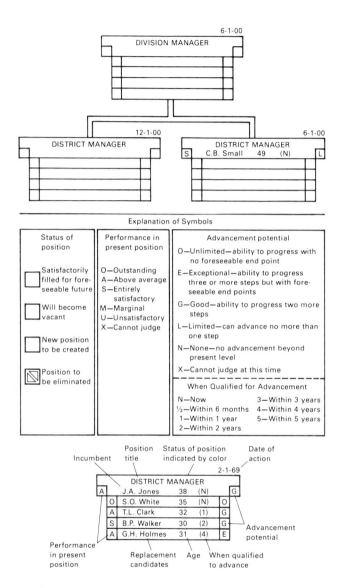

Fig. 8.1 *Sample replacement chart (From* Human resource planning *by J.W. Walker, Copyright © 1980, McGraw-Hill. Used with permission of McGraw-Hill Book Company.)*

- A high potential candidate may be qualified for more than one management position, but may be "boxed in" by the vertical, line-oriented replacement planning or, alternatively, may be named as a backup for several positions, giving a false impression of management depth.
- The planning is fragmented and vertically oriented; rarely is there provision for lateral or diagonal moves across organizational units.
- There is rarely any input from the individuals themselves regarding their own self-assessments and career interests.
- Most significantly, the charts rarely result in the moves planned or in other development activities; the process is often a static, annual paperwork exercise (Walker, 1980, pp. 284–285).

Another problem is a halo effect or self-fulfilling prophecy. Even when these charts are kept secret, special attention given to designated successors may lead to more career movement without necessarily providing benefits to either the individual or the organization.

Generating promotion lists. A less specific but similar procedure for formulating replacement charts is compiling promotion lists. Frequently done during annual meetings held by department managers or human resource development committees, each individual's advancement potential is discussed and those "ready now" for promotion are ranked on a promotion list. Separate lists may be kept for each organizational level or for only the top levels. There may be a single list at each level for the entire organization, or separate lists for each department. The lists are usually secret; many personnel may not be aware that the lists exist. While promotion lists have many of the same disadvantages as replacement charts, they provide more flexibility in that specific individuals are not designated as possible replacements for each position. This makes it possible to draw from a pool of prescreened candidates when making a staffing decision.

Planning for long-term succession.   Replacement charts and promotion lists are generally short-term planning efforts. The decision to place a person on the promotion list or replacement chart must be reviewed periodically. Long-term succession planning requires a more intensive review of job requirements and how they might change. Chapters 5 and 6 explored the advantages of ongoing, targeted career planning and development. This process involves assessing advancement potential early in the individual's career, formulating career plans in recognition of available opportunities, having a sequence of critical job assignments and training experiences geared to achieving the career target, and routinely re-evaluating and redirecting the career plans as necessary. In the process, the organization gathers information about individuals from a variety of sources, compiling a sound information base for making staffing decisions.

Job Matching Systems

Aligning individual abilities and interests with job requirements is the ultimate goal of most staffing decisions. A variety of techniques have been proposed (Stevens, 1979; Wellbank et al., 1978; Morrison & Holzbach, 1979). The basic design underlying these techniques is that an inventory of human resource talent is compared, person by person, with the job requirements. Individuals in the talent pool are generally those with high potential or those who have been rated ready for promotion or transfer. Searching the talent pool helps guarantee open job bidding by ensuring that all potentially qualified candidates are considered (Cascio, 1978). Large organizations utilize computerized information systems to accomplish the matching process, but a computer is not always necessary.

   An essential component in a job matching system is a job function code which applies not only to a broad cross section of positions but also to individual qualifications. That is, an individual's skills and abilities must be described along the same dimensions used to describe jobs. Therefore, the dimensions must be applicable to a variety of job functions. The following are examples of job matching systems used in two corporations.

A job-based career development and human resource management program.   Sears, Roebuck and Company formulated a system which integrates career planning and individual development with corporate human resource planning and development to satisfy organizational staffing needs (Wellbank et al., 1978). Sears' philosophy of management development is to rotate managers from job to job as they advance from the lower ranks. The company believes that a rational sequence of job assignments will reduce the time required to develop the necessary skills for a given target job, such as store manager. Implementing this belief demanded a systematic procedure for analyzing job requirements.

Sears uses a job evaluation system which measures three basic job competencies: know-how, problem solving, and accountability. Each of these job competencies has several sub-dimensions. Each job receives a total score and subscores. Consequently, it is possible to calculate changes in scores resulting from a proposed job transfer or promotion. This allows specifying the extent to which a new manager will need training in a new skill area.

The job evaluation system was used to construct possible career paths (see Chapter 5 for a discussion of career paths). Sears found, however, that the career paths did not always coincide with the paths actually followed by managers in the past. A revised set of career paths took practical constraints and additional company needs into account. These paths are viewed as a logical way to increase present managerial skills and develop new skills. Fast tracks (i.e., those paths that entailed the fewest moves to a target position) were then identified. These are particularly beneficial for grooming high potential managers and for developing females and minorities under the company's affirmative action programs. Rational lateral moves and even downward moves were also identified for those needing additional development and those wishing to develop expertise in a new functional area. Clusters of similar jobs and paths between clusters were identified to simplify the number of possible paths in the organization. Training necessary to prepare for specific jobs was specified from the job evaluation system.

This job-based career management system enables managers with vacancies in their units to search the organization's personnel files for individuals who are ready for a move into their vacancy. While this information would be supplemented by information on the employee's performance and career preferences, the matching procedure helps the organization make more accurate decisions by considering the future of the individual and the organization.

Job matching in the U.S. Navy.   The Navy has devised a matching procedure for laterally transferring management personnel (officers) in their early careers (Morrison & Holzbach, 1979). The procedure is crucial to the Navy's policy of changing officer assignments every three years. Officers who are due to rotate are represented by a "detailer." The detailer works with placement managers who are responsible for filling vacancies. The detailer meets with officers to discuss career goals and informs the officers about career opportunities. The placement manager and the detailer work together to negotiate an optimal match between the officer's preference, background, needs, abilities, and job requirements. Career counseling and provision of developmental opportunities are the responsibilities of the officer's current superior.

Job Posting

Job posting is a procedure which publicly posts position vacancies to encourage employees to apply for openings and prepare themselves for future openings (Connelly, 1975; Gruenfeld, 1975). Advising employees of promotional opportunities allows them to take the initiative in securing new positions for themselves. Obtaining a proper match between positions and employees depends on managers searching for candidates and on employees seeking new positions. A survey of life insurance companies indicated that job posting is used for senior managerial, technical, and clerical positions (Connelly, 1975).

Job posting should be accompanied by policies to ensure fair treatment of employees and to avoid possible dysfunctions. For example, several insurance companies reported that some employees did not apply for an opening in another department because they feared that their supervisor would be vindictive. This problem may be reduced by a policy that it not be mandatory for employees to notify their supervisor before applying for a position. Providing job counseling services in the personnel department may also encourage applications.

The insurance company survey demonstrated that job posting can increase the retention rate (60% for in-house hires versus 45% for those hired from outside). A job-posting system and self-nominations permit employees to seek broader experiences to develop their skills. Being turned down for a position can have positive aspects, if it leads to the recognition of needed skill development. In fact, some companies require that feedback be given to individuals rejected for a position. Overall, job posting can increase one's understanding of company procedures and facilitate communication up and down the organizational hierarchy.

In summary, formal staffing support systems aid organizational career management in several ways. Promotion and transfer policies and standard operating procedures encourage equal treatment of employees and help managers find and select the most qualified people. Human resource planning uses forecasts to determine steps for meeting future force requirements. Succession planning includes formulating replacement charts, promotion lists, and plans for long-term success. Job matching and job-posting systems help match people to jobs on the basis of abilities and interests.

INFORMAL SUPPORT SYSTEMS

Informal support systems for managing one's career are the social, professional, and patron relationships that provide information, guidance, emotional support, and sponsorship for individuals. The most common form of informal support comes from one's *peers* who often offer friendship, information, and act as sounding boards for one's career issues. *Role models* differ from peer supporters in that a role model may be any work associate—peer, superior, subordinate, or co-worker—whose behaviors, personal style, and attitudes are emulated (Shapiro, Haseltine, & Rowe, 1978). Role models can be helpful in guiding one's career development by exemplifying effective work behavior and attitudes; alternatively, inappropriate behaviors and attitudes can also be modeled or identified and avoided.

Peers and role models often influence individual career management, but they have little effect on how the organization manages one's career. In contrast, *sponsors* and *mentors* provide informal support through sharing career management information and influencing others in the organizational hierarchy. Sponsors and mentors can be instrumental in facilitating career advancement (Roche, 1979).

Peers and Role Models Assist in Career Management

The use of peers and role models in individual career management is not new. Employees have often learned from, and supported, each other as part of their formal development (e.g., unions, apprenticeships) and informal development (employment related groups, teams, or clubs).

Bandura (1971a) demonstrated that role modeling is a central element in social learning. Through a process of vicarious reinforcements, information relating to the probable consequences of a given pattern of behavior is conveyed to the observer (Bandura, 1971b). The role modeling that often results has been shown to be a factor in the development of effective work behavior patterns (Baron, Byrne, & Griffith, 1974; Weiss, 1977). Since the choice of role models is often based on the model's success and competence, role modeling can serve as a guide for individual development. To the extent that the organization fosters and encourages role modeling through supporting "buddy" or "peer pal" relationships, it would be facilitating career development. The research on role theory supports such developmental processes for role clarification and reducing role conflicts (Stumpf, Freedman, & Rabinowitz, 1981; Toffler, 1981; Van Sell, Brief, & Schuler, 1981).

The concept of work-role models has recently been expanded to include models of life-style and professional identity as well as on-the-job behaviors and characteristics (Shapiro, Haseltine, & Rowe, 1978). This has led some individuals to search for a total role model, one they view as an ideal example of how to be successful (Roeske & Lake, 1977). Such a search is seldom fruitful and can lead to unrealistic expectations regarding success in one's field. Bucher and Stelling (1977) suggest that *selective* role modeling, which involves focusing on specific behaviors and attitudes of many role models, is more productive. Selective role modeling permits one to learn from both "positive" and "negative" models; hence, one learns what to do as well as what *not* to do. Although role modeling is not likely to lead directly to attaining leadership roles, power, or authority, it does facilitate skill building, identity development, and individual career management.

Characteristics of Sponsor and Mentor Relationships

Sponsors are typically more involved in their protégé's career management than role models. They are advocates who praise their subordinates and help them obtain their desired positions.

The mentor–protégé relationship is even more intense. Mentors are often more powerful than sponsors in shaping their protégés' careers (Shapiro, Haseltine, & Rowe, 1978). Mentoring occurs when a talented junior person forms an attachment to a sensitive and intuitive senior person who understands and has the ability to communicate with the individual.

An example of mentoring is provided by the Jewel Companies, a Chicago-based chain of food stores and related businesses (*Harvard Business Review*, 1978). In a recent interview, the president and two former chief executive officers of Jewel described how they affected each other's lives and how the company's philosophy of management development maintained continuity over time. Jewel's philosophy is that all executives are responsible for assisting people down the line to be successful. The boss in a department is viewed as a "first assistant" to those who report to him or her. This was a revolutionary idea in the 1930s and '40s when subordinates were expected to follow their supervisor's directions without question. The key to implementing the philosophy is in locating bright individuals and giving them challenging opportunities while working with them so they may gain the skills necessary to do their jobs.

George Clements, former chairman of the Jewel Companies, described his early working relationship with Donald Perkins, the current chairman, as follows:

> *He was very mature. . . . he had a background of hard work, and he could work with people. If he had a question about somebody, he'd keep it to himself. He wouldn't wind that person down: he'd just forget it and work around it. When I realized that he had it—and that was early in his career—he was in his 20s—I never said anything, never told him, never told anybody. But I felt it was my job to give him experience around the organization, to do it carefully and try to teach him patience and take some of the Harvard influence out of him* (Harvard Business Review, *1978, pp. 93–94).*

Perkins was not Clements' only protégé. Perkins worked closely with several managers, following their progress and offering meaningful job assignments. The personal relationship with Perkins did not emerge until Perkins was appointed Executive Vice President.

Today, Jewel's management development philosophy is operationalized in a fairly systematic support system. Each management trainee is assigned to one of 170 operating company officers as a sponsor. The "apron strings" are cut when the individual is assigned to another supervisor, but the friendship ties that emerge during the sponsorship period often continue.

Describing the mentor–protégé relationship. The dynamics of mentor–protégé relationships have been examined by Kram (1980) in an intensive study of young managers and their mentors. Kram interviewed fifteen managers (eight men and seven women ranging in age between twenty-six and thirty-four) first to identify one or two senior managers whom they viewed as significantly influencing their development, and subsequently to learn about how their careers evolved. Interviews were also conducted with the senior managers.

Kram found that developmental relationships between junior and senior managers provide *career functions* and *psychosocial functions* that enhance the development of both managers. Career functions are those elements of the relationship that enhance career advancement. Examples are coaching, exposure to managers at higher levels, protection in the face of criticism from above, and challenging work assignments. Psychosocial functions are those elements of the relationship that enhance the feeling of self-competence and effectiveness as a manager. Examples are role modeling, counseling, and friendship.

The development of a working mentor–protégé relationship does not just happen. Roles and expectations need to be defined and clarified (Toffler, 1981). However, both the mentor and the protégé can benefit from the relationship (Klauss, 1981; Kram, 1980). While the younger person benefits by establishing a professional identity and launching a career, the senior individual benefits from the recognition and internal satisfaction of contributing to the development of a promising young manager.

A developmental relationship often changes over time as the parties develop in their careers (Kram, 1980). Organizational factors can influence the relationship by bringing people together or separating them. The mentor's advancement opportunities may decrease, thereby affecting his or her power and changing the psychosocial nature of the relationship. Affirmative action programs may encourage black-white and male-female mentor-protégé relationships, but such relationships may create social pressures that affect their continuity (Alderfer et al., 1980).

Mentor–protégé relationships also have been studied in a survey of 1250 executives across many companies (Roche, 1979). A mentor was defined for the respondents as a person who had a personal interest in their career and was prone to guide it. Nearly two-thirds of the executives indicated having had a mentor or sponsor and one-third of them had two or more mentors. Those who had a mentor earned more money at a younger age, were better educated, were more likely to follow a career plan, and sponsored more protégés themselves than executives who did not have a mentor. All the female respondents (less than 1% of the sample) reported having a mentor and averaged more mentors than men (three for women, two for men). Seven in ten of the youngest executives (those under forty) had protégés. This proportion dropped for those between ages forty and fifty-five, and rose again for executives who were fifty-five or older. This may indicate the desire of those nearing retirement to pass along knowledge. The study also suggests that mentoring may generate a chain effect in that those with two mentors had an average of three protégés. Thus, many executives in an organization may eventually benefit from the mentoring process.

In summary, sponsor and mentor relationships with junior individuals have several beneficial effects. The protégé and the organization take more active roles in career management. There is likely to be more career planning, as well as more protégé advancement possibilities and satisfaction with career progress. Developmental activities are likely to be more frequent and targeted to specific career objectives.

EXAMPLES OF STAFFING SUPPORT SYSTEMS

The number and diversity of both formal and informal staffing support systems suggest that any one organization or division is not likely to have enacted all such systems. The two cases provided below exemplify how two different organizations have designed a set of interrelated staffing support systems to meet their staffing needs. Neither case is necessarily "right" for other organizations; however, both systems suggest how staffing support systems can be used effectively.

A Centralized Staffing Decision System

Jack Morley is responsible for coordinating management movement in a national company at the third and fourth levels of management. He reports to a fourth-level manager in the personnel department, but he works closely with the personnel vice president and personnel assistant vice president.

Jack's job consists of three functions: monitoring position vacancies, tracking managers who can be promoted and released, and recommending candidates to fill position vacancies.

One element of Jack's job is to generate and update a list of promotable managers three times a year. A formal appraisal process is conducted in May. This entails asking all vice presidents throughout the company to identify individuals who are promotable to third and fourth levels within the next six months. No more than 10% of the people at each level can be designated promotable. The process is repeated informally four and eight months later. The appraisals are usually made by supervisors and discussed at departmental meetings with the higher level supervisor.

According to company policy, only individuals who have been identified as having high potential have a chance to be promoted to third level and above. The company's philosophy is to develop generalists; those who reach third level usually have had experience in at least three different departments.

Once every six months Jack forecasts upcoming job vacancies based on information provided by the company vice presidents and their department heads. This forecast is then circulated to the vice presidents who are asked to submit candidates for these openings.

When an opening occurs, candidates for promotion and transfer are identified from a number of different sources including the hiring supervisor, the promotion list, and the planning vehicle mentioned above. Another source is the Selected Management Roster. This is a list of third- and fourth-level managers who have high potential two levels above their present level. In addition, the personnel data base can be used to identify managers on the basis of a number of different characteristics (e.g., all those with marketing experience slated to go to another department). The data base includes the boss's rating of the individual's potential for advancement and the individual's expressed career interests.

Jack attends many staffing meetings held by the different departments, and these meetings provide an additional source of candidates. Career plans for lower level managers are discussed during these meetings. Many times these plans go beyond the information available in the personnel data base, and so the meetings serve as an informal source of candidates. Staffing problems that arise also indicate possible candidates. Such problems include medical hardships, geographic hardships (e.g., an employee prefers to transfer to a particular location for an important personal reason), EEO, and termination of rotational assignments.

Once Jack identifies viable candidates for a position and narrows the choice down to the most promising candidates, he presents this information to the supervisor with the vacancy (the hiring supervisor). Occasionally the hiring supervisor has little choice since EEO or the need to transfer someone who is leaving a rotational job may predetermine the decision. When the immediate supervisor has made a choice, Jack coordinates the release date with the new and old bosses. Also, he obtains approval from the personnel assistant vice president and the personnel vice president.

Jack is concerned about maintaining his integrity. Therefore, he tries to recommend candidates he knows will be acceptable to the hiring supervisor. He estimates that about 80% of the time the hiring supervisor selects one of the people he recommends as the top three candidates. There have been instances, however, when Jack's recommendations have been rejected or when the hiring supervisor's selection has been rejected by the personnel vice president. In some cases, the personnel vice president has tentatively approved candidates before they are recommended to the hiring supervisors.

One of the prime selection standards is that the successful candidate must have what Jack terms "saleability." This means that the individual must have general skills to do other jobs, thereby ensuring that he or she will not be placed in a dead-end position. To guarantee this, a vice president from a department other than the one with the new job assignment must support the person by agreeing to take him or her at a later date. Therefore, the candidate must have a favorable reputation with more than one vice president. This does not mean, however, that the candidate will necessarily go to the "backer's" department sometime in the future.

Promotions are subjected to more stringent scrutiny than lateral transfers. The question in the case of a possible lateral transfer is not how many other jobs the person can do, but rather, whether this is a good developmental move for the person. If all other things are equal, a lateral transfer entails less risk than a promotion since the candidate already has performed well at that level.

As an example, Jack described the following promotion decision. A vacancy arose on November 4th, when a third-level manager requested a maternity leave. Her plan was to return to the company at a later date, recognizing that she would probably be assigned to another position at that time. A final decision for a replacement was made ten days after her maternity leave request was filed, and the candidate selected took over on January 1st.

Jack identified seven candidates after informally talking with staff contacts. The promotability list was also a source, and, in fact, the final candidate was identified from this list. The candidates came from five different departments. Information about the candidates was obtained from (1) the area's administrative staff manager responsible for personnel matters, (2) the immediate supervisor of the vacancy, (3) that supervisor's boss, (4) the corporate personnel assistant vice president, and (5) the corporate personnel vice president. The candidate Jack recommended and the person ultimately selected was a second-level female who had eight years service with the company. It was necessary for her to relocate to take the position. The fourth-level manager who would be her boss had been her boss once before.

A Selection Committee Decision System

Dave Martin has been in his current position five years and has eighteen years service with the company. He was appointed to the fourth-level personnel planning committee fifteen months ago by his supervisor, the data systems vice president. The committee meets every other Friday, depending upon need.

Dave indicated that during the last year the committee made at least twelve promotion decisions and transferred at least as many managers in the process. Many of the moves involved chains of personnel changes. Career planning is a major responsibility of the committee, and they often transfer someone to enhance the individual's career development. Once every two years they evaluate the potential of all third-level managers in the company and make judgments about job moves that will enhance these managers' career development. The committee also obtains information from managers about their career interests. When a vacancy arises due to the termination of an assignment, a transfer within third level, or a promotion of a third-level manager to fourth level (a decision made by a higher committee), it is likely that Dave's committee will already have identified a suitable replacement for the position. The committee occasionally initiates personnel moves for developmental purposes. In general, the committee prefers to laterally transfer a third-level manager with fourth-level potential than to promote a second-level manager to third level when the manager is not necessarily fourth-level material.

Dave stated that his peers on the committee often influence his opinions, and he theirs. He routinely solicits opinions from the fourth-level managers he represents. Dave did not perceive a difference among committee members with respect to the influence they have over each other. Meetings are "open discussions" in the sense that there is much give and take. Dave described personnel decisions as an "interactive process," meaning that committee members negotiate with and attempt to convince each other as well as provide a check on each other's logic.

A major advantage of the committee process Dave cited is that it fosters interdepartmental personnel changes. Bringing in "new blood" develops fresh perspectives and demonstrates to employees that they do not have to wait until there is an opening in their department to be promoted.

The amount of time Dave devotes to committee work varies. Meetings last between four and six hours. Dave spends as much as six hours in preparation for about 25% of these meetings. This preparation involves meeting with people in the departments he represents.

Dave discussed a promotion decision involving the position of data systems staff manager. The vacancy arose on January 13th when the person occupying the position was promoted by Dave's committee to a high band third-level job in the data systems department. The specifications for the newly created vacant position detailed on the vacancy announcement indicated that data processing skills were of prime importance. In addition, the job required knowledge of the overall data systems operation, the ability to manage several high pressure assignments simultaneously, and a high level of interpersonal skill to coordinate the needs of different departments with the services offered by the data systems department. These qualifications were listed on the vacancy announcement along with the job responsibilities. The announcement labeled the job as "permanent," meaning that rotation out of the position would not be automatic but would be subject to the job incumbent's abilities, performance, and career interests. Therefore, no particular length of time for occupying the position was specified.

Since the position vacancy was in Dave's department, he was to represent the supervisor with the vacancy at the committee meeting on January 17th. Between January 13th and January 17th, Dave discussed the vacancy during two departmental staff meetings. The first meeting was with other fourth-level managers in the department but did not include the data systems vice president. However, the vice president attended the second staff meeting. Two potential candidates within the department were considered seriously by the fourth-level managers. One candidate had come into the data systems department via the comptrollers' organization and had an accounting background. He had worked in data systems administration but was currently in the hardware acquisition unit of the data systems department. The second candidate had been hired into the company as an experienced computer programmer but had little additional company experience. Both candidates had the necessary technical knowledge and could handle the pressure of multiple assignments. Also, both had advancement potential and were rated "promotable now with additional development necessary."

No other candidate was considered by the committee for this position at the January 17th meeting. The individual with the accounting background was promoted. The committee had been urged by the personnel department to look for a female; however, there were no qualified females available. The committee was considering candidates for three other positions on the same day that this decision was made, and a qualified female was found for one of these positions, satisfying the affirmative action deficiency in the job classification. In fact, the committee members spent most of their time during that meeting developing a chain of moves including the transfer of one female and backfilling the position with a promotion of another female.

Comments on the Examples

Both of the above cases are examples of centrally controlled staffing systems. In the first case, the personnel vice president and his staff maintain firm control over promotions. In the second case, promotions and transfers are a group decision. Both systems regularly gather information on employees' advancement potential and promotability. Jack Morley, who coordinates the staffing system in the first case, forecasts vacancies every six months and can begin searching for candidates before vacancies arise. Several standard operating procedures are at his disposal. The company has even operationalized the candidate's "saleability" by requiring that a vice president from another department agree to take the candidate at a later date. The committee system in the second case is less formal. The committee seems more concerned with each employee's career plans, and often makes transfers and promotions on the basis of the developmental needs of the employees as well as the more immediate needs of the business.

It should be noted that the committee system is in a smaller company (about 4000 management employees) that is located in a single state while the centrally controlled system under the personnel vice president is larger (about 17,000 management employees) and is a nationwide company. Consequently, the committee members are more familiar with the people they make decisions about than are Jack Morley and the personnel vice president. Also, relocating people costs less for the company and is easier for the employee in the smaller company. The type of staffing system that will work best in an organization depends on many factors including the organization's climate, size, economic conditions, etc. Research is needed to evaluate the effectiveness of different staffing systems under different conditions. In the final section, we suggest some general guidelines for staffing support systems based on the information presented in this chapter.

DEVELOPING STAFFING SUPPORT SYSTEMS: SUMMARY AND GUIDELINES

As the previous section suggests, there is no one "correct" staffing model. Systems vary in degree of centralization, formality, and the number of people involved. Even with such variation, it is possible to develop support systems to facilitate individual career planning and development as well as design human resource systems for effective organizational career management. Clear policies and procedures, human resource planning, and succession planning reduce the uncertainty individuals experience with respect to organizational career management, and thereby facilitate individual career management. Further, such staffing support systems should improve the organization's ability to meet future human resource needs.

Other staffing support systems such as job matching, job posting, and fostering mentor—protégé relationships encourage individuals to actively manage their careers within the organization. This should facilitate effective career progression from both the individual's and organization's perspective and reduce turnover of valued employees. Several guidelines for staffing support systems are suggested below:

1. *Improve managers' understanding of factors influencing staffing decisions.* Knowing what policies affect these decisions, who makes them, the standards for approval, and what factors limit the decision maker's discretion can help individuals behave in ways that lead to career progression. Moreover, such knowledge can provide managers with ideas about what they should do to make better staffing decisions. Vehicles to enhance understanding include published statements of company policies, career progression guidelines, and lists of standards for evaluating and promoting individuals.

2. *Involve managers at all organizational levels in the development of standard procedures.* This should result in a product that is realistic and acceptable to those who must use it. Training programs and follow-ups will be necessary to guarantee that the procedures are applied as intended.

3. *Establish uniform policies and procedures for making staffing decisions.* Such policies and procedures should deal with obtaining and comparing promotability ratings, establishing departmental and company-wide promotion lists, devising career paths, and delineating steps for releasing an employee from a current position. Some procedures, such as those dealing with company-wide EEO—AA targets, will be essential.

4. *Use standardized personnel forms and standardized methods of collecting promotion and transfer related information about candidates.* Meaningful comparisons will be possible, and the search and information handling components of the staffing decision process will be less demanding when similar types of clearly understandable information are available on all candidates. Moreover, uniformity will facilitate equal treatment of all candidates and provide documents for supporting the decisions made.

5. *Form a committee to make staffing decisions when the decision requires (a) information from different sources and/or (b) the acceptance or approval of a number of people.* Search committees are valuable when people are likely to disagree and candidates are not readily available. Committee members should be chosen on the basis of the amount of unique information and judgmental insight each member can contribute. Strategies which help the committee structure the task and improve relationships may be necessary for the group to work effectively.

Epilogue

At this point, an encapsulation of the book is in order. We also take this opportunity to highlight two sets of guidelines presented earlier.

The introductory section began by distinguishing between individual career management and organizational career management (Chapter 1). The cases of Len White and Metrobank (Chapter 2) provided a basis for understanding individual and organizational career issues.

The second section focused on individual career management through self-assessment (Chapter 3) and individual career issues with attention given to problems faced by minorities, women, and dual-career couples (Chapter 4).

Organizational career management programs were examined in the third section. These included programs for career planning (Chapter 5) and training and development (Chapter 6). Planning and development were depicted as a continuous cycle throughout a person's career. Numerous examples of actual programs were offered.

The final section examined organizational career management from the standpoint of staffing management positions from within the organization (Chapter 7) and support systems which facilitate the staffing process (Chapter 8).

Guidelines for individuals to follow in managing their careers include the following (see Chapter 3):

1. Develop a clear and accurate understanding of your skills, interests, and goals.

2. Seek accurate and timely information through both formal and informal systems as a basis for career planning and decision making.

3. Share preferences and goals with relevant supervisors and seek feedback on effectiveness and the feasibility of attaining career goals.

4. Remain flexible to unforeseen opportunities.

5. Reassess career plans and goals as a function of the developmental experiences undertaken and feedback on performance and potential.

6. Integrate individual and organizational goals whenever possible.

Guidelines for organizations to follow include the following (see Chapter 5):

1. Establish career paths to provide direction and guidance for career planning.

2. Provide regular and specific feedback to employees on their performance and potential, and communicate career management activities, programs, paths, and support systems clearly and routinely.

3. Design information systems which provide objective, accurate, and realistic information for use in staffing decisions.

4. Delineate individual and organizational responsibilities in the career management process.

5. Maintain continuity and flexibility in human resource programs.

6. Integrate the human resource functions and programs offered as part of a total career management program.

The above guidelines for individuals and organizations are goals. They reflect our biases, hopes, and aspirations. Although such goals are more easily stated than accomplished, their identification is a first step. The next step is yours!

Appendix A: A Profile of a Career Course

A recent survey by Hall (1982) indicates that there are several trends in the objectives and content of career-related courses. Courses are being offered at both the undergraduate and graduate level, and as company programs. Course objectives focus on developing skills in career management and problem-solving career issues through methods of self-evaluation, goal setting, and career planning and development (Hall, 1982).

Most courses and company programs do not have a single text; they typically require the participants to read two or three books from among the following: Bolles (1980), Burack and Mathys (1979a, b), Hall (1976), Hall and Hall (1979), Jelinek (1979), Kanter (1977), Kotter, Faux, and McArthur (1978), Morgan (1980), Schein (1978), Storey (1976a), Walker (1980), Wanous (1980). London and Stumpf (1982) can now be added to this list of available books.

Below is a list of topics often covered in one or more class sessions of a typical career course (Hall, 1982). A brief description of the topic follows each heading. The chapter of *Managing Careers* that corresponds to each topic is then noted along with the books listed above which provide content coverage. We list these books in order of their degree of content coverage.

Other topics covered in many career courses include organizational power, stress management, time management, résumé preparation and interviewing (Hall, 1982).

Topic	Description	*Managing Careers* Chapters	Other Content Sources
Overview of Individual and Organizational Career Issues	Presents key concepts with equal attention to both individual and organizational issues and perspectives.	1, 2	Wanous (1980) Jelinek (1979) Morgan (1980)
Self-Assessment, Objective Setting, and Individual Career Planning	Provides concepts and techniques for self-assessment. Use of experiential exercises for self-assessment and goal setting.	3 Appendix B	Kotter et al. (1978) Storey (1976a) Bolles (1980)
Individual/Organizational Fit; Career and Life-Style Choices	Provides concepts and techniques for analysis of organizations and positions. Examines career possibilities from several perspectives including advancement potential, life-style, and family.	2, 3	Kotter et al. (1978) Storey (1976a) Bolles (1980)
The Joining-Up Process and Socialization	Discusses organizational entry, job expectations, preferred job attributes, career issues for young managers, and early job experiences. Some attention to organizational socialization practices.	3	Wanous (1980) Schein (1978) Morgan (1980) Jelinek (1979) Hall (1976)

Career and Life Stages	Presents the career/life issues and concerns during early, mid, and late career stages. Focus is more on the individual than the organizational context.	4	Hall (1976) Schein (1978) Morgan (1980) Jelinek (1979)
Career Issues for Subgroups such as Minorities, Women, and Dual-Career Couples	Discusses discrimination and unfair treatment of minorities and women. Outlines special career development activities for subgroups to compensate for their unique issues.	4	Hall and Hall (1979) Morgan (1980) Jelinek (1979) Hall (1976)
Human Resource Planning and Career Planning Practices	Presents the concepts of human resource planning from the organization's perspective. Discusses individual and organizational responsibilities for career planning programs. Includes methods and techniques for program evaluation.	5, 8	Burack and Mathys (1979a, b) Walker (1980)
Training and Development Programs	Provides information on organizational training and development activities. Considers different de-	6	

*A recent book in this area is Wexley and Latham (1981).

Topic	Description	Managing Careers Chapters	Other Content Sources
	velopmental activities for individuals in different career stages and as a function of organizational needs.		
Organizational Promotion and Transfer Decisions	Discusses how organizations make decisions about their employees.	7	Kanter (1977) Storey (1976a)
Staffing Support Systems	Discusses the human resource systems used to facilitate career management. Covers such topics as succession planning, promotion lists, job posting, role models, sponsors, and mentors.	8	Kanter (1977) Storey (1976a) Walker (1980)

We recommend that *Managing Careers* be used with one or two other books depending on the focus of the course. If the focus is self-assessment and career planning, the Kotter et al., Bolles, or Storey workbooks would be appropriate. A course designed to provide a general overview of career issues might use *Managing Careers* in conjunction with Morgan's or Jelinek's book of readings. Hall's or Schein's book could be used with *Managing Careers* to provide additional detail on individual issues and career stages. If the course emphasis is human resource planning, our book could supplement the texts by Walker or Burack and Mathys (1979b). If the focus is on organizational career planning processes, our book could be used with Burack and Mathys (1979a).

DISCUSSION QUESTIONS

Class discussion and program assignments vary as a function of the emphasis taken in the course. Possible discussion questions (along with relevant chapter numbers from *Managing Careers*) include the following:

Chapters 1 and 2

1. What are the most important *individual* factors that have affected your career and are likely to affect your career in the future?

2. What *organizational* factors have affected your career?

3. How can individuals and organizations work together to manage careers to the benefit of both?

Chapter 3

4. In doing a self-assessment, why is it necessary to generate extensive information on oneself and to use several sources of information?

5. What questions should one ask when investigating a job opportunity?

6. How can organizational recruitment and selection practices be designed to help individuals make more effective career decisions?

7. From the organization's standpoint, analyze the pros and cons of developing specialists versus generalists who have had experience in many facets of the organization's operation.

Chapter 4

8. How have your career development issues changed over the last ten years?

9. What issues do (did) you see as critical to your career during the exploration and trial career stage? the establishment and advancement stage?

10. Minorities and females often perceive organizational barriers to their career progression. What effect will perceived barriers have on their motivation to manage their careers?

11. Treating different employees differently is common in most work organizations. How can one determine when such differential treatment is fair or discriminatory?

12. To what extent and in what ways should organizations become involved in addressing dual-career issues and nonwork activities?

Chapter 5

13. Consider your career plan for the next two years. Which responsibilities are yours? Which responsibilities should be assumed by your employer? Which responsibilities are shared?

14. Should organizations develop accelerated advancement programs? Discuss why or why not in terms of individual and organizational outcomes?

15. Why are few career planning programs evaluated? What could be done to encourage program evaluation?

16. What are the most common goals of career planning programs for the individuals involved? for the organization? What outcome measures are most relevant to these goals?

Chapter 6

17. Outline a sequence of job assignments and training courses that meet the guidelines for targeted development.

18. Discuss how one would analyze training needs for a department in your organization or one familiar to you.

Chapter 7

19. How should promotion and transfer decisions take into account individual career plans and development needs?

20. Discuss the guidelines managers should follow in filling job vacancies.

21. Use the components of the decision-making process (strategy formulation, search for alternatives, evaluation-choice, and planning for implementation) to describe how you found a job in the past. Would you do it differently in the future?

Chapter 8

22. Would you prefer to work for an organization with formal or informal promotion and transfer policies? Would you prefer an organization with centralized or decentralized staffing decisions? How about staffing decisions made by individuals or committees? Discuss the pros and cons of each alternative.

23. Discuss the career of a person who is successful in an occupation. How did that person learn the job? Who served as role models, sponsors, or mentors? Is the person a sponsor or mentor to others?

PROGRAM ASSIGNMENTS

Typical assignments include two or three of the following:

1. A self-assessment paper.
2. A personal career development plan.
3. A position analysis of one's target or entry level job.
4. A career analysis of someone in one's preferred field.

5. A literature review of a selected topic in career development.

6. The design and suggestions for implementation of a career planning/development program for one's employer.

7. The design of an empirical study to assess benefits of a career management program.

8. A critical analysis of specific career development practices in one's company.

Appendix B: Individual Career Management Exercises

As suggested throughout Chapter 3, self-assessment, setting objectives, developing plans, and taking career actions is a demanding process. It is never entirely complete since people and their situations frequently change.

Several exercises are suggested below to assist one in establishing the groundwork for career management. They are intended to be used in conjunction with guidelines and tables in Chapter 3. The exercises have been extensively used by the authors as well as others; for example, Bolles (1980), Kotter, Faux, and McArthur (1978), and Storey (1976a). Readers interested in a step-by-step workbook should see one of these sources.

Exercise 1: Assess Yourself

1. *Describe your life and career to date.* Be explicit. Start by describing yourself, your family, educational experience, jobs you have had, and career interests and concerns that have been salient at different times. Expand the above discussion until it is at least ten pages long.

2. *List your career decisions.* What have you done to manage your career to date? What work-role related decisions have you made? List them. If there are less than ten, expand the list since you probably left many out. After each decision, list the five most important issues or factors that led you to choose the direction you did over other available options. Now summarize how you feel about these decisions and their outcomes.

3. *Examine your values.* Based on the factors you listed above as influencing your career decisions, identify the underlying values you hold. For example, do your decisions favor economic gain, an aesthetic environment, social relationships, etc.?

4. *Examine your work tasks and interests.* Start by summarizing your last five major job/task assignments. What did you do in each assignment? Describe a typical day. What did you enjoy most? List the activities you enjoyed as well as those you avoided. Use the format suggested below.

Job or Task	A Typical Day Involved:	I Enjoy Most or Least:
1. _____	_____	_____
2. _____	_____	_____
3. _____	_____	_____
4. _____	_____	_____
5. _____	_____	_____

5. *Utilize additional resources.* Several standardized instruments are available for examining values and interests. While some are easy to self-administer, most benefit from the guidance of a counselor and an instructor's manual. The Allport-Vernon-Lindsey *Study of Values,* referred to in Chapter 3, is available through Houghton Mifflin, Hopewell, N.J. 08525 (800–225–1464). *The Strong-Campbell Interest Inventory* is available through NCS Interpretive Scoring Systems, Inc., P.O. Box 1416, Minneapolis, Minnesota 55440 (612–933–3649; 800–328–6759).

One's spouse, close friends, peers, supervisors, and subordinates also can be excellent sources of personal assessment information. Discussing oneself and one's career-related decisions, values, and interests with relevant others provides the opportunity to clarify aspects of self-assessment by obtaining multiple perspectives.

6. *Develop identity statements by analyzing the self-assessment information.* The information generated in steps 1–5 above must be synthesized into a useable set of identity statements. Examine the information and categorize it into about twenty areas. Follow the guidelines suggested in Chapter 3.

Exercise 2: Establish Objectives

1. *Specify personal objectives.* List five career-related things you want to attain in the next three years. List five more you want to attain before you retire. Consider your personal needs, career goals, and life objectives when constructing the above lists.

2. *Identify barriers to goal attainment.* Once you have specified your needs, goals, and objectives, identify possible barriers and obstacles to attaining these goals. Work with relevant others to clarify barriers.

3. *Translate goals into action steps.* Establishing goals and identifying barriers must be followed up with concrete action steps to attain these goals. Work with relevant others (e.g., peers, supervisors) to specify: (1) the work-roles and tasks you are seeking, (2) the social and political aspects of the positions you seek, (3) the demands the focal positions will place on your skills, personal time, and family, and (4) the sequence of possible assignments and developmental experiences that will prepare you to perform effectively and to achieve self-fulfillment.

Exercise 3: Assess Job Possibilities

Perform an analysis of a job you think fits the implications of your self-assessment. This should involve a systematic study of an actual position in order to discover and define the major task dimensions of the job and what the job calls for in terms of behavior and qualifications.

Your job assessment should include a specification of:

1. position title and its location on the organizational chart,
2. its primary functions,
3. the performance appraisal dimensions used,
4. a discussion of lateral and hierarchical relationships, and
5. the qualifications necessary for one to perform this position effectively.

To obtain the above information, generate a set of interview questions and then interview at least two people in the position you are analyzing. Supporting organizational documents should be helpful (e.g., their position description, organizational chart, etc.).

Repeat the above process for each job you plan to consider.

References

Abdelnour, B.T., & Hall, D.T. Career development of established employees. *Career Development Bulletin,* 1980, *2* (1), 5–8.

Acker, J., & Van Houten, D.R. Differential recruitment and control: The sex structuring of organizations. *Administrative Science Quarterly,* 1979, *24,* 152–163.

Ackerman, L. Career development: Preparing round pegs for square holes. *Training and Development Journal,* 1976, *30* (2), 12–14.

Adams, J.S. Toward an understanding of inequity. *Journal of Abnormal and Social Psychology,* 1963, *67,* 422–436.

Alderfer, C.P., Alderfer, C.J., Tucker, L., & Tucker, R. Diagnosing race relations in management. *Journal of Applied Behavioral Science,* 1980, *16,* 135–166.

Anderson, J.C., Milkovich, G.T., & Tsui, A. Intra-organizational mobility: A model and review. *Academy of Management Review,* 1981, *6,* 529–538.

Armstrong, J.S. *Long-range forecasting: From crystal ball to computer.* New York: Wiley, 1978.

Arvey, R.D. *Fairness in selecting employees.* Reading, Mass.: Addison-Wesley, 1979.

Bailyn, L. The slow burn way to the top: Some thoughts on the early years of organization careers. In C.B. Derr (Ed.), *Work,*

family, and the career: New frontiers in theory and research.
New York: Praeger, 1980, 94–106.

Bandura, A. *Psychological modeling: Conflicting theories.*
Chicago: Lieber-Atherton, 1971a.

Bandura, A. *Social learning theory.* Morristown, N.J.: General
Learning Press, 1971b.

Baron, R.A., Byrne, D., & Griffith, W. *Social psychology: Understanding human interaction.* Boston: Allyn and Bacon, 1974.

Barr, D.F. More needs analysis. *Training and Development Journal,* 1980, *34,* 70–74.

Bartolome, F., & Evans, P.A.L. Professional lives versus private
lives—Shifting patterns of managerial commitment. *Organizational Dynamics,* 1979, *7* (4), 3–29.

Bartolome, F., & Evans, P.A.L. Must success cost so much? *Harvard Business Review,* 1980, *58* (2), 137–148.

Beach, L.R., & Mitchell, T.R. A contingency model for the selection of decision strategies. *Academy of Management Review,* 1978, *3,* 439–449.

Beehr, T.A., Taber, T.D., & Walsh, J.T. Perceived mobility channels: Criteria for intraorganizational mobility. *Organizational
Behavior and Human Performance,* 1980, *26,* 250–264.

Benson, P.G., & Thornton, G.C., III. A model career planning
program. *Personnel,* 1978, *55* (2), 30–39.

Beyer, J.M., Stevens, J.M., & Trice, H.M. Predicting how federal
managers perceive criteria used for their promotion. *Public
Administration Review,* 1980, January/February, 55–66.

Bigoness, W.J. Effect of applicant sex, race, and performance on
employer's performance ratings: Some additional findings.
Journal of Applied Psychology, 1976, *61,* 80–84.

Blankenship, L.W., & Miles, R.E. Organizational structure and
managerial decision behavior. *Administrative Science Quarterly,* 1968, *13,* 106–120.

Blau, P.M., Gustad, J.W., Jesson, R., Parnes, H.S., & Wilcox, R.C.
Occupational choices: A conceptual framework. *Industrial
and Labor Relations Review,* 1956, *9,* 531, 536–537, 543.

Blauner, R. *Racial oppression in America.* New York: Harper & Row, 1972.

Blessing, B. *Career planning for the 80's: Fact, fantasy, future.* Princeton, N.J.: Blessing/White, 1979.

Boehm, V.R., & Hoyle, D.F. Assessment and management development. In J.L. Moses & W.C. Byham (Eds.), *Applying the assessment center method.* Elmsford, N.Y.: Pergamon Press, 1977.

Bolles, R.N. *What color is your parachute?* Berkeley, Calif.: Ten Speed Press, 1980.

Bowen, D.D., & Hall, D.T. Career planning for employee development: A primer for managers. *California Management Review,* 1977, *20* (2), 23–35.

Bray, D.W. Management development without frills. *The Conference Board Record,* September 1975, 47–50.

Bray, D.W., Campbell, R.J., & Grant, D.L. *The management recruit: Formative years in business.* New York: Wiley, 1973.

Bray, D.W., Campbell, R.J., & Grant, D.L. *Formative years in business: A long-term AT&T study of managerial lives.* New York: Wiley, 1974.

Bray, D.W., & Grant, D.L. The assessment center in the measurement of potential for business management. *Psychological Monographs,* 1966, *80* (17, Whole No. 625), 25p.

Bray, D.W., & Howard, A. Career success and life satisfactions of middle-aged managers. In L.A. Bond & J.C. Rosen (Eds.), *Competence and coping during adulthood.* Hanover, N.H.: University Press of New England, 1980, 258–287.

Brett, J.M., & Werbel, J.D. *The effect of job transfer on employees and their families.* Washington, D.C.: Employee Relocation Council, 1980.

Brewer, J., Hanson, M., VanHorn, R., & Mosely, K. A new dimension in employee development: A system for career planning and guidance. *Personnel Journal,* 1975, *54,* 228–231.

Brief, A.P., & Aldag, R.J. The "self" in work organizations: A conceptual review. *The Academy of Management Review,* 1981, *6,* 75–88.

Brush, D.H., & Schoenfeldt, L.F. Identifying managerial potential: An alternative to assessment centers. *Personnel,* 1980, *57* (3), 68–76.

Bryson, J.B., & Bryson, R. (Eds.). *Dual-career couples.* New York: Human Sciences Press, 1978.

Bucher, R., & Stelling, J. *Becoming professional.* Beverly Hills, Calif.: Sage, 1977.

Burack, E.H., & Gutteridge, T.G. Institutional manpower planning: Rhetoric versus reality. *California Management Review,* 1978, *20* (3), 13–22.

Burack, E.H., & Mathys, N.J. *Career management in organizations: A practical human resource planning approach.* Lake Forest, Ill.: Brace-Park, 1979a.

Burack, E.H., & Mathys, N.J. *Human resource planning: A pragmatic approach to manpower staffing and development.* Lake Forest, Ill.: Brace-Park, 1979b.

Burack, E.H., & Smith, R.D. *Personnel management: A human resource systems approach.* St. Paul, Minn.: West, 1977.

Bureau of National Affairs. *Employee promotion and transfer policies* (Personnel Policies Forum Survey No. 120). Washington, D.C.: Bureau of National Affairs, 1978.

Bureau of National Affairs. *Recruiting policies and practices.* Washington, D.C.: Bureau of National Affairs, 1979.

Byham, W.C., Adams, D., & Kiggins, A. Transfer of modeling training to the job. *Personnel Psychology,* 1976, *29,* 345–349.

Campbell, D.P. *Manual for the SVIB-SCII.* Stanford, Calif.: Stanford University Press, 1977.

Campbell, D.T., & Stanley, J.C. *Experimental and quasi-experimental designs for research.* Chicago: Rand McNally, 1966.

Campbell, J.P., Dunnette, M.D., Lawler, E.E., III, & Weick, K.E., Jr. *Managerial behavior, performance, and effectiveness.* New York: McGraw-Hill, 1970.

Career success at Exxon Corporation. *The Career Development Bulletin,* 1980, *2* (1), 1–2.

Carroll, S.J., Jr., & Tosi, H.L., Jr. *Management by objectives: Applications and research.* New York: Macmillan, 1973.

Cascio, W. *Applied psychology in personnel management.* Reston, Va.: Reston, 1978.

Cascio, W.F., & Silbey, V. Utility of the assessment center as a selection device. *Journal of Applied Psychology,* 1979, *64,* 107–118.

Cashel, W.S., Jr. Human resources in the Bell System. *Human Resources Planning,* 1978, *1,* 59–65.

Clark, H.L., & Thurston, D.R. *Planning your staffing needs: A handbook for personnel workers.* Washington, D.C.: Bureau of Policies and Standards, U.S. Civil Service Commission, 1977.

Cobrun, D. Job–worker incongruence: Consequences for health. *Journal of Health and Social Behavior,* 1975, *16,* 198–212.

Colarelli, S.M., Stumpf, S.A., & Hartman, K. *Towards a theory of career exploration.* Unpublished manuscript, New York University, 1982.

Colarelli, S.M., Stumpf, S.A., & Wall, S.J. Analyzing managerial jobs: Quick and clean. *Eastern Academy of Management Proceedings,* 1981, 80–85.

Connelly, S. Job posting. *Personnel Journal,* 1975, *54,* 245–247.

Cook, T.D., & Campbell, D.T. The design and conduct of quasi-experiments and true experiments in field settings. In M.D. Dunnette (Ed.), *Handbook of industrial and organizational psychology.* Chicago: Rand McNally, 1976, 223–326.

Crawford, J.D. Career development and career choice in pioneer and traditional women. *Journal of Vocational Behavior,* 1978, *12,* 129–139.

Crystal, J., & Bolles, R.N. *Where do I go from here with my life?* Berkeley, Calif.: Ten Speed Press, 1974.

Cyert, R.M., & March, J.G. *A behavioral theory of the firm.* Englewood Cliffs, N.J.: Prentice-Hall, 1963.

Dalton, G.W., Thompson, P.H., & Price, R.L. The four stages of professional careers—A new look at performance by professionals. *Organizational Dynamics,* 1977, *6* (1), 17–33.

Decker, P.J. Effects of symbolic coding and rehearsal in behavior-modeling training. *Journal of Applied Psychology,* 1980, *65,* 627–634.

Digman, L.A. How well-managed organizations develop their executives. *Organizational Dynamics,* 1978, *7* (2), 63–80.

Dimick, D.E. Factors associated with the importance of policy in personnel decisions. *Academy of Management Proceedings,* 1978, *38,* 202–205.

Doeringer, P.B., & Piore, M.J. *Internal labor markets and manpower analysis.* Lexington, Mass.: Lexington Books, 1971.

Drandell, M. A composite forecasting methodology for manpower planning utilizing objective and subjective criteria. *Academy of Management Journal,* 1975, *18,* 510–519.

Dunnette, M.D., Hough, L.M., & Rosse, R.L. Task and job taxonomies as a basis for identifying labor supply sources and evaluating employment qualifications. *Human Resource Planning,* 1979, 31–51.

Dyer, L.D. Job search success of middle-aged managers and engineers. *Industrial and Labor Relations Review,* 1973, *26,* 969–979.

Ebert, R.J., & Mitchell, T.R. *Organizational decision processes: Concepts and analysis.* New York: Crane, Russak, 1975.

1979 Employment and Training Report of the President, cited in Powell (1980).

Feldman, D.C. A socialization process that helps new recruits succeed. *Personnel,* 1980, *57* (2), 11–23.

Ference, T.P., Stoner, J.A.F., & Warren, E.K. Managing the career plateau. *Academy of Management Review,* 1977, *2,* 602–612.

Fernandez, J.P. *Black managers in white corporations.* New York: Wiley, 1975.

Fernandez, J.P. *Racism and sexism in corporate life.* Lexington, Mass.: Lexington Books, 1981.

Ferrini, P., & Parker, L.A. *Career change.* Cambridge, Mass.: Technical Education Research Centers, 1978.

Finkle, R.B. Managerial assessment centers. In M.D. Dunnette (Ed.), *Handbook of industrial and organizational psychology.* Chicago: Rand McNally, 1976, 861–888.

Freedman, R.D., & Stumpf, S.A. The usefulness of assessment centers in management education. *Eastern Academy of Management Proceedings,* 1981, 198–202.

Freedman, R.D., Stumpf, S.A., & Platten, P. An assessment center for career planning and change. *Journal of Assessment Center Technology,* 1980, *3,* 5–10.

Freedman, R.D., Stumpf, S.A., Weitz, E., & Platten, P. Degree of career change, detachment, and job outcomes. *Eastern Academy of Management Proceedings,* 1981, 117–122.

Gemmill, G., & DeSalvia, D. The promotion beliefs of managers as a factor in career progress: An exploratory study. *Sloan Management Review,* 1977, *18* (2), 75–81.

Gladwin, T.N., & Walter, I. *Multinationals under fire: Lessons in the management of conflict.* New York: Wiley, 1980.

Goldstein, I.L. *Training: Program development and evaluation.* Monterey, Calif.: Brooks-Cole, 1974.

Goldstein, I.L. Training in work organizations. *Annual Review of Psychology,* 1980, *31,* 229–279.

Goldstein, A.P., & Sorcher, M. *Changing supervisory behavior.* Elmsford, N.Y.: Pergamon Press, 1974.

Golembiewski, R.T. *Renewing organizations: The laboratory approach to planned change.* Itasca, Ill.: F.E. Peacock, 1972.

Gomez-Mejia, L.R., Page, R.C., & Tornow, W.W. Development and implementation of a computerized job evaluation system. *The Personnel Administrator,* February 1979, 46–55.

Granovetter, M.S. *Getting a job: A study of contacts and careers.* Cambridge, Mass.: Harvard University Press, 1974.

Gruenfeld, E.F. *Promotions: Practices, policies, and affirmative action.* Ithaca, N.Y.: Publications Division, New York State School of Industrial and Labor Relations, Cornell University, 1975.

Hackman, J.R., & Morris, C.G. Group tasks, group interaction process, and group performance effectiveness: A review and proposed integration. In L. Berkowitz (Ed.), *Advances in experimental social psychology* (Vol. 8). New York: Academic Press, 1975.

Hackman, J.R., & Oldham, G.R. *Work redesign.* Reading, Mass.: Addison-Wesley, 1980.

Halaby, C.N. Bureaucratic promotion criteria. *Administrative Science Quarterly,* 1978, *23,* 466–484.

Hall, D.T. A model of coping with role conflict: The role behavior of college educated women. *Administrative Science Quarterly,* 1972, *17,* 471–486.

Hall, D.T. *Careers in organizations.* Santa Monica, Calif.: Goodyear, 1976.

Hall, D.T., & Hall, F.S. What's new in career management. *Organizational Dynamics,* 1976, *5* (1), 17–33.

Hall, F.S. Developing and managing careers: A teaching perspective. In R.D. Freedman, C. Cooper, & S.A. Stumpf (Eds.), *Management education: Issues in theory, research, and practice.* London: Wiley, 1982.

Hall, F.S., & Albrecht, M.H. *The management of affirmative action.* Santa Monica, Calif.: Goodyear, 1979.

Hall, F.S., & Hall, D.T. Dual careers—How do couples and companies cope with the problems? *Organizational Dynamics,* 1978, *6* (4), 57–77.

Hall, F.S., & Hall, D.T. *The two-career couple.* Reading, Mass.: Addison-Wesley, 1979.

Hammer, T.H. Affirmative action programs: Have we forgotten the first-line supervisor? *Personnel Journal,* 1979, *58,* 384–389.

Hamner, W.C. Reinforcement theory and contingency management in organizational settings. In H.L. Tosi & W.C. Hamner (Eds.), *Organizational behavior and management: A contingency approach.* Chicago: St. Clair Press, 1974, 86–112.

Harlan, A., & Weiss, C. Moving up: Women in managerial careers. *The Career Development Bulletin,* 1980, *2,* 10–11.

Harvard Business Review. Everyone who makes it has a mentor, 1978, *56* (4), 89–101.

Hastings, R.E. Career development: Maximizing options. *Personnel Administrator,* 1978, *23* (5), 58–61.

Hellervik, L. *Clinical evaluations for career development.* Paper presented at the American Psychological Association Annual Meeting, Los Angeles, Calif., August 1981.

Helmich, D. Executive succession in the corporate organization: A current integration. *Academy of Management Review,* 1977, *2,* 252–266.

Hoffman, W.H., & Wyatt, L.L. Human resource planning. *Personnel Administrator,* 1977, *22* (1), 19–23.

Holland, J.L. *Making vocational choices: A theory of careers.* Englewood Cliffs, N.J.: Prentice-Hall, 1973.

Horwitz, J.B., & Stumpf, S.A. *Predicting preference, effort, and job choice: Expectancy theory or chance?* Paper presented at the 1981 American Institute for Decision Sciences Annual Meeting, Boston, Mass., November 1981.

Howard, A., & Bray, D.W. *Career motivation in mid-life managers.* Paper presented at the American Psychological Association Annual Meeting, Montreal, September 1980.

Howard, A., & Bray, D.W. Today's young managers: They can do it, but will they? *The Wharton Magazine,* 1981, *5,* 23–28.

Ilgen, D.R., Fisher, C.D., & Taylor, M.S. Consequences of individual feedback on behavior in organizations. *Journal of Applied Psychology*, 1979, *64*, 349–371.

Jacoby, J. Consumer and industrial psychology: Prospects for theory corroboration and mutual contribution. In M.D. Dunnette (Ed.), *Handbook of industrial and organizational psychology*. Chicago: Rand McNally, 1976, 1031–1062.

Jelinek, M. (Ed.). *Career management for the individual and the organization*. New York: Wiley, 1979.

Jones, E.W., Jr. What it's like to be a black manager. *Harvard Business Review*, 1973, *51* (4), 108–116.

Jurgensen, C.E. Job preferences (what makes a job good or bad?). *Journal of Applied Psychology*, 1978, *63*, 267–276.

Kabanoff, B. Work and nonwork: A review of models, methods, and findings. *Psychological Bulletin*, 1980, *88*, 60–77.

Kabanoff, B., & O'Brien, G.E. Work and leisure: A task attributes analysis. *Journal of Applied Psychology*, 1980, *65*, 596–609.

Kanter, R.M. *Men and women of the corporation*. New York: Basic Books, 1977.

Kaufman, H.G. *Obsolescence and professional career development*. New York: AMACOM, 1974.

Kellogg, M. Executive development. In D. Yoder & H.G. Heneman (Eds.), *ASPA handbook of personnel and industrial relations*. Washington, D.C.: Bureau of National Affairs, 1979.

Kirkpatrick, J.J. Occupational aspirations, opportunities, and barriers. In K.S. Miller & R.M. Dreger (Eds.), *Comparative studies of blacks and whites in the United States*. New York: Seminar Press, 1973, 357–374.

Klauss, R. *Mentors and senior advisors for executive development*. Washington, D.C.: W.S. Office of Personnel Management, 1981.

Kleinman, L.S., & Durham, R.L. Performance appraisal, promotion, and the courts: A critical review. *Personnel Psychology*, 1981, *34*, 103–121.

Klimoski, R.J., & London, M. Role of the rater in performance appraisal. *Journal of Applied Psychology,* 1974, *59,* 445–451.

Klimoski, R.J., & Strickland, W.J. Assessment centers—Valid or merely prescient. *Personnel Psychology,* 1977, *30,* 353–361.

Korman, A., & Korman, R.W. *Career success/personal failure: Alienation in management.* Englewood Cliffs, N.J.: Prentice-Hall, 1980.

Korman, A.K., Wittig-Berman, U., & Lang, D. Career success and personal failure: Alienation in professionals and managers. *Academy of Management Journal,* 1981, *24,* 342–360.

Kothari, V. The importance and application of promotional criteria as perceived by management, union, and employees. *Academy of Management Proceedings,* 1974, *34,* 37.

Kothari, V. Promotional criteria: Three views. *Personnel Journal,* 1976, *55,* 402–405.

Kotter, J.P., Faux, V.A., & McArthur, C.C. *Self-assessment and career development.* Englewood Cliffs, N.J.: Prentice-Hall, 1978.

Kram, K.E. *Mentoring processes at work: Developmental relationships in managerial careers.* Unpublished doctoral dissertation, Yale University, 1980.

Lang, J.R., Dittrich, J.C., & White, S.E. Managerial problem solving models: A review and a proposal. *Academy of Management Review,* 1978, *3,* 854–866.

Larwood, L., & Whittaker, W. Managerial myopias self-serving biases in organizational planning. *Journal of Applied Psychology,* 1977, *62,* 194–198.

Latham, G.P., & Saari, L.M. Application of social-learning theory to training supervisors through behavioral modeling. *Journal of Applied Psychology,* 1979, *64,* 239–246.

Latham, G.P., & Wexley, K.N. *Increasing productivity through performance appraisal.* Reading, Mass.: Addison-Wesley, 1981.

Latham, G.P., & Yukl, G. A review of research on the application of goal setting in organizations. *Academy of Management Journal,* 1975, *18,* 824–845.

Lawler, E.E., III. *Pay and organizational effectiveness: A psychological view.* New York: McGraw-Hill, 1971.

Levinson, D.J., et al. *The seasons of a man's life.* New York: Knopf, 1978.

Levinson, H. On being a middle-aged manager. *Harvard Business Review,* 1969, *47* (4), 51–60.

Lindblom, C.E. The science of muddling through. *Public Administration Review,* 1959, *19,* 79–88.

Lippman, S.A., & McCall, J.J. The economics of job search: A survey, Part I: Optimal job search policies. *Economics Inquiry,* 1976, *14,* 155–189.

London, M. Effects of information heterogeneity and representational roles on group member behavior and perceptions. *Journal of Applied Psychology,* 1977, *62,* 76–80.

London, M. What every personnel director should know about management promotion decisions. *Personnel Journal,* 1978, *57,* 550–555.

London, M., Crandall, R., & Seals, G. The contribution of job and leisure satisfaction to quality of life. *Journal of Applied Psychology,* 1977, *62,* 328–334.

London, M., & Stumpf, S.A. *Staffing management positions: Individual and organizational factors affecting the decision process.* Paper presented at the Academy of Management Annual Meeting, Atlanta, Georgia, August 1979.

London, M., & Stumpf, S.A. *Career planning and the promotion decision process.* Paper presented at the American Psychological Association Annual Meeting, Montreal, September 1980a.

London, M., & Stumpf, S.A. *Effects of candidate characteristics on management promotion decisions: An experimental study.* Unpublished manuscript, American Telephone and Telegraph Company, 1980b.

Lopez, F.E., Rockmore, B.W., & Kesselman, G.A. The development of an integrated career planning program at Gulf Power Company. *Personnel Administrator,* 1980, *25* (10), 21–29, 75–76.

Louis, M.R. Surprise and sensemaking: What newcomers experience in entering unfamiliar organizational settings. *Administrative Science Quarterly,* 1980, *25,* 226–251.

Luxenberg, S. Education at AT&T. *Change,* 1978/79 (December-January), 26–35.

Manhardt, P.J. Job orientation of male and female college graduates in business. *Personnel Psychology,* 1972, *25,* 361–368.

March, J.C., & March, J.G. Almost random careers: The Wisconsin school superintendency, 1940–1972. *Administrative Science Quarterly,* 1977, *22,* 377–409.

March, J.G., & Simon, H.A. *Organizations.* New York: Wiley, 1958.

Martin, N., & Strauss, A. Patterns of mobility with industrial organizations. *Journal of Business,* 1956, *29* (2), 107–110.

McCall, M.W., Jr. *The manager's job: Implications of diary and observational studies.* Paper presented at the American Psychological Association Annual Convention, New York, September 1979.

McCall, M.W., & Lombardo, M.M. *Looking Glass, Inc.: An organizational simulation* (Technical Report No. 12). Greensboro, N.C.: Center for Creative Leadership, 1978.

McClelland, D.C. Achievement motivation can be developed. *Harvard Business Review,* 1965, *43* (6), 6–14, 178.

McGhee, W., & Tullar, W.L. A note on evaluating behavior modification and behavior modeling as industrial training techniques. *Personnel Psychology,* 1978, *31,* 477–484.

Miller, D.B. Career planning and management in organizations. *S.A.M. Advanced Management Journal,* 1978, *13,* 33–43.

Mintzberg, H. *The nature of managerial work.* New York: Harper & Row, 1973.

Mintzberg, H., Raisinghani, D., & Théorêt, A. The structure of "unstructured" decision processes. *Administrative Science Quarterly,* 1976, *21,* 246–275.

Miret, P. The creation of a system of personnel management forecasting: Technology or sociology. In D.T. Bryant & R.J. Niehaus (Eds.), *Manpower planning and organization design.* New York: Plenum, 1978.

Mitchell, J.L., & McCormick, E.J. *Development of the PMPQ: A structural job analysis questionnaire for the study of professional and managerial positions* (PMPQ Report No. 1). West Lafayette, Ind.: Purdue University, Department of Psychological Sciences, 1979.

Morgan, M.A. (Ed.). *Managing career development.* New York: Van Nostrand Reinhold, 1980.

Morgan, M.A., Hall, D.T., & Martier, A. Career development activities in industry: Where are we and where should we be? *Personnel,* 1979, *56,* 13–30.

Morrison, J.H. Determining training needs. In R.L. Craig (Ed.), *Training and development handbook: A guide to human resource development.* New York: McGraw-Hill, 1976.

Morrison, R.F., & Holzbach, R.L. *Molding the individual and the organization.* Paper presented at the Academy of Management Annual Meeting, Atlanta, Georgia, August 1979.

Moses, J.L. The assessment center method. In J.L. Moses and W.C. Byham (Eds.), *Applying the assessment center method.* Elmsford, N.Y.: Pergamon Press, 1977.

Moses, J.L., & Byham, W.C. (Eds.). *Applying the assessment center method.* Elmsford, N.Y.: Pergamon Press, 1977.

Moses, J.L., & Ritchie, R.J. Supervisory relationships training: A behavioral evaluation of a modeling program. *Personnel Psychology,* 1976, *29,* 337–343.

Nadler, D.A. *Feedback and organization development: Using data-based methods.* Reading, Mass.: Addison-Wesley, 1977.

National Commission on Working Women. *An overview of women in the workforce.* Washington, D.C., Center for Women and Work, September 1979.

Near, J.P., Rice, R.W., & Hunt, R.O. The relationship between work and nonwork domains: A review of empirical research. *Academy of Management Review,* 1980, *5,* 415–429.

Newell, A., & Simon, H.A. *Human problem solving.* Englewood Cliffs, N.J.: Prentice-Hall, 1972.

O'Reilly, C.A., III. Personality–job fit: Implications for individual attitudes and performance. *Organizational Behavior and Human Performance,* 1977, *18,* 36–46.

Ouchi, W.G. *Theory Z: How American business can meet the Japanese challenge.* Reading, Mass.: Addison-Wesley, 1981.

Ouchi, W.G., & Jaeger, A.M. Type Z organization: Stability in the midst of mobility. *Academy of Management Review,* 1978, *3,* 305–314.

Owens, W.A., & Schoenfeldt, L.F. Toward a classification of persons. *Journal of Applied Psychology Monograph,* 1979, *65,* 569–607.

Page, R.C., & Gomez, L.R. *The development and application of job evaluation and staffing systems using the position description questionnaire* (Personnel Research Report 162–79). Minneapolis, Minn.: Control Data Corporation, January 1979.

Payne, J.W. Task complexity and contingent processing in decision making: An information search and protocol analysis. *Organizational Behavior and Human Performance,* 1976, *16,* 366–387.

Pedigo, P., & Meyer, H. *Management promotion decisions: The influence of affirmative action restrictions.* Paper presented at the Academy of Management Annual Meeting, Atlanta, Georgia, August 1979.

Pinto, P.R. Career development trends for the 80's: Better managers, higher productivity. *Training/HRD,* April 1980, *31,* 33.

Pitts, R.A. Unshackle your 'comers.' *Harvard Business Review,* 1977, *55* (3), 127–136.

Posner, B.Z. Comparing recruiter, student, and faculty perceptions of important applicant job characteristics. *Personnel Psychology,* 1981, *34,* 329–340.

Powell, G.N. Career development and the woman manager—A social power perspective. *Personnel,* 1980, *57* (3), 22–32.

Quinn, R., Tabor, J., & Gordon, L. *The decision to discriminate: A study of executive selection.* Ann Arbor, Mich.: Survey Research Center, Institute for Social Research, 1968.

Raia, A.P. *Managing by objectives.* Glenview, Ill.: Scott, Foresman, 1974.

Reid, G.L. Job search and the effectiveness of job-finding methods. *Industrial and Labor Relations Review,* 1972, *25,* 479–495.

Rice, R.W., Near, J.P., & Hunt, R.G. Unique variance in job and life satisfaction associated with work-related and extra-workplace variables. *Human Relations,* 1979, *32,* 605–623.

Riger, S., & Galligan, P. Women in management: An exploration of competing paradigms. *American Psychologist,* 1980, *35,* 902–910.

Robinson, R.B., Jr., & Glueck, W.F. *Career development and organizational effectiveness: An analysis of the literature.* Paper presented at the Southern Management Association Annual Meeting, New Orleans, La., November 1980.

Roche, G.R. Much ado about mentors. *Harvard Business Review,* 1979, *57* (1), 14–31.

Roeske, N.A., & Lake, K. Role models for women medical students. *Journal of Medical Education,* 1977, *52,* 459–466.

Ronen, S. *Flexible working hours: An innovation in the quality of work life.* New York: McGraw-Hill, 1980.

Rosen, B., & Jerdee, T.H. The influence of sex role stereotypes on evaluations of male and female supervisory behavior. *Journal of Applied Psychology,* 1973, *57,* 44–54.

Rosen, N., Billings, R., & Turney, J. The emergence and allocation of leadership resources over time in a technical organization. *Academy of Management Journal,* 1976, *19,* 165–183.

Rosenbaum, J.E. Tournament mobility: Career patterns in a corporation. *Administrative Science Quarterly,* 1979, *24,* 220–241.

Rothstein, W.G. The significance of occupations in work careers: An empirical and theoretical review. *Journal of Vocational Behavior,* 1980, *17,* 328–343.

Rynes, S.L., Heneman, H.G., III, & Schwab, D.P. Individual reactions to organizational recruiting: A review. *Personnel Psychology,* 1980, *33,* 529–542.

Saklad, D.A. Manpower planning and career development at Citicorp. In L. Dyer (Ed.), *Careers in organizations.* Ithaca, N.Y.: Cornell University, 1976.

Sarachek, B. Career concerns of black managers. *Management Review,* 1974 (October), 17–24.

Schein, E.H. *Career dynamics: Matching individual and organizational needs.* Reading, Mass.: Addison-Wesley, 1978.

Schmitt, N. Social and situational determinants of interview decisions: Implications for the employment interview. *Personnel Psychology,* 1976, *29,* 79–102.

Schwab, D.P. Recruiting and organizational participation. In K. Rowland & G. Ferris (Eds.), *Human resource management.* Boston: Allyn and Bacon, 1982.

Shapiro, E.C., Haseltine, F.P., & Rowe, M.P. Moving up: Role models, mentors, and the "patron system." *Sloan Management Review,* 1978, *19* (3), 51–58.

Shaw, M.E. *Group dynamics: The psychology of small group behavior.* New York: McGraw-Hill, 1975.

Shrode, W.A., & Brown, W.B. A study of optimality in recurrent decision making of lower-level managers. *Academy of Management Journal,* 1970, *13,* 389–402.

Simon, H.A. *Models of man.* New York: Wiley, 1957.

Smith, E.J. The working mother: A critique of the research. *Journal of Vocational Behavior,* 1981, *19,* 191–211.

Soelberg, P.O. Unprogrammed decision making. *Industrial Management Review,* 1967, *8,* 19–29.

Stein, R.T. *A job analysis of Looking Glass, Inc.* Greensboro, N.C.: Center for Creative Leadership, 1980.

Stevens, T. Beyond job posting. *Career Development Bulletin,* 1979, *1* (2), 4–5.

Storey, W.D. *Career Dimensions I, II, III, and IV.* Croton-on-Hudson, N.Y.: General Electric Company, 1976a.

Storey, W.D. *Self-directed career planning at the General Electric Company.* Paper presented at the Academy of Management Annual Meeting, Kansas City, Mo., August 1976b.

Storey, W.D. Which way: Manager-directed or person-centered career pathing. *Training and Development Journal,* 1978, *32* (1), 10–14.

Strong, E.K., Jr. *Vocational interests of men and women.* Stanford, Calif.: Stanford University Press, 1943.

Stumpf, S.A. Career roles, psychological success, and job attitudes. *Journal of Vocational Behavior,* 1981a, *19,* 98–112.

Stumpf, S.A. *The effects of career exploration on organizational entry and career related outcomes.* Working paper, New York University, 1981b.

Stumpf, S.A., & Colarelli, S.M. Career exploration: Development of dimensions and some preliminary findings. *Psychological Reports,* 1980, *47,* 979–988.

Stumpf, S.A., & Colarelli, S.M. The effect of career education on exploratory behavior and job search outcomes. *Academy of Management Proceedings,* 1981, 76–80.

Stumpf, S.A., Colarelli, S.M., & Hartman, K. *Development of the Career Exploration Survey (CES).* Unpublished manuscript, New York University, 1981.

Stumpf, S.A., & Dawley, P.K. Predicting voluntary and involuntary turnover using absenteeism and performance indices. *Academy of Management Journal,* 1981, *24,* 148–163.

Stumpf, S.A., Freedman, R.D., & Rabinowitz, S. *Role perception relationships with facets of job satisfaction and performance indices as moderated by hierarchical level.* Unpublished manuscript, New York University, 1981.

Stumpf, S.A., Freedman, R.D., & Zand, D.E. Judgmental decisions: A study of interactions among group membership, group functioning, and the decision situation. *Academy of Management Journal,* 1979, *22,* 765–782.

Stumpf, S.A., Greller, M., & Freedman, R. Equal employment opportunity regulation and change in compensation practices. *Journal of Applied Behavioral Science,* 1980, *16,* 29–40.

Stumpf, S.A., & London, M. Clustering rater policies in evaluating candidates for promotion. *Academy of Management Journal,* 1981a, *24,* 752–766.

Stumpf, S.A., & London, M. Management promotions: Individual and organizational factors affecting the decision process. *Academy of Management Review,* 1981b, *6,* 539–550.

Stumpf, S.A., & Rabinowitz, S. Career stage as a moderator of performance relationships with facets of job satisfaction and role perceptions. *Journal of Vocational Behavior,* 1981, *18,* 202–218.

Stumpf, S.A., & Zand, D.E. *Assessing the anticipated effectiveness of judgmental decisions. Journal of Management,* 1981 (in press).

Stumpf, S.A., Zand, D.E., & Freedman, R.D. Designing groups for judgmental decisions. *Academy of Management Review,* 1979, *4,* 589–600.

Super, D.E. *The psychology of careers.* New York: Harper & Row, 1957.

Super, D.E. A life-span, life-space approach to career development. *Journal of Vocational Behavior,* 1980, *16,* 282–298.

Super, D.E., Crites, J., Hummel, R., Moser, H., Overstreet, P., & Warnath, C. *Vocational development: A framework for research.* New York: Teachers College Press, 1957.

Super, D.E., & Hall, D.T. Career development: Exploration and planning. In M.R. Rosenzweig & L.W. Porter (Eds.), *Annual Review of Psychology,* 1978, *29,* 333–372.

Taylor, R. Preferences of industrial managers for information sources in making promotion decisions. *Journal of Applied Psychology,* 1975, *60,* 269–272.

Terborg, J.R. Women in management: A research review. *Journal of Applied Psychology,* 1977, *62,* 647–664.

Terborg, J.R., & Ilgen, D.R. A theoretical approach to sex discrimination in traditionally masculine occupations. *Organizational Behavior and Human Performance,* 1975, *13,* 352–376.

Thompson, J.D. *Organizations in action.* New York: McGraw-Hill, 1967.

Thornton, G.C., III. Differential effects of career planning on internals and externals. *Personnel Psychology,* 1978, *31,* 471–476.

Thornton, G.C., III. Psychometric properties of self-appraisals of job performance. *Personnel Psychology,* 1980, *33,* 263–272.

Toffler, B.L. Occupational role development: The changing determinants of outcomes for the individual. *Administrative Science Quarterly,* 1981, *26,* 396–418.

Tornow, W.W., & Pinto, P.R. The development of a managerial job taxonomy: A system for describing, classifying, and evaluating executive positions. *Journal of Applied Psychology,* 1976, *61,* 410–418.

Tversky, A. Intransitivity of preferences. *Psychological Review,* 1969, *76,* 31–48.

U.S. Bureau of the Census. *Statistical abstracts of the United States:* 1979 (100th ed.), Washington, D.C., 1979, 417.

Ullman, J.C., & Gutteridge, T.G. The job search. *Journal of College Placement,* 1973, *33* (3), 67–72.

Vaillant, G.E. *Adaptation to life.* Boston: Little, Brown, 1977.

Van Maanen, J., & Schein, E.H. Career development. In J.R. Hackman & J.L. Suttle (Eds.), *Improving life at work: Behavioral science approaches to organizational change.* Santa Monica, Calif.: Goodyear, 1977.

Van Sell, M., Brief, A.P., & Schuler, R.S. Role conflict and role ambiguity: Integration of the literature and directions for future research. *Human Relations,* 1981, *34,* 43–71.

Vardi, G. Organizational career mobility: An integrative model. *Academy of Management Review,* 1980, *5,* 341–355.

Veiga, J.F. Do managers on the move get anywhere? *Harvard Business Review,* 1981a, *59* (2), 20–22, 26–38.

Veiga, J.F. Plateaued versus nonplateaued managers: Career patterns, attitudes, and path potential. *Academy of Management Journal,* 1981b, *24,* 566–578.

Vroom, V.H., & Yetton, P.W. *Leadership and decision-making.* Pittsburgh, Pa.: University of Pittsburgh Press, 1973.

Walker, J.W. Let's get realistic about career paths. *Human Resources Management,* 1976, *55* (Fall), 2–7.

Walker, J.W. Personal and career development. In D. Yoder & H.G. Heneman, Jr. (Eds.), *Training and development.* ASPA Handbook of Personnel and Industrial Relations (Vol. 5). Washington, D.C.: Bureau of National Affairs, 1977.

Walker, J.W. *Human resource planning.* New York: McGraw-Hill, 1980.

Walker, J.W., & Gutteridge, T.G. *Career planning practices: An AMA survey report.* New York: AMACOM, 1979.

Wall, S.J., Awal, D., & Stumpf, S.A. Conflict management: The situation, behaviors, and outcome effectiveness. In D. Ray (Ed.), *The relationship between theory, research, and practice: An assessment of fundamental problems and their possible resolution.* Mississippi State, Miss.: Southern Management Association, 1981, 253–255.

Wanous, J.P. Realistic job previews: Can a procedure to reduce turnover also influence the relationship between abilities and performance? *Personnel Psychology,* 1978, *31,* 249–258.

Wanous, J.P. *Organizational entry: Recruitment, selection, and socialization of newcomers.* Reading, Mass.: Addison-Wesley, 1980.

Wanous, J.P., Stumpf, S.A., & Bedrosian, H. Job survival of new employees. *Personnel Psychology,* 1979, *32,* 651–662.

Webb, E.J., Campbell, D.T., Schwartz, R.D., & Sechrest, L. *Unobtrusive measures: Nonreactive research in the social sciences.* Chicago: Rand McNally, 1981.

Webber, R.A. Career problems of young managers. *California Management Review,* 1976, *18* (4), 19–33.

Weiner, Y., & Schneiderman, M.L. Use of job information as a criterion in employment decisions of interviewers. *Journal of Applied Psychology,* 1974, *59,* 699–704.

Weiss, H.M. Subordinate imitation of supervisor behavior: The role of modeling in organizational socialization. *Organizational Behavior and Human Performance,* 1977, *19,* 89–105.

Wellbank, H.L., Hall, D.T., Morgan, M.A., & Hamner, W.C. Planning job progression for effective career development and human resources management. *Personnel,* 1978, *55* (2), 54–64.

Wexley, K.N., & Latham, G.P. *Developing and training human resources in organizations.* Glenview, Ill.: Scott, Foresman, 1981.

White, M.C., DeSanctis, G.L., & Crino, M.D. A critical review of female performance, performance training, and organizational initiatives designed to aid women in work-role environment. *Personnel Psychology,* 1981, *34,* 227–248.

White, T. *Career planning workshop.* Division 14 workshop series, American Psychological Association Annual Meeting, Montreal, September 1980.

Yoder, D., & Heneman, H.G., Jr. (Eds.). *Staffing policies and strategies.* Washington, D.C.: The Bureau of National Affairs, 1974.

Yohalem, A. *The careers of professional women: Commitment and conflict.* Montclair, N.J.: Allenheld, Osmun, 1979.

Zand, D.E. *Information, organization, and power: Effective management in the knowledge society.* New York: McGraw-Hill, 1981.

Zedeck, S. An information processing model and approach to the study of motivation. *Organizational Behavior and Human Performance,* 1977, *18,* 47–77.

Name Index

Subject Index